THE
DEPARTED

For Melanie

Also by Michael Williams:

On the Slow Train
On the Slow Train Again

Steaming to Victory

THE TRAINS NOW DEPARTED

Sixteen Excursions into the Lost Delights of Britain's Railways

MICHAEL WILLIAMS

arrow books

Arrow Books
whose ad

Michael Williams has asserted his right to be identified as the Author of this Work in accordance with the Copyright, Designs and Patents Act 1988.

Grateful acknowledgement is made to: Argyll Press for permission to excerpt from *Waverley Route* by David Spaven; Countryvise publishing for permission to excerpt from *Seventeen Stations to Dingle* by John Gahan; Ian Allen publishing for permission to excerpt from *Night Ferry* by George Behrend and Gary Buchanan, *The Titled Trains of Great Britain* by Cecil J. Allen and *The Stanmore and Eden Valley Railways* by Peter Walton; Irwell Press for permission to excerpt from *An Illustrated History of the North Cornwall Railway* by David Wroe; Oakwood Press for permission to excerpt from *The Stratford-Upon-Avon and Midland Junction Railway* by J.M. Dunn; Orion Publishing Group in regards to *The Ward Lock Red Guide to Lynton and Lynmouth* by Reginald J. W. Hammond.

Every effort has been made to trace copyright holders and to obtain their permission. The publisher apologises for any errors or omissions and, if notified of any corrections, will make suitable acknowledgement in future reprints or editions of this book.

First published by Preface Publishing in Great Britain in 2015
First published in paperback by Arrow Books in 2016

www.penguin.co.uk

A CIP catalogue record for this book is available from the British Library.

ISBN 9780099590583

Illustrations by Mai Osawa
Maps by John Gilkes

Typeset in Centaur MT by Palimpsest Book Production Ltd, Falkirk, Stirlingshire
Printed and bound in Great Britain by Clays Ltd, St Ives plc

Penguin Random House is committed to a sustainable future for our business, our readers and our planet. This book is made from Forest Stewardship Council® certified paper.

MIX
Paper from responsible sources
FSC® C018179
www.fsc.org

Contents

The Slow and Dirty it may have been for some, but the old Somerset & Dorset remains, for its many devotees today, the most romantic and alluring of all the vanished lines of Britain. Did its origins in Glastonbury help weave the spell?

The exotic life and death of the Night Ferry from Victoria to the Continent, haunt of spies, diplomats, starlets and sultans. Even in today's Eurostar era, its memory stands proud as Britain's only truly international train.

A saunter through Metro-land to the London Underground's farthest outpost. It's buried under weeds today, but once the Pullman trains ran from here, serving the most splendid of breakfasts to commuters up to Baker Street.

Beeching butchered the bleak Stainmore line over the Pennines, in its day the highest in England. But the old viaducts still stand tall, and the tales of the tough men who worked it live on as the stuff of legend.

The Flying Scotsman, the Cornish Riviera, the Coronation Scot — such speed, such luxury! In days gone by almost every main line had its named expresses. These glamorous trains are a fast-receding memory in the corporate world of today's franchised railways.

Introduction:
The romance we lost

Sometimes you come across a lofty railway viaduct marooned in the middle of a remote country landscape. Or a crumbling platform of some once-bustling junction buried under the buddleia. If you are lucky you might be able to follow some rusting tracks or explore an old tunnel leading to . . . well, who knows where? Listen hard. Is that the wind in the undergrowth? Or the spectre of a train from a golden era of the past panting up the embankment?

These are the ghosts of the trains now departed – lines prematurely axed often with gripping and colourful tales to tell, marvels of locomotive engineering prematurely sent to the scrapyard, and architecturally magnificent stations felled by the wrecker's ball. Then there are the lost delights of train travel, such as haute cuisine in the dining car, the grand expresses with their evocative names, and continental boat trains to romantic far-off places. Such pleasures have all but vanished in our modern homogenised era of train travel.

But why should nostalgia be on anyone's mind in this age of fast, state-of-the-art trains, which routinely whisk us efficiently all over the developed world at speeds of up to 200 mph. Is it merely fanciful and indulgent to summon up some 'lost age' of the railways when more of us are choosing to use the rail network than at any time in history. Trains today, the mantra goes, are faster, more frequent and better than ever. Why bother about the past?

Well, for many of today's train travellers 'faster, more frequent and better' is too often a euphemism, in corporate railwayspeak, for 'worse'. It is sometimes tempting to wonder if, deep in every railway operations HQ, there is a department whose sole job is to think up ways of corroding the experience of passengers (or 'passenger experience' if you go along with the jargon.) Here are seats that don't line up with the windows, garish plasticky train interiors, an incomprehensible fares system, ticket collectors who assume everyone is a criminal, a cacophony of endless announcements about 'the next station stop' and 'suspicious packages', and of course the extinction of many of the things that once made rail travel joyous – restaurant cars with white tablecloths and silver service, obliging porters, staffed stations, waiting rooms with blazing fires, a comfy compartment you could snuggle in, luggage in advance . . . I'm sure you can devise your own list. No wonder the universe of railways of the past seems rose-tinted.

But let's not get carried away. There are many tangible things we have lost over the years that it is unreasonable to expect to recover in the modern age. Nor would we want them. That romantic little branch line train was often as illusory as George Orwell's 'old maids bicycling to holy communion through the morning mist'. As Paul Theroux wrote,

There is an English dream of a warm summer evening on a branch line train. Just that sentence can make an English person over 40 fall silent with the memory of what has now become a golden fantasy of an idealised England: the comfortable, dusty coaches rolling through the low woods, the sun gilding the green leaves and

striking through the carriage windows; the breeze tick-
ling the hot flowers in the fields, birdsong and the
thump of the powerful locomotive; the pleasant creak
of the wood panelling on the coach; the mingled smell
of fresh grass and coal smoke; and the expectation of
being met by someone very dear on the platform of a
country station.

The reality was that the train was often a draughty superannuated relic fit only for the scrapyard, used by a handful
of passengers each week and leaching a steady stream of
money from the public purse. No one could reasonably
expect to revive such services.

Likewise, present-day 'railwayacs' and 'locoists' wax sentimental about the colourful liveries and polished brasswork
of the steam engines of yore. We may enthuse about the
'Blackberry Black' of the London & North Western at
Euston or the 'Improved Engine Green' of the London,
Brighton & South Coast Railway (which was actually yellow),
much as a design guru might fuss over a Farrow & Ball
paintcard. Yet the truth is that, lovely though they seem in
retrospect, steam locomotives were labour-intensive and
inefficient machines, and by the 1950s it had become difficult
to attract staff to work with them. As for the competition
– seen even now as a virtue of the 'buccaneering' old days –
the reality was that many British towns and villages ended
up with more stations and railway services than they could
ever possibly need, the result being failure and eventual
closure. To recreate any part of this world today would be
absurd.

Yet most of us British, I think, cannot help but view the
railways through a prism of nostalgia. The mood seems to
be everywhere. Here is Michael Portillo, ubiquitous on our
living-room TVs, brandishing his Bradshaw and seemingly

endlessly roaming the rails and catching the *zeitgeist* with his *Great British Railway Journeys*. Pete Waterman is there too, rejoicing in the greasy world of the steam engine, while Dan Snow adds the gloss of the celebrity historian.

So what is it about trains that makes us so rheumy-eyed? Is it that, as the nation that invented the railway, we are pining in a postmodern world for our lost industrial heritage? In the introduction to their anthology *Train Songs* the poets Sean O'Brien and Don Paterson reckon that the appeal of the railways is precisely to do with their relationship to time. 'The train moves into the future on its iron road while provoking a complex nostalgia that has accompanied it since birth,' they write. 'Almost as soon as the railway arrived in Britain it began to depart. After the railway boom of the 1840s the empire of the tracks seems always to have been defending and withdrawing from its own frontiers.'

A cocktail of loss stirred with the recall of vanished pleasure is ever present in the literature of rail travel – moments fleetingly experienced and then lost for ever. Here is Auden's 'Night Mail' ever hurrying on with 'letters of thanks, letters from banks, letters of joy from girl and boy'. For Edward Thomas it was the sublime moment when his express train paused at Adlestrop and 'for that minute a blackbird sang'. Philip Larkin momentarily peeks from a train into the romantic lives of strangers in 'The Whitsun Weddings'. For Thomas Hardy life is never the same after a snatched kiss at the barrier in 'On the Departure Platform'. 'Each a glimpse and gone for ever!' as Robert Louis Stevenson puts it in his famous 'From a Railway Carriage'.

Much more than merely agents of commerce and industry, the railways are loved because they encapsulate the whole gamut of human life and experience. They are the focus of emotions and the stuff of memories. The railway station, observe social historians Jeffrey Richards and John Mackenzie, is a gateway through which people pass 'in profusion on a variety of missions – a place of motion and emotion, arrival and sorrow, parting and reunion'. It is a place of 'countless stories' – of drama, mystery and adventure.

Yet many of these stories belong to a world long gone – lyrically described by Gilbert and David St John Thomas in their charming book *Double Headed*:

Railways are in a world of their own; they are segregated from the rest of the nation, and yet they serve it. They are self-contained, definable, understandable even by attentive amateurs and therefore welcoming to escapists; yet they are ubiquitous, infinitely diverse, complex within their own limits and wrapped in their own mystique. They have their own language, their own telephone network, their eating houses, factories and estates; they have their own slums, palaces, mausoleums and rustic beauty; they offer majesty and meanness, laughter, wonder and tears.

Not much of this could be said of the railways of today. It is hardly surprising then that we should invest so much emotion in romantic nostalgia. Who could disagree with that most poetic of railway historians Cuthbert Hamilton Ellis when he wrote (in 1947),

Surely it was always summer when we made our first railway journeys. Only from later boyhood do we remember what fog was like at Liverpool Street . . . or how the Thames Valley looked between Didcot and Oxford when there was naught but steel-grey water upon the drowned meadows. No, it was always summer! Sun shone on the first blue engine to be seen, a Somerset & Dorset near Poole; there was sunshine most dazzling

5

on a Great Western brass dome; the sun shone on an extraordinary mustard-coloured engine of the London, Brighton & South Coast.

'Nostalgic?' asks Hamilton Ellis. 'If so, why not?'

And why not, indeed? This sense of what the railways of the past signify to us has been heightened recently by a renaissance of railway enthusiasm. Gone are the days when those with an interest in railways were derided as trainspotters, anoraks or rivet counters, and mocked in the routine of almost every second-rate comedian on the stand-up circuit. The mark of respectability came in autumn 2014 when the National Railway Museum staged an exhibition called Trainspotting, at which various celebrities 'came out' to declare their interest in what twenty years ago was the preserve of the nerd.

Actually, railway enthusiasm never really went away and – despite the mockers – has a long and noble history. The first railway enthusiast can be reckoned to be the actress Fanny Kemble, who in 1830, at the age of twenty-one, just before the opening of the Liverpool & Manchester Railway, charmed George Stephenson into letting her ride with him on the locomotive. The engine, she gasped, was 'a magical machine, with its flying white breath and rhythmical, unvarying pace'. Recognition of what was to become a national pursuit initially came when Stephenson's 1825 engine *Locomotion* was put on public display on a plinth at Darlington station in 1857. Soon, upright professional men were indulging their hobby in a manner not dissimilar to butterfly collecting or philately. By the turn of century they had their own magazine and their own place to go in London, the Railway Club – as smart an institution in its own way as the Garrick or the Oxford and Cambridge.

Before its decline into unfashionability in the 1980s trainspotting had been a national cult in which men and boys turned out in all weathers on platforms all over the land, accompanied by their bible – a well-thumbed copy of the Ian Allan *Locospotters' Guide*. I recall having to fight my way to the ends of the platforms at King's Cross and Paddington through throngs of boys with notebooks and lapels plastered with enamel badges of their favourite engines. Then we discovered Pink Floyd and girls – and all grew up.

These days things have come full circle, with hedge fund managers in the City indulging their baby-boomer passions by spending millions buying and restoring vintage express steam locomotives to run on the main line – motivated not by profit but by the sheer joy of the thing. This is probably not surprising, since railway enthusiasm is the ultimate nostalgia in the imagination of what Orwell called a 'nation of collectors'. And why should such pleasures have to be defended? As the historian Roger Lloyd wrote in his book *The Fascination of Railways*, 'I have never met a lover of railways who felt the slightest need to produce any justification for his pleasure. Why should he?' The National Railway Museum even had the confidence to commission some verse from the poet Ian McMillan giving trainspotting a modern family feel:

It's a life filled with moments that ring like a bell,
With elation the thrill of the chase;
It's a smile from your dad that says 'Yes, all is well'
As he matches the grin on your face.
This is a hobby that never will pall.
Tomorrow's a spotting day. Well, aren't they all?

In this spirit I have chosen sixteen icons through which I unashamedly celebrate the lost delights of Britain's railways. The following chapters are not primarily about old engines, though there are plenty here. Nor do they represent a critique of Richard Beeching, whose 1963 report led to the slashing of the national rail network – although there are many lines here over which his shadow fell. Rather, in the 'journeys' of my title I've undertaken an odyssey which took me from Preston to Paris and Baker Street to Bangkok to celebrate the best of what has gone from our railways. I'm entirely with the railway historian Bryan Morgan when he writes in his evocative book *The End of the Line* that 'the words on an Ordnance Map "Track of Old Railway" have the power deeply to move me, and when I discover the scar itself I have to discover where it is going and what is left of its furniture'.

And so I walked over the crumbling viaducts of what was once the highest railway in England; I uncovered the furthest outpost of the London Tube buried in the undergrowth of the Buckinghamshire countryside. I rode today's fastest train from Scotland to London to summon up the great days of the Anglo-Scottish expresses. I trudged through the back streets of provincial towns to stand on the sites of old stations where the hopes and dreams of Victorian visionaries were raised and dashed. I relived the world of Rowland Emmet and William Heath Robinson on the tracks of some of the most eccentric railways ever built. I sat in a car park by the sea where the laughter once echoed from happy excursionists piling off trains from Lancashire and Yorkshire factories and mills. In all these journeys I've tried to re-inhabit the essential character of the railways as they once were and to distil the romance that has been irretrievably lost.

Maybe surprisingly, I didn't generally find what I sought on Britain's preserved 'heritage' railways – booming though they are, with 108 of them currently flourishing and attracting more than seven million visitors each year. It's true that without them none of today's children would ever imbibe the distinctive sounds and scents of the steam age. Yet to me their reality, with a few exceptions, seems not quite genuine. I'm with Muriel Searle, author of *Lost Lines*, who wrote, 'The trains puff satisfactorily enough but are dedicated to pleasure instead of running a genuine everyday transport service, for which they were built. They carry tourists, but no farmer to market or housewives to the shops, pet dogs on leads, but not crates of live hens; a modicum of holiday baggage in some instances, but not punnets of Cheddar strawberries to Bristol or crates of Clark's shoes to John o' Groats.'

For me the essential flavour of the railways of the past is often best divined standing on some overgrown embankment, beneath the ruins of an ivy-covered viaduct or amid the last fragments of some grand city terminus such as the old Euston or the demolished Birmingham Snow Hill or Nottingham Victoria, gently reconstructing the humanity and the grandeur that was once there. If you wait long enough between somewhere and nowhere, the past can often return with surprising clarity. Even a high-speed journey to Paris on the Eurostar helped resurrect for me the ghosts of the glamorous days of the old boat trains. Likewise a delicious lunch on one of today's weekday trains to the West Country was a journey back to the great days of the splendid restaurant cars of the golden age.

Meanwhile, we must be cautious about over-egging the nostalgia. Compared with the 'good old days' there is so much that is better about the modern railway. As I write this, sitting in front of me is the *ABC Railway Guide* from February 1953, with its well-worn buff cover and adverts for Lemon Hart Rum and *Punch* magazine — as familiar in the homes of our parents as an old Bible or prayer book. We may regret their passing, yet it paints a dismal picture of the train services of even the recent past. Back then the railway journey from Euston to Manchester, for example, took around four hours with gaps of up to two hours between trains. Today there are three trains every hour taking half the time. Name almost any journey on the main lines of Britain and the story is mostly the same.

As well as being faster, today's trains are infinitely safer and cleaner too – air-conditioning rather than smuts in the eye. Even the remotest branch lines have it better, with regular timetables and no more wondering when the train will come on a windswept platform in the middle of nowhere. Electronic information is ubiquitous, and if you fancy it, all today's train companies have real-time train information on their websites and apps, as well as Twitter feeds. The world defined by the *ABC Railway Guide* is already in the trash.

For all this, though, we may wonder if in fifty years' time we would ever be able to speak lovingly of today's railways with the warmth of Hamilton Ellis in the concluding words of *The Trains We Loved*:

> These were the trains we loved; grand, elegant and full of grace. We knew them and they belonged to the days when we first gazed on the magic of cloud shadows sweeping over the Downs, when we first became fully aware of the smell of a Wiltshire village after rain, or when we first saw a Scottish mountain framed in a double rainbow so vivid that no painter dared to try to record it . . . They were the days when the steam locomotive, unchallenged, bestrode the world like a friendly giant.
>
> If this is your world, read on.

Chapter One

The Holy Grail of lost railways

The Slow and Dirty it may have been for some, but the
old Somerset & Dorset remains, for its many devotees
today, the most romantic and alluring of all the vanished
lines of Britain. Did its origins in Glastonbury help
weave the spell?

Blinking through the darkness, I'm half a mile on foot
into one of the longest and most notorious railway
tunnels in Britain, deep under the hills south of Bath. But
the only puffing to be heard is from cyclists exultantly
whisking through the gears, Chris Hoy-like, as they swish
along the old trackbed. This is a miraculous transformation
of an old railway line, in which the Combe Down Tunnel

of the old Somerset & Dorset Joint Railway has been turned into Britain's most unusual cycle way. Who would imagine that this was once such a smoky and ash-filled inferno that train crews would pee on the coal to keep down the dust before entering and lie on the floor with their overalls over their faces to prevent suffocation.

But then there has always been a magic about the old S&D – still nearly fifty years after its closure the holy grail for enthusiasts of abandoned railways. The most romantic, the most alluring in the tug of its nostalgia, this most magical of lines is associated too with the magical village of Glastonbury. Never mind the Settle & Carlisle, the Liverpool & Manchester, the Stockton & Darlington or any other famous railways with double-barrelled names you care to mention, the Somerset & Dorset rides high permanently in the pantheon of nostalgia.

All those other 'joint' lines with similar names have melded into the mists of time. Who now remembers the old Midland & South Western Junction, lovely though it was, running in rural splendour through the spine of southern England? The venerable Midland & Great Northern, full of Norfolk seaside memories of yore, still has its loyal following. But, ah, the S&D! At the mention of the name, grown men and women go misty-eyed and fumble for their Specsavers wipes. Where were you that early spring day in 1966 when the S&D shut for ever? You can be sure that every rail enthusiast worth their enamel badges has a view.

So how can it be that a rail byway – chronically loss-making for most of its life and dubbed the Slow and Dirty or Shabby and Doubtful by its passengers – should acquire such mythical status? Never mind that this seventy-one-mile backwater from Bath to Bournemouth was briefly dubbed the Swift and Delightful by one employee. (It was reckoned that he had either received a bung from the management or was declared insane shortly afterwards.) It is a story of high drama and big personalities, whose names still resonate today.

Here is proud Victorian entrepreneur James Clark, inventor of the sheepskin slipper, who founded the eponymous family shoe firm in 1825, still one of Somerset's most important industries. It was Clark's vision in seeking an outlet to transport his products from Glastonbury to the sea that led to a proposal for the establishment of the line in 1851. On the other side is another old Somerset dynasty, the Waugh family. The novelist Evelyn Waugh's grandfather spoke out against the railway after the army of navvies engaged in its building had terrified the family nanny while out for a walk with the pram. Add too one of the unsung visionaries of the Victorian era. Robert Read, the company secretary of the railway, with his big beard and sparkling eyes, may not be much remembered now, but without him the railway could not have been built, and would not have survived into the twentieth century and thus into today's mythology.

At the risk of heresy, we may even include the good Lord himself. According to Somerset legend, after the Crucifixion, Joseph of Arimathea, uncle of Jesus Christ, sailed up the Bristol Channel into an inland sea that extended to Glastonbury – the mythical Avalon – where he planted his staff, which became the Holy Thorn. There are those who reckon that he may even have brought his nephew along in person during the lost years between Jesus' boyhood and ministry. Could 'those feet in ancient time' that walked in Blake's words 'on England's mountains green' have trodden what would one day become the tracks of the Somerset & Dorset Joint Railway? There are some diehard S&D fans so unswerving in their faith they would probably swear it to be true!

Even so, there wasn't much glory or holiness about the S&D's progenitor, the little Somerset Central Railway, built across a bleak turf bog the fourteen miles from Highbridge to Glastonbury. The sneerers derided it as going 'from nowhere to nowhere', although this didn't deter a vast procession on its opening day – 17 August 1854 – carrying banners proclaiming 'Railways and Civilisation' and 'Where ther's a will ther's a way' [*sic*] winding around the ruins of Glastonbury Abbey to a spacious tent where a 'cold collation' was served to 500 people, followed by three hours of speeches, along with 800 'working class dinners' served in yet another tent.

But these were optimistic times, and before long the line was heading from somewhere to somewhere. The tracks were extended to the tiny port of Burnham-on-Sea, with a steamer link across the Bristol Channel to Cardiff. Robert Read, driven by his family motto '*Res non verba*', was dreaming of even bigger things, with an eye on the neighbouring Dorset Central, whose tracks were working their way north from near Poole. But could the two ever meet up to create a major route running from the Bristol Channel to the English Channel – particularly when built in the opposing gauges of Britain's two greatest railway engineering geniuses: Brunel's 7 feet ¼ inch and Stephenson's 4 feet 8½ inches?

An ingenious solution was found in laying one set of tracks within the other – a bit like one of the madcap schemes from Heath Robinson's surreal 1935 cartoon book *Railway Ribaldry* – although it didn't need to last for long, as Brunel's dream of a broad-gauge Britain was dead by the 1870s. Meanwhile, the Somerset & Dorset Joint Railway, as it had become, was not just running coast to coast, but even advertising a service from the Bristol Channel to France, leaving Burnham at 8 a.m. and docking in Cherbourg at 6 p.m., just ten hours later. It was an astonishing achievement for a little undertaking with just one main line, and a journey time that could not be achieved even by the most ambitious of high-speed trains today.

But there were even grander plans still. Work began in

1872 on an extension to Bath, creating a money-spinning link from a tiny junction bearing the quaint name of Evercreech with the Highbridge branch, linking in at Bristol with the Midland Railway main line to Birmingham to the north. In the middle of nowhere it might have been, but little Evercreech Junction – in the minds of the dreamers – was to become the Clapham Junction of the west. And there would be a tantalising harvest of black gold to be reaped in the rich coalfields around Radstock along the way. At least that was the idea.

But it was one thing building a railway across a former seabed on the Somerset levels, and another blasting a route over the formidable Mendip Hills, where 3,000 men smashed their way through rock, twisting and turning to find negotiable gradients to Masbury summit, 811 feet above sea level. It was a fearsome and audacious enterprise that terrified the locals. Arthur Waugh, Evelyn's father, whose own father was a country doctor at Midsomer Norton, painted a vivid picture of the construction in his autobiography, *One Man's Road*, recalling how the peace of his favourite walk, which he took regularly with his nanny, was shattered, with the countryside scored by 'a long and scarlet wound and loud explosions . . . Several of our favourite trees were lying on the ground; the earth was turned up; boards, wheelbarrows and the boots of loud, rough-voiced men had beaten down the primroses into a pulp of red soil.' A swarm of navvies apparently shouted profanities in the wake of the perambulator, forcing the horrified and red-faced nanny to flee in embarrassment.

The new line was judged by others an engineering triumph, but the builders of the original dead-flat railway may not have appreciated the degree to which Somerset is one of Britain's counties of greatest geological contrast. This is a rare place where mushy sea-level bogs jostle shoulders with bleak and unforgiving rocky hills. The cost of two years' blasting, the construction of seven viaducts and four tunnels, along with many cuttings and embankments, as well as buying new engines, exhausted the company's finances. Crushed by the sheer weight of their overambition, the directors were forced to sell out, doing a deal with the mighty Midland Railway to partner with the London & South Western Railway. This was a marvellous chance for the brass-nosed money men of Derby to extend their empire deep into the south-west, much to the fury of the Great Western, whose turf was being invaded.

Ironically, this shotgun marriage spawned a moderately successful railway, with beer, coal, bricks and other hardware carried from north to south as well as a burgeoning holiday trade taking advantage of growing leisure time for the toiling masses. For the workers in the mills of Lancashire and metal-bashing factories of the Black Country, the S&D was the conduit to a precious week's holiday on a sandy beach in the sunny south. A journal kept in 1910 by J. Thornton Burge, the stationmaster at Templecombe, published in the *Railway and Travel Monthly*, records no fewer than 200 trains and engines passing his signal box in twenty-four hours on a peak summer's day.

Even so, the charms of the S&D remained those of a predominantly rural backwater. Because of the line's isolation the staff were a close-knit bunch. 'Family spirit' were words constantly used in personal recollections by employees along the line. It was a quality that defined the ethos of the railway, since fathers, sons, uncles and cousins staffed the engines, the signal boxes and the booking offices and handed their jobs down through the generations. Drivers were even allowed to have their own personal engines and would take them to the railway's works at Highbridge for repair and collect them afterwards.

As well as keeping morale high, the closeness of the community allowed much flexing of the rule book. A favourite jape among crews was to grease the rails of the opposite track while in a cutting and then to discharge a vast cloud of steam. When the next train in the opposite direction hit the cloud, its wheels would spin helplessly. When the steam cleared their colleagues were also helpless – but this time with laughter. Crews were especially fond of their jimmies, home-made hooks that held down the blast pipes of the engines to improve their performance – highly illegal, of course. Alan Hammond records in his book *The Splendour of the Somerset & Dorset Railway* how a locomotive was driven through an engine-shed wall one day when the chairman of British Railways Western Region was doing an inspection. The damaged bricks were swiftly put back in place and nothing was ever said.

This is not to downplay two very serious accidents on the line. On 7 August 1876 fifteen people died in a head-on collision between Radstock and Wellow, and on 20 November 1929 the crew of a goods train was overcome by fumes in Combe Down Tunnel, killing the driver and two other staff. The train ran out of control, crashing into the entrance of Bath goods yard. But mostly the safety record was good, with one locomotive superintendent, Alfred Whitaker, inventing a much admired system in which a token could be passed on automatically from the locomotive to the signalman, thus avoiding two trains being on the same section of single track at the same time.

For most of its existence life along the line generally bumbled along in its usual slow and dirty way. A train would sometimes come to a halt in the middle of nowhere, much to the bemusement of passengers, while its crew picked mushrooms in a line-side field before frying them with bacon and eggs on a hot shovel in the firebox. Another perk for staff was the clutches of eggs retrieved from bird crates after their live cargoes had been released from pigeon trains.

There were other oddities. If you listened carefully outside the waiting room at remote Masbury station you might discern the strains of 'Praise my Soul, the King of Heaven' as the porter played the harmonium at Sunday evening services there. The community surrounding little Shoscombe and Single Hill Halt was still inaccessible to buses until 1966, and for thirty-six years you would have found the Misses Tapper, later Mrs Beeho and Mrs Chivers, ready for a chinwag in the booking office, which they ran like a community centre.

But somehow there was more to the S&D than another secondary railway marooned in yokel world. There was always that dash of quinine, that twist of lime that gave the railway its distinctive flavour. The liveries, for instance, were among the smartest of any railway in Britain, with engines and carriages alike painted in smart Prussian blue lined out in gold, contrasting with polished brass set off with a smart crest and scarlet buffer blocks. The staff meanwhile turned out in snazzy green corduroy.

Unusual among country railways, the S&D had its own dedicated express train – although the description is something of a misnomer, since the famous Pines Express, carrying holidaymakers from the Midlands and the north, took more than seven hours for the 248½-mile journey from Manchester to Bournemouth. Named in 1927 after the pine trees that are said to lend the resort its health-giving air, the train meandered through Birmingham and Gloucester before joining the S&D at Bath, where the Mendips led to some spectacular displays of fire and steam from locomotives storming Masbury summit with their heavy loads. Who would want to change trains in London when you could go direct by the Pines Express?

Few engines were powerful enough to tackle this mighty train single-handed, and some astonishing locomotive combinations were turned out – unique on Britain's railways. Here was a modern Southern Railway West Country Class Pacific bunkered up to an elderly ex-Midland Railway 4F freight engine of Victorian provenance, or perhaps a tiny Edwardian 4-4-0 locomotive of a type which had mostly been consigned to museums. At the end of the 1950s there was a living cavalcade of British engineering history on view in all its glory for anyone who cared to spectate at the lineside on a summer Saturday morning. The locomotive department even threw into the mix the eleven distinctive 2-8-0 freight locomotives specially designed for the line by the Midland in 1914, which for years had trundled humble goods trains over the Mendip banks. Like the anthropomorphic creations of the Reverend W. Awdry's *Thomas* books, these suddenly discovered fame on passenger services, outclassing engines half a century younger.

It was only at the very end that someone discovered an engine that could tackle these weighty summer passenger trains unaided. But the BR 9F 2-10-0 freight locomotives, built in the 1950s, arrived on the scene too late. The times were a-changing, as the motor factories of the Midlands churned out ever more affordable Austins, Morrises and Hillmans, and the final Pines over the S&D ran on 8 September 1962 – appropriately in the charge of 9F 2-10-0 *Evening Star*, the last steam locomotive built by British Railways and resplendent in green passenger livery. Subsequently rerouted via Oxford, the Pines lingered on for another five years, but its glory was gone.

By this time the long slow loss of the S&D's identity had become inexorable. The winding down of the north Somerset coalfield, which at one time had produced 200,000 tons a year, was a major factor in its decline. In 1973 the field would close completely, like the S&D before it. Although the line had retained some autonomy after 1923, when Britain's railways were grouped into four big companies, the Prussian-blue locomotives were painted over with unlined black and the brilliant coaches covered in a rather drab Southern Railway green. The S&D locomotive works at Highbridge was shut, and new-fangled road vehicles steadily ate into the market for transporting milk and farm goods. Although the long-distance passenger services prospered after nationalisation in 1948, the outlook for local trains was bleak. The service to Burnham and to the cathedral city of Wells was withdrawn on 29 October 1951, the Wells branch latterly carrying a grand total of six passengers a day.

There was a bittersweet poignancy to the celebration of the railway's centenary in 1954, since, in their hearts, everyone knew that a way of life that had lasted so long was nearly at an end. More than 100 of the 250 living descendants of founder James Clark, many of them still employed by the family firm, travelled on a special train from Glastonbury bearing 800 people. Some were in period costume, bewhisk-ered and crinolined. The driver and fireman were bearded and bowler-hatted. The sun shone, the drinks flowed and a jolly time was had by all. But a dozen years later the Somerset & Dorset would be dead and gone.

Further life was sucked out of the line when British Railways Western Region took over in 1963, rationalising services even more. Many said this was final revenge by functionaries up at Paddington for the deal done with the Midland behind the old Great Western's back the previous century. Cynics predicted the S&D was condemned to become a withered arm of the Western Region – a moribund and hopelessly uneconomic branch line. They were right. And so the scene was set for the fall of Beeching's axe.

As closure loomed, official sabotage became the order of the day. Freight trains were diverted and maintenance was abandoned. Weeds ran riot on the tracks and in the flower beds of once immaculate platforms. Locomotives plodded on with minimum repairs, and when they failed they were scrapped. Timetables were made as inconvenient as possible. As Kenneth Hudson reported in 1965 in the BBC programme *How to Kill a Railway*, 'Utterly meaningless connections continued to feed non-existent passengers into a "ghost" Pines Express' long after the train was discontinued. The inevitable closure was announced for 3 January 1966 – a catastrophe for communities along the line but also for the railwaymen who for generations had given years of loyal service.

Emotions ran high, and angry staff took matters into their own hands. On New Year's Day a farewell rail tour double-headed by two big Class 8F locomotives was brought to a halt by the signals at Binegar. The crew stepped down into the frosty darkness to encounter local signalman Ernie Cross, standing resolutely between the tracks and brandishing a statement which he flourished in front of the cameras of the assembled press. But his one-man protest against the 'vicious attitude' of railway managers was futile. Although the closure was delayed by the failure of a replacement bus to materialise, it was ruthlessly pushed through just weeks later.

The end couldn't have been more dispiriting. The last weekend of 5 and 6 March was for the railway's historian Robin Atthill 'a traumatic experience for all who had worked on the line or lived near it and loved it'. As the line played out its final hours 111 years after its birth, it was not just the last call for the Somerset & Dorset, but the end of steam in the West Country, and for many it signified something even more profound – the extinguishing for ever of all that was romantic about the railways of Britain.

In a bid to cling on to the final elusive moments two thousand people travelled over the line aboard chartered specials pursued by streams of cars through the byways of Somerset and Dorset. 'Every bridge, every cutting,' Atthill reported, 'was manned with onlookers who had made the most complicated cross-country journeys and infiltrated into the most impossible lanes to reach a bridge or crossing.'

The fields were black with figures rushing across country bearing cameras and tripods and tape recorders to get their pictures of the two burnished green Southern Pacifics on perhaps the grandest special ever to run on the railway. The locomotives spouted columns of fire into the darkening sky as they breasted the 1:50 gradient up to Masbury summit. By contrast, the last of the service trains, one carrying a coffin, wheezed with the weight of the hordes bidding their farewells. Some wondered whether, in their run-down state, the filthy and clapped-out locomotives would even make it to the end of the day.

Many other devotees had already said their private farewells. 'I had made my own last journey earlier in the week,' Atthill recorded, 'on an afternoon of brilliant sunshine and sharp showers. At almost every station there were old friends finishing their last week's work; dead engines filled the siding at Bath; in the shedmaster's office, the portrait of Alfred Whitaker [the old locomotive superintendent] still glowered from the wall; soon after four o'clock a porter moved along the platform with a long pole, turning up the gas lights.' Within days the line would be snuffed out. No longer slow and dirty but sabotaged and defeated.

Charmed it may have been during its lifetime, but how do we explain the modern magic of the S&D, which remains the most fabled of railways half a century after it closed. This Delphi of railway enthusiasm, this holy grail for gricers, has a lure at least as strong as its grander contemporaries such as the Settle & Carlisle or West Highland Line, which were saved from closure and are still alive today. If anything, its spiritual power grows more alluring as its physical presence crumbles ever more relentlessly into the landscape —

whittled away irreversibly by the elements. The Somerset & Dorset Joint Railway dead captures the imagination as potently as when it was alive, inspiring countless hundreds of articles in railway journals and with at least six preservation societies devoted to its resurrection in some form. At the last reckoning the Somerset & Dorset Heritage website listed fifty-five current titles about the line for sale. Surviving artefacts have found themselves in the auction room stratosphere, with a Bath Green Park 'totem' station sign under the hammer for more than £5,000 at the end of 2014.

Perhaps the key lies in that it outlived many of its rivals and that its demise coincided with the vast swell of nostalgia that came to a climax as the Beeching closures were implemented, symbolising the end of an era for the country railway and the age of timelessness and lost innocence it seemed to represent. Then there were all those lovely station names, just reeking of Olde England: Corfe Mullen, Shillingstone, Blandford Forum, Sturminster Newton, Shepton Mallet, Midsomer Norton, Edington Burtle – and of course Glastonbury with its eternal lure.

The mood was captured by the comic duo Michael Flanders and Donald Swann with their song 'Slow Train' in 1963 – an elegy for the lost world of the country railway – whose opening lyrics ran, 'No more will I go from Blandford Forum and Mortehoe/ On the slow train from Midsomer Norton to Mumby Road'.

In the same year Poet Laureate John Betjeman made a classic BBC film – *Branch Line Railway* – about a Somerset & Dorset journey, filmed in grainy black and white and tinged with his characteristic note of melancholy. Riding the train to Burnham in his battered homburg and shabby raincoat, he eulogised, 'Forget motor cars. Get rid of anxiety. And here to the rhythm of the Somerset & Dorset Joint Railway dream again that ambitious Victorian dream which caused this long railway still to be running through deepest, quietest, flattest, remotest, least spoilt Somerset.'

The image was burnished too by a gloriously eccentric amateur photographer called Ivo Peters, scion of the family soap-making business, who spent the post-war years chasing up and down the line in his beloved 4.25-litre Mark VI Bentley with his elderly medium-format camera. Peters produced one of the finest-ever picture portfolios of railways in the landscape – endowing the iconography of the Somerset & Dorset with an enduring lustre. Fittingly, after he died in 1989 his ashes were scattered on Masbury summit.

Nor must we overlook that other important ingredient in the S&D mix – the nostalgic power of the childhood seaside holiday, with its capacity to bathe memory in a veneer of sunshine that never quite fades. I recall as a teenager in the 1960s escaping the tedium of a Bournemouth boarding-house holiday with my parents with a trip along the S&D from Bournemouth West to Evercreech Junction. It was an undistinguished journey behind a dirty British Railways Standard tank engine at the end of its functioning life, but I can summon with total recall the shaft of sun through the compartment window in which the dust rising from the ancient seats seemed to do a dance as the brilliant summer light shimmered through the line-side trees.

Some other essential elements may be stirred into the alchemy. There have been few railways in England where heavy expresses were worked so hard over such difficult terrain. Unlike many comparable railways in their declining years, the line stayed purely steam-operated to the end, unpolluted in the minds of enthusiasts by the new diesels that heralded the coming era of standardisation. And right up to closure, as Betjeman's charming film showed, the railway was a perfect period piece. There would be a coal fire burning in the waiting room at Evercreech Junction, and in spring a bowl of primroses always graced the beeswaxed Victorian table.

There was no better way, as one writer put it, to escape into the Victorian era than to spend a winter's afternoon at Bath Green Park station. So perfect was the atmosphere that on the day closure was announced it was being used as a set for a film of Robert Louis Stevenson's comedy *The Wrong Box*, the consummate stand-in for a Victorian London terminus.

The mood still abounds, as I enjoy the coolness of the old station after my long walk along the trackbed on my way back from Combe Down Tunnel and beyond. The Green Park buildings have been preserved, and the elegant sixty-six-foot arched roof now doubles up as a shelter for the car park of the Sainsbury's supermarket built in the old goods yard. This was always an airy and elegant station, with its imposing booking hall and grand Victorian lavatories. Aesthetes claim its handsome classical facade of Bath stone makes a far more fitting contribution to the city's architectural landscape than the Jacobean gables and mullions of Brunel's Great Western main-line station along the road, although the short platforms were unpopular with trainspotters, who could find their coveted quarry out of sight at the front of long summer trains.

These days the old booking office is a restaurant, while chic shops reflecting the laid-back image of modern Bath occupy the old platform offices. I'm desperately thirsty after my trek over the track, but instead of a greasy railway buffet cuppa I can choose from a vast range of exotic beverages, including an 'Indian roadside tea' or a 'quenching coconut juice'. I select the latter from the organic juice bar in what was once the station tea room – where once the smell of boiled cabbage might have predominated. But stop! Hark for a moment . . . Is that hissing coming from the cappuccino machine? Or is that the engine at the head of the afternoon train? All stations to Midford, Masbury and Midsomer Norton. Destination: the mists of time.

Chapter Two

Final ticket for the boat train

The exotic life and death of the Night Ferry from Victoria to the Continent, haunt of spies, diplomats, starlets and sultans. Even in today's Eurostar era, its memory stands proud as Britain's only truly international train.

Who-oo-osh! Our Eurostar train – all 800 high-tech tons of it and three quarters of a mile long – accelerates like a rocket out of London's St Pancras. Motors whirring, it shoots out from underneath Sir William Barlow's great arched roof, and before long we're flashing through the outer fringes of east London. We're over the Dartford Crossing in a trice and soon the orchards of Kent pass by at 186 mph in a blur of apple blossom. A hot cheese toastie is in prospect, in the exotically-named Café Metropole – otherwise known as the buffet car. Could there be a more desirable way to get to Paris than aboard this marvel of high-speed rail technology – fast, efficient, super-smooth, connecting the capitals of England and France in just over two hours? And all with a bit of fake gallic glamour.

But for all the slickness, there's something indefinable missing. Aboard these silky Class 373 Eurostar trains it's easy to nod off – no more perfect opportunity than in the blackness of the Channel Tunnel. Suddenly I'm dreaming, but not about tackling a rubbery chunk of *fromage* in the minimalist Philippe Starck decor of the 20.06 to Paris; instead I'm far away, having polished off a splendid silver-service supper on a starched white tablecloth in an elegant dining car heading for an exotic foreign city.

In this journey of dreams, we had sauntered down Platform 2 at Victoria to take the 10 p.m. Paris train. We'd perhaps already enjoyed a Tom Collins in the American Bar at the Savoy before indulging in a snifter at the station's Grosvenor Hotel. The supper prepared by a French chef in the restaurant car, washed down with champagne and claret, was exquisite. As for the company, it seemed both mysterious and glamorous – surely that chap with the distinctive dark-haired lady at the next table in the dining car can't be the Duke of Windsor? That swarthy fellow whispering conspiratorially to his companion – he looks uncannily like a creation of Ian Fleming.

Never mind – it's time for bed and the short walk along the corridor to a cosy berth, where the black-gloved conductor asks if sir or madam needs anything else, before we slip between crisp white cotton sheets. Faintly, amid our dreams, in the middle of the night there are some clanks and clangs and what sounds like the moan of a steamship's hooter and the soothing slap of waves on a shore. Though the train appears curiously to have stopped, we feel ourselves being rocked ever so gently back to sleep.

We awake to a timpani of thuds, rattles and clangs, along with a hiss of steam. There's a plaintive sigh of escaping air from the rattling brake system and we emerge, with a slight thump, over a wobbly bridge-like contraption, past an unmistakably French gendarme in his distinctive uniform. In the grey dawn there's the rumble of a mighty French Pacific, product of the world's greatest modern steam-engine designer, André Chapelon. It backs onto the front with the alien owl-like shriek of its whistle. The driver – with his beret and goggles, looking for all he's worth like Jean Gabin in *La Bête Humaine* – helps set the scene.

With a whiff of Disque Bleu floating on the air, there's the hum of commuter voices on the platform, since this is the fastest service of the day up to Paris. Racing through the flat country of the Nord, we are sped on our way by the many crossing keepers, often exquisitely manicured black-clad ladies of indeterminate age. And there is no mistaking where we are. On the sides of houses are louche-sounding advertisements for Dubonnet or Byrrh ('the best liqueur') or maybe for Dubonnet's great rival St Raphael Quinquina.

Paris is in sight now, and with a discreet '*Pardon, Messieurs et Mesdames*' the conductor glances at our passports. Luxuriously, unobtrusively unheralded by the bureaucracy of immigration and unsung by any public-address system, we arrive under the great roof of Paris's Gare du Nord. The conductor unfolds a chamois to clean the soot off the door handles before we alight. Joy of joys, this is the first time we have had to leave our carriage since we tucked ourselves in somewhere in the Garden of England.

But this is no fantasy of a jaded modern rail traveller. This seeming idyll is how it once was aboard what remains, at the time of writing, the only truly international train in history ever to operate between England and the Continent. The Night Ferry, which ran between London's Victoria and Paris, Brussels and Basle, was not some throwback to a vanished Victorian era; this was a grand train offering the ultimate in modern comfort: travel between London and the heart of Europe without ever having to leave your bed. Its last service ran as recently as 30 October 1980.

Of course, there have been other boat trains – and glamorous ones too. None more so than the Golden Arrow, which also ran between Victoria and Paris, with its famous umber and cream art deco Pullman cars and haute cuisine menus. Then there was the Emerald Isle Express, connecting London with the Holyhead boat to Dun Laoghaire in Ireland, and the Hook Continental – infinitely glamorous, despite its mundane name – which conveyed its passengers comfortably to Holland from Liverpool Street via Harwich. But none could match the mystique of the Night Ferry, whose comfy sleeping cars rolled effortlessly onto specially adapted ships in the middle of the night, speeding on to their destinations on the opposite side of the Channel to arrive in time for breakfast. And nobody ever had to leave the warmth and comfort of their bed.

When the train was launched in 1936 it seemed such an obvious and brilliant idea. Yet astonishingly the idea of a roll-on, roll-off train had been tried in Britain only once before – back in time on 3 February 1850, when the directors of the newly opened Edinburgh, Perth & Dundee Railway were the first passengers to go to sea in a railway carriage, making an historic journey from the Scottish capital to Perth. When they got to the banks of the Forth, their train ran down a specially built drawbridge laid with track, known as a linkspan, connecting with another set of rails on the deck of the 389-ton ferry *Leviathan*. After the four-and-a-half-mile crossing to Burntisland on the other bank, the train was drawn off using a similar linkspan arrangement. Unfortunately, the twenty-foot tidal fall meant that the pitch of the drawbridges was too steep for the safety of passengers, although the *Leviathan* ran for another forty years, successfully transporting freight wagons until the opening of the great Forth Railway Bridge in 1890.

The idea of train ferries across the Channel might have seemed an obvious one. But the reality was endlessly delayed by plans to build a Channel tunnel, which were so plausible that digging on both sides of the Channel actually started in 1880. This was abandoned only because of British security fears, as war seemed to be on the horizon. Ironically, it was the military supply demands of World War I that finally got the cross-Channel train ferries going, with the first running from Southampton to Dieppe in December 1917, followed by Richborough in Kent to Calais, and Newhaven to Dieppe in February 1918. But although empty passenger carriages destined for use as hospital trains were conveyed on ferries across the Channel, there were still no services carrying real people.

Fast-forward to a very extravagant and lavish party in the port of Calais on 9 December 1922, attended by two of the grandest British grandees of railway travel, Sir Herbert Walker, chairman of the newly formed Southern Railway, and Lord Dalziel, chairman of the management committee of the Compagnie Internationale des Wagons-Lits, which in its short history ran some of the most sumptuous, luxurious and sybaritic trains in history. The champagne in Calais was flowing for the company's relaunch of one of the world's most star-studded services, the Calais-Méditerranée Express, otherwise known as the Blue Train – Le Train Bleu. This was the fabled night express that conveyed some of the world's richest people from northern Europe to the French Riviera.

There was only one engineering firm in the entire world which could supply new carriages for the launch quickly enough, and that was the Leeds Forge Company, which had pioneered the use of pressed steel – much lighter than the wood traditionally used for building railway carriages. The company engineered forty luxury sleeping cars of all-steel construction, the most comfortable ever built. And there was no better way to ship them over to the Continent than aboard one of the specially equipped wartime train ferries.

The CIWL was the brainchild of an obscure Belgian, Georges Nagelmackers, who had been sent by his family to the United States in the 1860s to recover from a broken love affair. Instead he transferred his affections to luxury trains. So impressed was he with the ultra-comfortable night trains of George Pullman, American founder of the famous Pullman Car Company, that he vowed to bring similar luxury to Europe. Soon after its foundation in 1874, the Compagnie's WL trademark, brandished by two lions, had become the favoured brand of luxury travel, patronised by kings and presidents, princes, sheikhs and sultans.

The Compagnie was never defined by any borders, and its coaches ran magisterially across Europe, either as entire formations, such as the Orient Express, or attached to normal service trains. Although it never owned any locomotives, its trains, like the Nord Express from Paris to St Petersburg, or the Sud Express from Moscow to Vladivostok, became the stuff of legend, with carriages decorated by Lalique and publicity produced by Cassandre. Peking, Baghdad, Cairo, Tehran and Bucharest were among the roll-call of exotic destinations included on their routes.

How logical it seemed back in the 1920s to add another great international express – between the English and French capitals – to the stable, especially as the technology was there to make the crossing between England and France.

And British-built sleeping cars had already done the trip. But who could have forecast that the great financial crash was about to unfold, and it took years of dreaming and planning to build a ferry dock suitable for the trains at Dover, where the connection would be made to Dunkerque and then on to Paris. The engineering problems were enormous, compounded by the twenty-five-foot rise and fall of the tide at Dover, the rough Channel seas and fissures in the porous chalk beneath the dock. When finally completed, the *Railway Gazette* pronounced it one of the great engineering achievements of the day.

Even so, there was an embarrassing mishap when the inaugural VIP train ran from Paris on Tuesday 13 October 1936. *Quelle horreur!* One of the brand-new sleeping cars, carrying no less a panjandrum than the British foreign secretary, Sir John Simon, derailed on the quayside at Dover after being shunted off the *Hampton Ferry*, although there were no injuries. The first public train the following evening had a trouble-free passage, although it must have made a slightly odd sight, with the modern sleeping cars, specially built to fit the smaller British loading gauge, double-headed by two decidedly elderly locomotives, an L1 class 4-4-0 No. 1758, piloting a Victorian D1 Class 4-4-0 No. 1470. The return first class fare, including the sleeping car conductor's gratuity, was £9. 4s. od.

And there was such excitement! 'Emotionally moving,' is how the train's historians George Behrend and Gary Buchanan describe it in their book *Night Ferry*:

> At long last, the comfort, convenience, elegance, allure
> and above all safety and privacy of international over-
> night rail travel by Wagons-Lits 'Grand International
> Express' extended to England . . . In the 1930s the Great
> European Expresses were the accepted ways of European

travel. From Calais, sleeping cars departed nightly for Istanbul, Rome, Trieste, San Remo, Monte Carlo, Nice, Cannes and Bucharest. Thrice weekly they ran to Karlovy Vary (Carlsbad), Warsaw and on to the Russian frontier . . .

So what a thrill to step aboard in London! To see the same glamorous gold and blue cars, with their foreign French wording, drawn up at Victoria, made many rub their eyes in disbelief. On the waist at one end were the words 'Voiture-Lits I-II Classe' and at the other end 'Sleeping Car I-II Class', while above the windows were the proud words: 'Compagnie Internationale des Wagons-Lits et des Grands Express Europeens'.

You could almost smell the continental air as you passed through the tiny passport control room onto Platform 2 at Victoria. You surrendered your passport and your ticket (always known as a *bulletin*) at the door of the *voiture* to a conductor standing to attention, immaculate in brown uniform with gold piping and brass buttons, cap as flat as a French army officer's with a shiny black peak. And, of course, black gloves. There was a personal number on his lapel and discreetly pinned on the left breast pocket a badge with a small chevron marking every five years of service.

What a contrast to the scruffy porters of the domestic railway with their rolled-up sleeves and waistcoats. As one writer put it, 'You feel your journey has really started as soon as you step inside your cosy compartment – T. S. Eliot's "little den".' Even the business tycoons relaxed, especially if the conductor had discreetly popped the cork on a quarter-bottle of champagne. On the table was a little booklet, introducing the train, with all the connections from Paris, as well as a woodcut of Notre-Dame and a recommendation for a famous city-centre rotisserie. There was also a rather severe customs declaration form in four languages. It warned that you would be fined if you struck any item out. Many passengers were perplexed to be asked whether they 'had brought a carpet on the train', but woe betide any reckless passenger who deleted the question.

The complement of the Night Ferry is described in all its grandeur by Cecil J. Allen in his book *The Titled Trains of Great Britain*, written in 1946:

> The formation of the train from Dover to Victoria at peak periods rises to as much as two French vans and ten sleeping cars, all of International Sleeping Car Company's stock working through from Paris to London; then attached at Dover, a restaurant and kitchen car, buffet car, corridor first, two corridor seconds, another restaurant and kitchen car, and a first-class brake – twelve Continental and seven SR vehicles, making this about the heaviest passenger train in Great Britain.

Snuggled into your berth at Victoria, you would soon be on your way – the only sign that this was to be a very unusual train journey indeed were life jackets in the luggage rack and netting to stop luggage falling out in rough seas. You had to hope that the noticeboard on the platform announcing the condition of the Channel did not read, 'Heavy swell tonight'. Unusually too, for such a glamorous train, there would be nobody to see you off – bar a solitary railway policeman – and not a window to open, such were the strict requirements of the British customs.

Nor was it possible to see the train's two locomotives, way out in the darkness at the far end of the platform. If you had, you might have wondered, in the early days, why they should have been of such extreme vintage for such a state-of-the art train, causing them to puff and grunt, issuing huge billows of smoke and steam as each locomotive's four modest driving wheels got a grip on Grosvenor Bridge as they steamed out of the terminus. The answer was that the Southern Railway did not have a single modern locomotive powerful enough to pull the train single-handed.

To get over the problem, in 1939, Oliver Bulleid, the Southern's ingenious chief mechanical engineer, designed the revolutionary streamlined 2-8-2 Mikado locomotive specially for the Night Ferry. Sadly, war intervened, but if it had gone ahead, it would have been one of the most sophisticated and powerful steam locomotives ever built. Luckily, the Ministry of War Transport permitted Bulleid to build his big Merchant Navy Class Pacifics, all named after shipping lines, which soon became regulars on the train. How appropriate to be steaming towards Dover and beyond hauled by No. 21C1 *Channel Packet* or sister engines with famous nautical names such as *Cunard Line* or *French Line CGT*. Soon the lights of the London suburbs would recede and the cool Kent night air would waft through the tiny louvres of the non-opening windows.

Now the dining car beckoned, with plenty of time for a feast. Although the crossing was a mere eighty-seven miles from London, the journey to Dover Marine station would take nearly two hours. In the parlance of Pullman dining, dinner might consist of Soup of the Day with Golden Croutons, Roast Sussex Chicken & Sauté Potatoes, *Petits Pois*, Fruit Salad and Double Devon Cream and the Cheese Board. It might sound utilitarian today, but even in the post-war years it was an experience of positively gourmet quality. The Wagons-Lits conductors would also bring beer, spirits and champagne from the diner and serve you in your cabin, as British customs would not admit anything stronger than mineral water to be brought beforehand into the cabins.

By the time they reached Dover, passengers were starting to doze off, lulled on their way through the Kent countryside by the gentle rhythm of the track under the sleeping cars' firm suspension – helped on, no doubt, by the excellence of the fine wines in the dining car. With many in their slumbers, not all were able to appreciate the civil engineering marvels of the massive new ferry dock, specially constructed at Dover, that made their journey possible.

There was a short pause on the quayside as the less exalted passengers got off to walk along the covered passage to the ferry. Meanwhile an ancient tank engine would edge down, propelling its 'swinger' onto the sleeping cars. The swinger, nicknamed Queen Mary after the famous liner, was an old coach underframe with a cabin mounted at one end to protect the shunters from the elements. Ever so gently, the engine eased its charges down the special track to the linkspan. Passengers with keen hearing would know they were aboard by the echo from the ship's covered deck. Sometimes on warm summer nights an elegant crowd in silk dressing gowns would alight and head for the ship's cocktail bar for a nightcap or three, while the crew attended to the complex engineering that would soon allow the ship to be on its way.

The enclosed dock, which allowed the trains to run onto the ships no matter the height of the tide, had taken three years of work by a team of divers operating round the clock. More than 400 feet long and 70 feet wide, it initially defied almost every effort to seal it and hold back the rough waves of the Channel. There was even an outlandish proposal to freeze the encroaching seawater. Eventually the dock floor had to be laid with five-foot-deep concrete, reinforced with old rails and steel girders while still underwater.

Berthing ships locked on to a screw below the waterline, allowing the rails on the linkspan to line up accurately with the deck – with two tracks on the quay branching into four on board, each track accommodating four sleeping cars. Each carriage was secured to the deck with eight chains, the springs on the bogies having been tightened down. There was enough choppiness on most cross-Channel journeys without bouncing coach bogies adding to the general air of seasickness. Pits were installed in the decks beneath the coaches so that the washbasins and toilets could continue to discharge – although the slopping effluent must have been vile in high seas.

Throughout the sea journey scrupulous silence was supposed to be maintained. But although the crew crept around on their duties, this was not always to the satisfaction of the passengers. When one woman complained about the noise of the chains being attached to the coaches, she was told curtly, 'Madam, men have been known to sleep in the heat of battle.' But it was a rare passenger who was not eventually soothed to sleep by the lullaby of the ship's turbines. Although the train ferries were not equipped with stabilisers or modern devices like bow thrusters, the regular captains, like the legendary Len Payne or Tommy Walker, were masters at keeping their vessels stable in the roughest seas.

Not many would be awake when the sound of heavy chains announced arrival at Dunkerque at 4.30 in the morning. But it was always a delicate business getting the ferry into the lock, particularly in a heavy swell, which prevented the lock gates from being opened easily. But if you had slept through this, your instincts might have been teased awake by the unmistakable sounds of France, when, in steam days, a giant o-8-o locomotive would grip the train and haul it up the linkspan.

'With some exceptions,' as Behrend and Buchanan describe it colourfully, 'French engines did not puff like British ones.

They ran on briquettes of pressed coal dust and moved quietly, belching black smoke . . . Their drivers wore berets and goggles . . . the brakes were Westinghouse air type, and on Pennsylvania carriage bogies, created that special noise – a romantic descending musical chromatic scale.' The authors continue with their description of an old France which has now almost vanished: 'For some travellers all was strange: the language, the motor cars driving on the right; the frightful smell of drains, particularly pungent in Dunkerque's docks, mingled with other French smells that time and television advertisements have lessened – the aroma of mixed garlic, *papier-mais* cigarettes and much rough wine.'

Soon the tank would be replaced by one of the top-link André Chapelon Pacifics from the Paris La Chapelle shed for the run up to the capital. With their huge smoke deflectors, these locomotives were the monarchs of the French tracks – each one so cherished that it was only permitted to be driven by one man, a veritable aristocrat of the tracks, whose name was painted on the cab. He could often be seen lovingly oiling his steed before departure. And so, to a chorus of seagull shrieks, the heavy train would pull slowly out as passengers dozed, drowsy with the rhythm of the rail joints. Shrouded in morning mists, the coal-mining country of northern France would give way to dewy fields, with great teams of Percheron carthorses, ploughing or haymaking or harvesting, according to the season.

You could have your tea or coffee in bed served by your conductor, but most people in the heyday years of the train rose for *Le Meat Breakfast*, as Wagons-Lits called it. The atmosphere in the dining car (in post-war years a luxurious vehicle originally built for the French president's train) is described by George Behrend and Gary Buchanan in *Night Ferry*:

The metal floor plates [of the gangways] slid against each other as you exchanged the quiet of the Wagons-Lits for the cheerful clatter of the Wagon-Restaurant: its lofty ornate ceiling made the sleepers with their narrow loading gauge seem curiously English, whereas in London they looked so very French.

Classical dining car ritual stayed unchanged from 1890 to 1960. On the tables baskets of wrapped biscottes and bottles of Worcester Sauce reflected the international Wagons-Lits style. Soup cups were used at breakfast for serving tea, coffee or chocolate. Connoisseurs of Wagons-Lits would purloin a few wrapped sugar knobs from the silverine bowl – these were by Beghin of Thumieres. *Ouefs sur le plat* with ham arrived in an almost red-hot metal platter straight off the coal-fired range, placed on a second plate above that on the table to prevent scorching of the cloth.

The writers, clearly in awe, continue: 'Cereals and fruit juices were available, and baskets of hot toast, croissants, brioches and of fresh fruit were brought round. There was no air conditioning or sound-proofing, and the vestibules made a roar like a thousand waterfalls, while the 'thrump' over crossings and the piercing screech of the whistle created that sense of urgent elation which was *Le Meat Breakfast* . . .'

With the waiters bobbing along, swaying with the motion of the train and brandishing steaming silver-plated pots of coffee and hot milk, regular passengers would play the game of spotting the nationality of the diners. The man looking with disgust at the fried eggs drowning in HP sauce was almost certainly French – perhaps one of the many government couriers who used the train regularly. You could bet that the bleary-eyed young couple staring with incredulity at a glass pot containing an orange substance marked 'Olde

English Marmelade (Made in France)' were from England – possibly one of the many honeymoon couples who took their first journey into married life aboard the Night Ferry. At the end of the meal the *serveur-receveur* (leading attendant) made out the bill, with the *chef de brigade* trotting along behind, with his tin tray of monies and his exchange-rate card.

Behrend and Buchanan recount a delightfully Gallic restaurant car scene aboard the train one day:

> There was a large man (past middle age now) who protected his then anonymous but still substantial shirt-front with his napkin as he sat drinking chocolate. He seemed to know all about Wagons-Lits, for by fiddling a ring behind the *brise-bise*, and pulling on the top handle at the same time, he let in some fresh air – and smuts – into the saloon. An elderly Frenchman opposite at once drew down the blind and there was an altercation during which the *chef de brigade* slammed the window shut again. The large man looked quizzically at the little oblong box on the wall with 'Reclamations, Complaints, *Reclami*' on it, for nobody had ever been known to put a thing in it.

Soon the French customs inspectors would tiptoe along the corridor and ever-so-politely inspect passports and baggage. In the days when the train first ran, Paris had no sprawling suburbs and the countryside ran right up to the city, so the first sign of arrival would be the city's ancient open-deck green buses. And in a trice passengers would be there – with all the thrill of arrival in a great foreign terminus – joining travellers from the other Wagons-Lits night trains from northern Europe. Oh joy to be an Englishman abroad, as *monsieur le conducteur* performed the ritual of electrically lowering the carriage steps to let passengers alight on the low French platforms of the Gare du Nord.

And so it was, throughout the life of the train, although services were suspended during the war, not running again until December 1947. In many respects the immediate post-war years were the heyday of the Night Ferry. Jetliners were in their infancy, and most cross-Channel travel was still by train and sea. The Night Ferry became more popular but never lost its aura of exclusivity. Among the little luxuries of the post-war era were the small wrapped parcels of Palmolive soap, complete with the train's monogram, which were supplied to passengers even though soap was rationed to the general British public.

The train also boasted a treasure trove of multilingual staff. According to the *Railway Gazette*, the management hired fluent speakers of French, Flemish, Dutch, German, Italian, Spanish and English 'as well as eastern dialects'. Whether there were Japanese speakers is not recorded, but the train often carried large parties of Japanese, apparently because they preferred railway travel to planes when they came to Europe. From the beginning of June 1957 a London–Brussels sleeping car was added to the complement and shunted onto a Belgian local express for the run up to the capital via Lille. By its twenty-first birthday in October 1957 the train had carried half a million passengers in its sleeping cars.

In line with its exotic character, the Night Ferry had many idiosyncrasies – not least the number of international celebrities (though they may not have been called that at the time) who valued the attentions of the staff and the privacy. One of the train's special charms was that, in addition to the eight compartments in each coach, there was an odd and somewhat mysterious ninth compartment, slightly smaller than the others and with no intercommunicating door to the compartment next door. The entrance door opened at an angle and had a lock with a chain fastening that allowed it to be secured slightly ajar. This ninth compartment was much in demand from diplomats, king's and queen's messengers and anyone else whose business required them to be wary of strangers knocking at the door. And it was popular with those on Her Majesty's Secret Service . . .

The train was not just fit for queen's messengers but the ultimate royal presence. Travelling privately in 1948, the young Princess Elizabeth, who would become queen four years later, made her very first trip to France aboard the Night Ferry. Exiled in France after his 1936 abdication, her uncle the Duke of Windsor was a frequent Night Ferry passenger, making private visits to see his mother Queen Mary back in the UK. Returning to France in the winter of 1949, he was among a group of passengers obliged to get up in their pyjamas and change trains at the unearthly royal hour of 4 a.m., when the Night Ferry derailed as the coaches were docking in Dunkerque. The procedures for disembarking the coaches from the ship were quite sophisticated, with the linkspan that connected the train to the dockside able to accept a seven-degree list to accommodate the swell of choppy water. Even so, the bogies jumped the grooved rails in the roadway alongside Mole No. 4 and wobbled along the road on their flanges before being brought to a halt. The comments of His Royal Highness on that freezing night were not recorded.

Rather like the London theatres, which have traditionally kept a couple of seats empty in case of an impromptu visit from a member of the royal family, a reserve car stood by for VIPs who wanted quick access to the train. One evening Lord Rothermere, the multi-millionaire tycoon proprietor of the *Daily Mail* newspaper empire, demanded from Thomas Cook a sleeper berth even when the train was full. Such was his perceived importance that the reserve car was brought specially out of the depot to accommodate him, along with supplies of crisp, starched sheets and pillowcases and soft, fluffy towels appropriate to the press mogul's mighty status.

A similar honour was accorded to Prime Minister Winston Churchill in 1954. Wanting to visit Paris, he pronounced that he would join the train at Sevenoaks Tubs Hill station, close to his Chartwell home in Kent. Customs officials were horrified and insisted the entire station was closed by the police to all but Churchill's party while the Night Ferry pulled up specially to let him get on board.

The staff of the train was organised according to a strict hierarchy. Each conductor answered to the conductor of Car No. 1, who was the *chef du train* and carried a forty-eight-page aide-memoire outlining what to do in almost any circumstance – including the sending of a telegram to the director general personally in case anybody died en route, an eventuality that never happened despite the Agatha Christie-like atmosphere aboard. However, there was a serious accident involving the train on 26 July 1963, when electric locomotive No. E5021 crashed through the buffer stops at Victoria on arrival, showering the two ladies in the Fullers confectionery kiosk immediately behind the buffers with sweets and cigarettes. Many of the forty-six people in the sleeping cars were thrown to the floor, and the Brussels car was lifted right up in the air, although nobody, fortunately, was killed.

On one occasion in 1939 Lord Chief Justice Hewitt arrived in London on the Night Ferry and was escorted through customs by Donald White, Thomas Cook's senior interpreter, who was a well-known figure. The customs man was being somewhat officious in examining suitcases, and Donald White hissed in his ear, 'That is the lord chief justice.' His Lordship looked him sternly in the eye and remarked sternly, 'Do not think that will save you when you come before me.'

The magic and aura of the Night Ferry even captivated Germany's wartime high command. In 1940, after the

Dunkerque evacuation, Hitler gave orders not to damage the linkspan because he intended to use the Night Ferry in the invasion of Britain. Even in 1944, when it was clear the Nazis had no hope of ever invading, local commanders did not dare go against the Führer's orders, and the linkspan remained intact while Dunkerque's other docks and quays were wrecked.

For all its life the Night Ferry was an enclosed world of its own, characterised by the charming Gallic argot used by the staff. Thus the bellows connection between the carriages was known as a *soufflet*, the trolley for light refreshments as a *vente ambulante* and the conductor's hat as a *képi*. More poetically still, the steam pipe used to heat the carriages was a *conduite blanche*. However, French translations did not always evoke magic – particularly the prosaic Ferry du Nuit, as the train was described in French timetables.

As with most things associated with the loss of glamour from train travel at the end of the post-war era, the first sign of the lights dimming for the Night Ferry came with the arrival in the early 1960s of Richard Beeching as chairman of British Railways, and rationalisation became the order of the day. There was less freight for the rail-equipped ferries, and certainly less sentiment for the great romantic days of the past. The train had already lost some of its cachet. In the winter of 1961 the prime minister Harold Macmillan and a large official party used the Night Ferry to make an official visit to Paris. But much to their irritation they got there half an hour late, due to thick fog at Dunkerque. Never again was the train used for official visits. Henceforth, these were made by air, and under Harold Wilson's premiership even queen's messengers took to flying in 1966.

Paradoxically, the abandonment of its services by ministers and civil servants lent the train a new and exotic glamour. Minus the deadening presence of officialdom, its snug compartments and dining-car cubbyholes became an even more attractive haunt for the shady demi-monde of double agents, drug smugglers, money launderers, philanderers and adulterers, which had always been attracted to the train's anonymity and pervading air of discretion. On 8 March 1953 the *Reynolds News* newspaper reported

> Customs men in London have uncovered a plot by international racketeers to smuggle drugs on the Night Ferry trains from Paris to Victoria. The drugs have been found in axle boxes on Continental-style coaches. Special precautions are now being taken to search the coaches. They are taken to the sidings outside Victoria, near Grosvenor Road, for inch-by-inch examination after the passengers have left. The Customs men were given the tip-off by a 'squeaker' that the Dope smugglers are operating somewhere between Paris and Dunkerque. Marijuana is the chief drug being smuggled. There is a big demand for this among addicts in London and other big cities, where it is made into cigarettes costing from 5s each upwards.

The last steam-hauled train ran on 1 January 1962, but services got a boost, being taken over by powerful Class 71 electric locomotives. These had been phased in from 1959 as part of the Kent coast electrification, having been specially built for the heavy loads of the remaining non-multiple-unit trains such as the Night Ferry and the Golden Arrow. As a non-standard design, only able to work over the third-rail electrified lines of the Southern Region, these handsome locomotives were useless anywhere else in Britain.

It was lucky that the Night Ferry had such good friends in high places, and so it was able to continue with majestic disdain. One of its most ardent supporters was the British ambassador to France. Sir Nicholas Henderson had also served in Warsaw, Copenhagen and Bonn, and was passionate about the joys of the Night Ferry. Its survival was also helped by the endless vacillation of politicians in both Britain and France over the prospects for a Channel tunnel. Announced with a fanfare by the Conservative transport minister Ernest Marples on 6 February 1964, hopes that the tunnel might open by the end of the following decade were dashed when Anthony Crosland, environment minister in a later Labour government, announced unilaterally on 20 January 1975 that all preliminary work would cease and the equipment be sold off.

The train had another revival in the late 1960s with the introduction of a through sleeping car to Basle in Switzerland. The first coach from Victoria to Basle ran on 16 December 1967, and the press noted at the time that the price of a double sleeping berth to Paris now cost less than a single room in Victoria's Grosvenor Hotel. But the enterprise was less successful than it might have been had there been a through coach to Chur for St Moritz or Interlaken for the Bernese Oberland. The journey of sixteen hours and twelve minutes from London was a long one, and worse, the compartments had no spaces for skis. To the disappointment of its fans, the service didn't last long, with the very last through coach from Basle to London running on 1 March 1969. At the time of writing there is still no international train from Britain that travels beyond France and Belgium – and the Night Ferry's status as Britain's only truly international train remains unchallenged although a Eurostar service to Amsterdam is on the cards.

In 1976 Wagons-Lits celebrated their centenary with a special '100-WL 1876–1976' logo printed on menus, soap packets and vanity kits. But joy quickly turned sour in a row over renewal of the company's contract, and it withdrew from involvement in the train at the end of that year, quitting British operations for good and passing it over to the state-run British Railways and SNCF of France – inevitably shedding much of its glamour in the process. By now the sleeping cars were senescent – some were more than forty years old – and it was BR policy not to run anything over thirty years old without special permission.

In January 1980 car No. 3792, which had been withdrawn in 1974 and restored at huge expense, was presented to the National Railway Museum in York, and visitors could not believe that cars identical to this relic still ran out of Victoria every night on their way to Paris and Brussels. The regulars didn't mind – occupancy rates for the overnight sleeping car journeys were running at 60 per cent – a figure that would be the envy of many luxury hotels.

Meanwhile, there were other endings that were a portent of the closure to come. The very last episode of the famous BBC sitcom *Steptoe and Son* featured the Night Ferry. Screened on Boxing Day 1974, it shows rag-and-bone man Harold dispatching his father abroad so that he can have Christmas alone with his girlfriend – in Bognor Regis. But sharp-eyed viewers may have noticed that the coaches were showing signs of their years.

By the end of the 1970s British Railways were no longer putting much effort into publicising the train, and some ticket offices even denied its existence. The Paris–Dunkerque breakfast car was withdrawn and replaced by a snack-vending machine, although hot meals were restored after furious protests by passengers. Another blow came when computer-aided automatic landing was introduced for planes at Heathrow Airport, diminishing another source of revenue for the train, since it was always well patronised on foggy winter nights when there were likely to be severe air delays.

The first intimation that the end was nigh for the Night

Ferry came in the underhand manner typical of the way British Railways announced closures during the period. Fearing a backlash following the abandonment of two other luxury trains – the Brighton Belle and the Golden Arrow in 1972 – the news was slipped out in an answer to a press question by BR chairman Sir Peter Parker at the opening of a new British Railways office in Paris on 4 March 1980. The train was losing £120,000 a year, he said, and there was no money to replace the life-expired sleeping cars. The Dover–Dunkerque night ship would still run, he purred reassuringly, though passengers would have to board on foot. This would not be very pleasant on a cold winter's night.

So efficient was the diversionary spin of BR management that when the press arrived to interview passengers on the very last train – the 21.25 London Victoria to Paris on the night of 31 October – several didn't even know it was finishing. The departure was certainly low key, with seven sleepers headed by a humble mixed-traffic diesel locomotive No. 33 043, although depot staff had fittingly lugged out one of the old headboards carried by the steam locomotives of the 1950s to fix to the front. Seated passengers had for some time been required to travel separately on a conventional electric multiple-unit train, so heavy locomotives were no longer required.

Station staff expressed their sadness by posting a special message on the departure indicator reading, AU REVOIR, MON AMI. THE LAST NIGHT FERRY SLEEPING CAR TRAIN TO PARIS AND BRUSSELS WILL LEAVE TONIGHT AT 21.25 FROM PLATFORM 2. BON VOYAGE. The illuminated modernity of the sign provided a poignant contrast to the ancient sleeping cars at the platform, which showed streaks of rust on their blue and gold bodywork. Souvenir hunters had long stripped them of anything worth taking. The very last act in a unique rail operation that had begun more than a century previously took place when the empty sleeper cars from the inbound train were run back as a ghost train across the Channel on the Night Ferry's timetable, where they were handed back to Wagons-Lits. Most were sold off for scrap, but a handful soldiered on for many years, before rotting away into the undergrowth in a siding at Les Ifs in Normandy.

There was one slim hope of reviving the Night Ferry. In 1977 the American shipping tycoon James Sherwood had bought at auction some redundant Wagons-Lits coaches from the Orient Express, spotting a gap in the market for the revival of luxury international train travel. 'The railways of the British Isles seem to have lost their way,' he said, 'when it comes to long-distance sleeper travel. Filthy trains with surly overpaid staff, who in some cases have been paid to look the other way while passengers are robbed.' His vision paid off when he launched the Venice–Simplon Orient Express in 1982, which today still represents the gold standard in luxury international train travel.

Sherwood considered the possibility of reintroducing the Night Ferry along similar lines to the VSOE.

I am often asked why I committed £11 million of my shareholders' funds to restore the British and continental rakes of the Venice–Simplon Orient Express. Many perceive it as a grand folly, but nothing could be further from the truth. In the 1960s passenger travel by sea was nearly extinguished by air competition, and conventional wisdom said that the day of the great luxury liner was gone. Today, there are far more luxury cruise vessels in operation than in the heyday of sea travel in the 1930s. My perception was that the affluent tourist wanted the adventure of taking the Orient Express to Paris and Venice.

Could he work the same trick with the London–Paris night train? The idea was to use the VSOE rake from Victoria to Dover Western Docks, transferring there to luxury sleepers operated by SNCF. The sleepers would be winched with jacks onto one of the newest of the cross-Channel train ferries – the *Vortigern*, built in 1969 – an operation that would be totally silent. Aboard ship, the cabins would be air-conditioned, and the sleeping cars would be transferred to the rails at Dunkerque for a fast run up to Paris. But alas it was all a dream. The *Vortigern* ended her days as a rust bucket flogging round the Greek islands before being scrapped in India in 2005, and the British train ferry is no more.

Today's VSOE passengers have to alight from their cocoon of 1920s luxury at Folkestone and climb aboard buses which transfer them to a shuttle train for their journey through the Channel Tunnel because fire regulations do not permit the through running of vintage carriages. Although the process is smoothed by an excellent glass or two of Orient Express wine, it is an understatement to say that essential elements of the romance have been lost.

But the ghosts of the past are not quite laid to rest. Sometimes on a clear night at Victoria's Platform 2 you can half-close your eyes, stare up at the Edwardian roof and imagine. Is that the moon winking at you through the glass? Or is it a ghostly glimmer of that famous neon lunar sign that for many years greeted arriving Night Ferry passengers? No matter, perhaps. The frisson of excitement surrounding the Night Ferry's departure on its glamorous journey to Paris and beyond will haunt evenings at Victoria for as long as the memory of Britain's first international train stays alive.

But there's a postscript to this story. After putting the Eurostar through its paces thirty-five years after the very last Night Ferry departed on its final journey, I pause for a rest in a delightful square near the Place de Clichy – a timeless area of the City of Light, evoking the spirit of the old Paris of boat-train days. Could the high-tech modern equivalent in any way compare?

The warmth of this early-March day is drawing out the cherry blossom while the *propriétaire* of a corner *épicerie* is putting out his wares after a lunchtime siesta. Down the street I spot an old-fashioned model train shop of the kind that is almost extinct in Britain, and there in the window – as if by way of temptation – is a 1950s tinplate model of the Night Ferry, resplendent in blue and gold, made by that oh-so-Gallic firm of Jouef, beloved of post-war French schoolboys.

Tearing off the brown-paper wrapping after I arrive back home in London, this miniature Night Ferry turns out to be powered by clockwork, but sadly does not exactly run like clockwork. Watching it wobble around my kitchen table, it makes me think. Perhaps it is kindest to this grand old icon to leave it where it belongs – in the past. Heresy though it may be, should we just admit that the Eurostar has left it behind?

Chapter Three

Kippers and champagne on the Tube

A saunter through Metro-land to the London
Underground's farthest outpost. It's buried under weeds
today, but once the Pullman trains ran from here, serving
the most splendid of breakfasts to commuters up to
Baker Street.

'Junction, mate? Don't make me laugh. It might call itself
a junction, but there ain't been no junction there for years.
I can tell you – it's a thirty-minute walk after you get off
my bus and there ain't another one back for hours. OK, if
you insist . . . But don't say I didn't warn yer . . .'

Charming chap, the driver of the number 60 Arriva Shires
and Essex bus from Aylesbury, heading for the deliciously

named destination of Maids Moreton. Sadly, I shall never get there since I have pressing business beforehand. The engine hums with irritation as I haul myself down from the step to the roadside in the seeming middle of nowhere in the undulating countryside of the Vale of Aylesbury – which despite its proximity to the M25 still exudes the ancient tranquillity of timeless rural England.

It is the hottest day of the year so far and getting hotter. The late-spring breeze after a diesel-filled hour grinding through the hamlets of Buckinghamshire smells especially fragrant. An armada of cabbage white butterflies follows me as I set off, OS Map 192 for Buckingham in hand, heading for one of the most mythical railway junctions in British railway history.

Mythical? Well, listen to this. Here is 'a country with elastic boundaries which each visitor can draw for himself, as Stevenson drew his map of Treasure Island. It lies mainly in Bucks; but choice fragments of Middlesex and Hertfordshire may be annexed at pleasure. As much of the countryside as you can comfortably cover on foot from one . . . station to another you may add to your private and individual map.'

The words are not mine but from the publicity of the Metropolitan Railway, famously celebrated for building the world's first underground line, and which also, uniquely, created an image of a country railway that was an advertising man's dream of bucolic bliss. It even had its own name – Metro-land. This fantasy of idyllic arcadian living, cooked up in the early years of the twentieth century, was one of the world's earliest brand images. (As with all good brands, the hyphen is important, and 'Metroland' as a single word only came later on.)

What an extravagant dream! This prototype of marketing packages extended to more than just promoting the coun-tryside on the fringe of London around the Chiltern Hills where the railway was busy underwriting the development of new housing estates. This was a vision of a suburban utopia surrounded by green fields and woods, with quiet well-ordered avenues of houses with grass verges, art deco sunshine patterns in glass doors and rosy-cheeked children played in gardens, eternally guarded from the reality of modern life by genial gnomes and pixies.

If there was ever a Shangri-La pertaining to this Metroland paradise, it was Verney Junction, an obscure railway platform in the middle of nowhere, created by dreamers. In its heyday Verney was the furthest-flung destination of the Tube, served not by plodding stopping trains but by comfortable expresses hauled by powerful steam locomotives conveying well-heeled commuters dining in style aboard Pullman cars down from the City and West End.

Grand indeed. But not much evidence of it today, or of Pullman-style luxury, as I arrive sweating at a nondescript cluster of a dozen houses where all is drowsy and shuttered. The hissing of the tea urn in the station buffet here is long gone. But after the weary trudge from the bus, how about a modest glass of water? The old railway hotel, the Verney Arms, once the hub of this tiny community, where important chaps from the City might down a large nightcap before heading home to the wife and kids, has seemingly been turned into an Italian restaurant. And is closed – not even the most modest of small espressos to be had here. Pressing my nose against a dusty window, not a sign of when it might open again. As for shops, I might as well be on another planet.

Maybe there's salvation to be found in a riffle through Google on my iPhone. Oops! Top hit for local entertainment is the 'Verney Junction swingers'. Swingers? What could this mean? Anthropologists of twenty-first-century Britain might claim this tells you everything about outer-suburban life in modern Bucks. But fortunately there's not much swinging apparent here so early on a weekday morning. I think I'll leave it for another day.

Maybe Verney was just a dream, like Alice's train from *Through the Looking Glass.* Tempting to think so. Yet buried under the foot-high grass can be discerned the remains of a platform. And the solid-looking architecture of that building over there? Could that have been the stationmaster's house? Otherwise little remains of what was once an important terminus with three platforms and all the paraphernalia of a commodious country junction – waiting rooms, ticket and parcels office and signal box. So no dream this – the name lives on today in maps and bus timetables, even though the last train departed nearly half a century ago.

A clue as to how this surreal rural outpost of the world's first urban railway could ever have come into existence lies in the blind and almost suicidal panic with which new railways were promoted in the railway mania of the middle of the nineteenth century. Like every economic bubble since, investors scrambled to put their money into rival schemes vying often to connect the same places no matter how economically or socially viable they might be. It was a boom in which the reputations and fortunes of promoters were either transformed beyond dreams or cruelly shattered.

With the economy booming and interest rates low, the new-fangled railways seemed to many like an ideal way to get rich quick. There was a stampede of railway schemes, some quite unsustainable and preposterous. In 1845 and the following two parliamentary sessions no fewer than 650 Railway Acts were passed, authorising the construction of nearly 9,000 miles of track – today's system is 10,072 miles by comparison. If all had been built, the capital required would have been more than one and a half times the country's gross national product – putting into perspective the current controversy over HS2, the proposed high-speed line to the north of England, which even on wildest projections would consume only a fraction of today's GNP.

By 1910 railways criss-crossed every part of the land, with not even the smallest agricultural hamlet in England beyond walking distance of a station. The madness is summed up by David St John Thomas in his classic book *The Country Railway*: 'Given the financial crises, inefficient and overworked engineers and malpractices, combined with the total lack of experience, local jealousies and quarrels between neighbouring companies trying to defend their territories rather than open up the region, and occasionally prepared to resort even to sabotage, the wonder is that the system developed at the lightning pace it did.'

In their own way, all these factors played their part in the spectacular rise and tragic fall of Verney Junction. But the directors of the Metropolitan Railway were not entirely crazy. After all they had managed to create the first and the greatest of the urban railways that transformed the emerging cities of the world in the nineteenth century. So what were they doing planning a terminus some fifty miles from London in the middle of nowhere? At first the Met's ambitions were small, born out of the desire of the Great Western Railway, which had built its London terminus at a rather inaccessible spot called Paddington, to get its passengers into the City as swiftly as possible. The result was a railway tunnel to Farringdon, the world's first undergound railway. Despite the fug, filth, noise and steam, the new line was a huge success, and almost ten million passengers were carried in the first year.

Buoyed with confidence, the railway rapidly drove west to Hammersmith – no flyovers and traffic congestion there in those days, rather a kind of arcadia of orchards and strawberry fields. The nascent railway forged east too, to Moorgate Street in the heart of the City. But it was another extension, to St John's Wood in the smart suburbs of north-west London in 1868, that offered a glimpse of an empire that might just be possible one day, the ultimate railway promoter's dream.

Enter Sir Edward Watkin, one of the greatest visionaries of the Victorian railway world, who became chairman of the Metropolitan Railway in 1872. After a humble start in the goods office of the London & North Western Railway, Watkin become chairman of both the South Eastern Railway and the Manchester, Sheffield & Lincolnshire Railway, and one day had a dream. What if you could link these powerful passenger and goods undertakings with a line through London, creating a mighty transport spine that could even, one day, pass from Dover under the English Channel to the Continent?

The Met pushed Watkin's dream forward, as its engineers drove ever harder into the suburbs. Soon the single-track line from Baker Street to St John's Wood was doubled, and by 1879 commuter trains were speeding to Kilburn, Willesden and out into Middlesex, urbanising the landscape as they went. Goodbye to the countryside and the olden days of bucolic bliss. Poignantly, as one commentator noted, until the railway came, the charms of Kilburn were linked to its 'proximity to the country . . .Within half an hour's walk the pedestrian is among trees and fields and pleasant places.' Some contrast to the gritty and ugly urban landscape that Kilburn eventually became.

A year later the line had reached Harrow-on-the-Hill, one of London's loveliest old villages with its ancient public school and church spire, landmarks for miles around. A few years previously the country around here had been noted for 'high yields of wheat and bean crops'. The world was moving on too at Kingsbury and Neasden down the new line, which had once been 'intersected by green lanes and field paths bordered by flowering hawthorn hedges while the River Brent meanders through'. From Harrow the new line drove on to Pinner in 1885 and Rickmansworth in 1887, arriving in Chesham, almost thirty miles from Baker Street, in 1889. In 1892 the Metro-land semis were starting to besiege Aylesbury.

By now the Metropolitan's image-makers were busy turning what many saw as the despoliation of pristine rural England into an asset. 'The extension of the Metropolitan Railway from London to Pinner, Northwood and Chesham has opened up a new and delightful countryside to the advantage of picturesque seekers; ancient houses and old-world ways,' enthused one publicity handout. 'Within 50 minutes from Baker Street and for the cost of less than a florin [10p], if the visitor be economically disposed, he can enjoy a feast of good things, fresh air, noble parks, stately houses, magnificent trees and sylvan streets.'

With the sylvan theme never far away, the Edwardian spin doctors up at HQ in Baker Street went on over the next decades to deploy every modern trick in creating one of the great advertising myths – even today the word Metro-land is shorthand for a social world that can be summoned up in an instant. A pity that its inventor, James Garland, the chief copywriter in the Met's marketing department, has vanished into obscurity, unlike other heroes of the London Tube such as Frank Pick, who pioneered the house style, and Harry Beck, who designed the famous Tube map. Legend has it that Garland was ill in bed with flu when 'Metro-land' came to mind. Lazarus-like apparently, he leaped out of bed and rushed into the office to convey the good news.

Garland's mission statement was unashamedly elitist. Never mind the thousands of low-income clerks who might have benefited from the new trains and the housing estates that were springing up around the new stations as the railway pushed through Middlesex into Hertfordshire and Buckinghamshire; the Met's eyes were turned firmly upmarket. It was the managerial class and bowler-hat brigade of the City that the railway had in mind: 'The strains which the London business or professional man has to endure,' soothed the Met's publicity, 'can only be counterbalanced by the quiet restfulness and comfort of a residence of pure air and rural surroundings.'

Soon Metro-land imagery was everywhere. By World War I the songwriter George R. Sims, author of the popular ballad 'It was Christmas Day in the Workhouse', had written it up in verse: 'I know a land where the wild flowers grow/ Near, near at hand if by train you go/ Metroland, Metroland.' Another music publisher brought out a 'Vocal One-Step' called 'My Little Metroland Home', with words by Boyle Lawrence and music by Henry Thrale. By the 1920s the word was so ingrained in the British psyche that it featured in Evelyn Waugh's famous novel *Decline and Fall* (1928), in which the Honourable Margot Beste-Chetwynd takes Viscount Metroland as her second husband – his 'funny name' deriving from his fiefdom on the Metropolitan Railway. The idea was still being celebrated in late-twentieth-century fiction. In Julian Barnes's first novel *Metroland* (1980), which opens in the 1960s, the clever-clever sixth-former who says things like 'J'habite Metroland' in his orals is riding lawlessly in first class when he becomes the captive audience of an 'old sod . . . dead bourgeois' who gives him a rundown of the distinguished history of the line.

Reinforcing the notion with its own magazine, *Metro-land* (available for a penny at booking offices), the Baker Street spin doctors under the leadership of Robert H. Selbie, the Met's brilliant general manager, effectively manufactured a

magic ´land – the stuff of dreams. Who could resist this
nostalgic paradise of harmonious living and sylvan pleasures
available to everyone – provided they had the money? Not
only could the ideal mock-Tudor home be yours (bought,
of course, from the Metropolitan Railway Estates company),
but for the weary commuter here too were long Sundays
that offered an opportunity to stroll in hay fields and beech
woods and the sight of vast sunny skies reaching down to
the soft grass of the Chiltern Hills. To make sure the message
was never missed, the legend 'Live in Metroland' was even
etched in the brass door handles of the trains.

Although it was born out of instantly manufactured
nostalgia, Metro-land went on in later years to be surrounded
by a genuine nostalgia of its own, most famously celebrated
by Sir John Betjeman, the poet laureate from 1972, whom
The Times once described as the 'Hymnologist of Metroland'.
The mood of the railway was famously captured in his
poems from 1954 in the collection *A Few Late Chrysanthemums*.
'Middlesex' perhaps catches it best:

> Gentle Brent, I used to know you
> Wandering Wembley-wards at will,
> Now what change your waters show you
> In the meadowlands you fill!
> Recollect the elm-trees misty
> And the footpaths climbing twisty
> Under cedar-shaded palings,
> Low laburnum-leaned-on railings
> Out of Northolt on and upward
> To the heights of Harrow hill.

Even this was outpaced in gushing nostalgia by Betjeman's
later eulogistic television documentary *Metro-land*, made by
the BBC in 1973. The poet, by this time a national institu-

tion, makes it as far as the ruins of Verney Junction, although with slightly more to discover than there is today, and concludes, 'The houses of Metro-land never got as far as Verney. Grass triumphs, and I'm rather glad.' He was right. By this time the mythology had soured and it was all too late; as Dennis Edwards and Ron Pilgrim put it in their book *The Golden Years of Metroland*, 'The Metropolitan Railway created a whole new world, but in doing so destroyed acres of beautiful countryside and a way of life that was quiet, peaceful and essentially English.'

None of this bothered the Met back in the 1890s as it drove relentlessly north on past Aylesbury into ever-remoter countryside, buying up the Aylesbury & Buckingham Railway as a short cut. Here was a magical moment for a moribund country railway, if ever there was one. The struggling Aylesbury & Buckingham was conceived out of a hotly fought battle to get the railways into Aylesbury – then, as now, a thriving market town on a branch of the Grand Union Canal, which the railways were keen to put out of business. The mighty London & North Western Railway was first in, with a branch from the Euston to Birmingham main line at Cheddington in 1839. Its twenty-three-year monopoly was smashed by the Great Western Railway, arriving from High Wycombe in 1863. But there was still a tantalising opportunity for a new north–south line through the rich Vale of Aylesbury.

The big idea first came along in 1860, with a proposal to link up southwards to the London & North Western Railway at Tring, connecting into its great London terminus at Euston. From the north, the trains would connect into the Buckinghamshire Railway, running cross-country from Bletchley to Banbury via Buckingham. Predictably, the mighty L&NWR vetoed the idea. But this didn't stop local land-owners from pressing ahead with the northern section. It was effectively a game of musical chairs, and who could possibly stand in the way of the Marquis of Chandos, who became the third and final Duke of Buckingham and Chandos in 1861, and Sir Harry Verney, MP for Buckingham?

The Duke of Buckingham had an especially colourful heritage. Richard Plantagenet Campbell Temple-Nugent-Brydges-Chandos-Grenville (1823–89), only son of the second Duke of Buckingham and Chandos, was in serious financial difficulties by the middle of the nineteenth century. His father had spent heavily on artworks, womanising and attempting to influence elections, and by 1847 had been nicknamed the greatest debtor in the world. Most of the family's 55,000-acre estates and their London home at Buckingham House were disposed of to meet debts, and the family seat at Stowe was seized by bailiffs as security and its contents sold. The only property remaining in the control of the Grenville family was the family's relatively small ancestral home of Wotton House and its associated lands around Wotton Underwood in Buckinghamshire, and the Grenvilles were looking for ways to maximise profits from the remaining farmland and seeking business opportunities in the emerging fields of heavy industry and engineering.

So with noble, and maybe some ignoble, backing a new line opened in 1868 from Aylesbury to Verney Junction, through the sleepiest of stations at Quainton Road, Grandborough Road and Winslow Road ('Road' being railway promoters' shorthand for a station that was usually a daunting hike from the local village or town). The duke was appointed chairman and Sir Harry vice-chairman of the new concern.

For years nobody much came or went on the little trains. The single track was so flimsily constructed that only the most delicate of locomotives – two light 0-4-2 saddle tanks

– were used to operate it. Even these had to be borrowed from the Great Western Railway because the line had spent all its money on construction and had none left over. They tugged behind them some antiquated coaches discarded from a railway in the West Midlands. But all that changed when the mighty Met swept up the line in 1892. The track was relaid and doubled, and when through services to London began, the trains got heavier and the locomotives more powerful, as befitted a proper main line. What a sight some of them were, right up to the end – perhaps one of the Metropolitan's big H Class 4-4-4s on the up Pullman, or the state-of-the-art K Class, built in 1925, on a heavy freight rumbling down from Neasden – and all exotic quarry for trainspotters, who loved the idea of steam on the Undergound.

But the Met's intrepid advance didn't last long. The brand new trunk line of the Manchester, Sheffield & Lincolnshire Railway was powering towards London along a parallel trajectory to the west, joining the Aylesbury & Buckingham at Quainton Road, and cutting the blood supply from Verney Junction as a potential route to the north.

Poor Verney, stranded in the middle of nowhere and left to wither – not a town, nor a village, nor even a hamlet, but somewhere in the middle of a field. There was no local population to serve a station, no shop, church or chapel, and even the most ruthless of Metro-land estate agents never thought the hinterland promising enough to build any homes. But it did at least lie on the route of the existing 'Varsity Line' – which meandered across the country from Oxford to Cambridge – at its junction with the line to Buckingham. This was where a dream died. A couple of platforms were built where the two lines met, linked to the outside world by a dirt track. The best that could be hoped for was that the platforms might be filled by passengers changing trains. At least the station had a noble name, christened after the local landowner Harry Verney, who was Florence Nightingale's brother-in-law. Curiously, Verney had another station named after him – at Calvert on the Great Central Railway nearby. He had changed his name from Calvert to Verney after inheriting his cousin's baronetcy.

For decades the trains stopped but few people ever got on or got off, although Verney Junction was always a cheery place. One of the engine drivers, Sam Grigg, described it in his memoir *Country Railwaymen*:

> Somehow the station always seemed to have staff that made it a place to remember. A traveller who had to change at Verney Junction could have an experience that would remain in his memory. A well-kept station can be an asset to the countryside; Verney was an asset to the rural and beautiful Buckinghamshire landscape. There were many summers in which a waiting traveller would pace the platforms and admire mermaids guarding the pool of goldfish. There was the windmill, the seal, stork and elves, all standing passively by, hardly likely to do other than delight any passer-by. A gardener would rejoice in the well-trimmed bushes, flowers and lovely standard roses. In the winter time there were compensations at Verney; a small, cosy waiting room with a bright fire, shining windows and polished floor, and that window gave a fine view of a wide expanse of countryside.

But the shadows were starting to lengthen. In 1933 the Metropolitan Railway was absorbed into London Transport, which concluded that its main job was to run Tube trains beneath the busy streets of the metropolis rather than pour money into an isolated country railway for the sake of a handful of passengers and a few milk churns.

So on 4 July 1936 passenger services from Quainton Road to Verney Junction were withdrawn, leaving the steadily rusting tracks open just for the occasional goods train. No longer would the porter cry, 'Hurry along for the London train' – even though sometimes there was not a soul there at all to hurry! No more would the stewards aboard the Pullman cars in their crisp starched jackets lay out the white tablecloths and light the stove to grill the kippers and kidneys that were the breakfast favourites of stockbrokers on their way up to London, the passengers all naturally acknowledged by name every morning.

The line to Verney was not the only antique curio hereabouts that London Transport inherited from the Metropolitan. A few stops up from Verney at Quainton Road it was still possible until 1936 to change onto the Brill branch – even more superannuated and lost in obscurity than the 'main line' to Verney. At the branch line platform, at the head of a creaking carriage and forgotten by almost everyone at HQ, could be found one of the ancient tank engines that had been pensioned off from service under the streets of London when the inner section of the Metropolitan Railway was electrified.

In its brief sixty-four-year life the Brill branch had progressed from being a primitive horse tramway, known to locals as the Wotton Tramway, or simply the Tram, to an artery of the London Underground. Extending for just seven miles, the line was originally the private fiefdom of the Duke of Buckingham, whose estate it was designed to serve and over whose land it ran for almost its entire length. Brill, the tiny hamlet that formed the destination, was famed for its ancient windmill – frequently cited in Metropolitan Railway literature – but not much else. The few houses could certainly have done nothing much for passenger revenues. At first horses were used to pull the wagons over tracks formed of sleepers laid longitudinally to save money but which hardly made for a comfortable journey. Maybe this did not matter, since the only passengers were workmen on the estate, but soon villagers were clamouring for a ride, and the railway purchased a coach from the Great Western Railway, which passengers had to share with milk churns, chickens, barrels of beer, pigeons and any other goods that turned up for the train.

Even more eccentric was the first locomotive, acquired from Aveling & Porter of Rochester in Kent, a company famed for its traction engines and road rollers – from which, to the casual eye, this snorting chain-driven behemoth looked indistinguishable. When the railway opened to the public in 1872 the number of passengers carried was tiny – only six or eight a day. This may not have been unconnected with the stench from the vast amounts of manure that were transported – 3,200 tons in 1872 alone. Worse, contemporary reports referred to vast piles of the stuff in fields all along the line side.

One of the curiosities of the era is a printed book, *The Rules and Regulations for the Conduct of the Traffic and for the Guidance of Officers and Men engaged on the Wotton Tramway*, written by the line's general manager R. A. Jones and published under the aegis of 'His Grace, the Duke of Buckingham and Chandos, Proprietor'. It included a table of fines for errant staff. The driver could be fined a shilling (then a substantial sum) for not having his engine ready, and he would have to forfeit half a day's pay if he were late at Quainton Road. Guards faced similar penalties, with the loss of half a day's pay if the train were more than ten minutes late setting off. All this may have seemed unnecessary on a railway with no signals and which only had one steam engine, but the duke, who in his day had been chairman of the mighty London & North Western Railway, was having no truck with anything less than the highest main-line standards on his own little line.

According to a timetable from the 1880s, the average speed between Brill and Quainton was 4 mph, due to the necessity of stopping at five intermediate stations and many farm gates, which the fireman had to jump down from the engine to open and close. Even so, derailments were frequent, and on 8 March 1883 there was an appalling tragedy. The lady's maid of the Duke of Buckingham's daughter was walking along the line with two other lady's maids near Wotton, having disembarked from the evening train to Quainton. The engine driver pooped the whistle, but Maria Nichols lingered a moment too long and was fatally injured by the locomotive.

For most of the time nothing much happened to disturb life in the verdant backwoods along the Brill branch. But it had a couple of brief flirtations with greatness. In 1874 Baron Ferdinand de Rothschild bought the site of what was to become one of the great stately homes of England at Waddesdon Manor. Many of the construction materials arrived over a spur at Westcott station from the Brill branch. Such was the lavishness and authenticity of this attempt to recreate a great chateau that teams of Percheron mares from Normandy were employed to haul the loads from the railway up to the summit at Lodge Hill, where the manor was built. The future King Edward VII came here by Metropolitan Railway, using the special station built for the house at Waddesdon Manor on the Verney Junction line. The locals marvelled as he passed by in a special saloon coach built for the Rothschilds, drawn by a tank locomotive decorated on each side with Prince of Wales feathers.

Less successful was a plan in the 1880s to turn the Brill branch into a main line running from Aylesbury and Oxford. The track was relaid and some new locomotives acquired, but the dream expired with the death of the Duke of Buckingham in 1889. The Brill line slumbered on into the twentieth century, its tranquillity undisturbed, sustained by a little freight from a tile- and brickworks near Brill and the conveyance of picnickers to a beauty spot at the aptly named Wood Siding. Sitting in the dappled sunshine of a glade under the trees alongside the little wooden platform there it was possible to imagine momentarily that London was on the other side of the universe.

The last train on the Brill branch wound its leisurely way through the countryside on 30 November 1935, and the following poignant note appeared in *The Times* on 2 December.

> On Saturday night for the last time an antiquated little tank engine drew an equally antiquated passenger coach along the seven-mile line between Quainton Road and Brill. The train contained officials of the Metropolitan Railway Company, including an assistant superintendent. It stopped at each of the five stations on the line. Documents, records and all valuables from each station were placed in the guard's van and the station lights were put out and the train steamed to its destination at Quainton Road.

The little Brill branch had simply run out of puff.

In the spring of 1936 auctioneers moved along the railway, station by station, selling everything off at knockdown prices. At Brill the booking office and waiting room with lean-to lavatory were a snip at six pounds. At Wood Siding the lovely old station sign was knocked down for just three shillings. What a bargain for some fortunate farmer the water tower at Wotton must have been. Going, going — it went for just ten shillings. Luckily, no fewer than two locomotives have survived to this day — a triumph of preservation given how tiny and obscure the railway was. Who would have imagined that Aveling & Porter No. 807 would have lived on from those early days in 1872? And when Metropolitan Railway A Class 4-4-0 tank locomotive No. 23 retired from life underground after the Met was electrified in 1905–6, how lucky it was pensioned off to the Brill branch, where it ducked the blowtorch and is now a celebrity resident of the London Transport Museum in London's Covent Garden.

As for the rest of the branch, there is scarcely a trace of it today, although the station at Quainton Road is lovingly preserved as the Buckinghamshire Railway Centre and a shrine to all things Metropolitan. Even with the help of OS Map 94 from 1919, unearthed by foraging through the shelves of the Aylesbury Oxfam shop, I could find little sign of the course of the old Brill railway trackbed. The large oak tree that shaded the simple platform at Wood Siding is still spreading its boughs, and memories live on in place names, such as Tramway Farm, Tram Hill, but almost everything else has disappeared.

After the Brill line was obliterated, the Verney line dragged on for a little longer. Scheduled passenger services had gone, and the infrastructure quietly continued to moulder. During 1939 the cranes moved in to reduce most of the line to single track, and the signalling was removed, turning what was once intended to be a great main line into a long siding. The Second World War brought a reprieve, and the line up to London was busy with shunters bustling around on coal trains to Baker Street. There was even the odd passenger service in 1943 and 1944 for wartime workers, though these were a well-kept secret.

But the end was inevitable, as it was for many country railways that sleepwalked through the war. A wartime connecting line had been built at Shepherd's Furze Farm near Claydon, linking the Great Central line to the north with the Oxford–Cambridge route, creating an alternative route for freight trains to the capital. For years the surviving double-track section from Winslow Road to Verney Junction was a Valhalla for old rolling stock, which rusted peacefully, hoping to dodge the inevitable, until somebody finally remembered its existence and sent it to the scrapyard. The last of this section of track was lifted in 1957.

The remaining passenger services were dwindling away too. On 7 September 1964 the Verney Junction to Buckingham service closed, despite a brave experiment with some ultra-modern diesels – the Buckingham to Banbury section had already gone in 1961. How incredible it must seem to today's commuters in the Vale of Aylesbury that the university town and former administrative centre of Buckinghamshire – now rail-less – was once served by some of Britain's most modern post-war trains.

Poor Verney was a junction no more, and soon there would be no trains either. Passenger services on the Verney section of the old Varsity Line ceased as the New Year dawned on 1 January 1968. Occasional freight trains would rumble by, shoving the weeds aside, but this was always a special location in the middle of nowhere – a 'place of refinement' as one historian put it. There was never a moment more evocative than nightfall, when the platforms were lit by the soft yellow glow of the oil lamps, their wicks neatly trimmed daily by the porter. The down outer home signal at the Metropolitan Railway junction would drop for the arrival of the London train as regularly as the signal box cat would tiptoe across the long lattice bridge for its supper.

And what memories of the grand journeys that could once be taken from here. Close your eyes for a minute and imagine the train home to Verney on the evening commuter run from Baker Street, perhaps aboard Pullman car *Galatea* or *Mayflower*, richly endowed with comfortable armchairs set out in small saloons rather like a gentleman's club. Or even one of the theatre trains, late on a Saturday evening. 'The scheme of decoration of the cars is that of the latter part of the eighteenth century,' enthused the *Railway Magazine* of the day,

> with remarkable artistic effect. The mural scheme is composed of panels of fine fiddle-back mahogany or wainscot oak, inlaid with enrichments of the period it represents on a ground of fine quartered veneer. On the eight glass-topped tables with which each car is supplied there is a tiny portable electrolier of a very chaste design. In addition to those lights, there are, at intervals, wall brackets affixed to the panelling. Quite handy to the passenger are the bell pushes and the lamp switches. These and the number frames are all of ormolu, finely chased and gilded.

The luxury didn't stop there. 'Even the blinds, which are of green and silk damask, have been specially woven, and above each blind is an ormolu baggage rack with finely chased ornamentation and panels of brass *treillage*. The floor covering is of a luxurious pile carpeting, a harmonious colour blend with the beautifully upholstered armchairs that are covered in morocco.'

Busying itself at the head of the train might have been one of the Met's massive K Class tank locomotives resplendent in its brick-red livery, set off with polished brass. The fireman would be stoking hard, ready for the off and the long climb up through the tunnels to Finchley Road. The historian of the Pullman Car Company, Charles Fryer, described the journey evocatively, not only reflecting Pullman's mission statement as 'luxury, service and privilege' but also attitudes of class and sex that are now frozen in the aspic of the past:

To me it seemed the every acme of luxury travel, utterly beyond my means . . . only possible to the top brass of the business world, whom I saw boarding their cars and settling into their armchairs. In the cramped six-aside accommodation of a Metropolitan compartment coach, I would daydream about what it might be like to belong to the higher echelons.

There they sat, the weary tycoons, each in his Louis Quinze chair at his own table, fingering the wine list. Softly across the carpeted floor an attendant approached them. What would Monsieur like to drink? A gin and tonic, perhaps, after the labours of the day? Each having been supplied with his own expensive beverage, their portly frames relaxed as they scanned *The Times* or the *Telegraph*. Isolated from the common herd, from the junior clerks and girl typists who thronged the platforms or squeezed into crowded compartments in front or behind, they could just stare out from plate-glass windows like goldfish from bowls and just ignore the lesser bourgeoisie.

The only hardship suffered by the Met's pampered customers was the necessity for bladder control, as the toilets were closed while the trains were in the tunnels of the London section. From there onwards there would be no stop for half an hour.

During that time they would mostly nod off. Then . . . away into the heart of Metroland, halting at Chorley Wood, Chalfont, Amersham, Great Missenden, Wendover, Stoke Mandeville and Aylesbury. At each of these, a tycoon or two would ease himself from his seat, retrieve his briefcase and umbrella, have the door opened for him by an attendant, step out on to the platform and walk a few yards to the waiting limousine, thence to be chauffeur-driven to his mock Tudor mansion among the beechwoods. To be one of *them* now, instead of just a scrubby junior clerk.

Indeed. Many worlds away this afternoon I'm beating a sweaty path through thigh-high weeds along the old track alignment back to the junction at Quainton Road, where it's not going to be much fun standing in the sweltering heat waiting for one of the rare buses back to civilisation. How foolish you might think for the railways ever to venture this way and expect to thrive. And yet the latest news is that this quiet part of Buckinghamshire is soon to get not only one new railway, but two.

The former Varsity Line is due to be restored and electrified all the way from Oxford to Bedford as part of a new east–west trunk route. And the path of the new HS2 is planned to pass on its ultra-fast way to the north just a few decibels away from where the Verney Arms now sleeps. But under the new plans there will be no more stopping trains at Verney Junction on either line. Perhaps it's for the best. While the new trains race by, the quiet old junction and its Metro-land memories will continue to slumber among the brambles.

After all, despite all the technology and speed, what modern train could trump the reassuring moment when the steward on the 17.42 from Baker Street to Verney Junction nudges your elbow to ask, 'Would you fancy a touch more angostura in your gin, sir?'

Rest in peace, old railway.

Chapter Four
The railway that touched the sky

Beeching butchered the bleak Stainmore line over the
Pennines, in its day the highest in England. But the old
viaducts still stand tall, and the tales of the tough men
who worked it live on as the stuff of legend.

Eat your heart out, Settle & Carlisle Railway, with all
your plaudits as the most scenic line in England, plus
all your dramatic viaducts and sensational Pennine moorland
scenery. How marvellous that you were saved from the
Beeching closures and now stand as a beacon in the revival
of historic world railways, never mind being lauded on TV
by celebrity broadcasters. But here's a rival, even grittier, just

as daring in its engineering and certainly more defiant in its determination to keep the trains running through hostile northern Pennine scenery. However, unlike its distinguished counterpart, it's gone. Dead and silent. The Stainmore railway, running for sixty-six miles east to west across northern England through the harsh landscapes of Cumberland, Westmorland and Durham, was, until it closed in 1962, the loftiest and most dramatic main line in England. Here was the highest summit on an English main line and at one time the highest mainline station too. This sensational and beautiful railway also had one of the finest views from a carriage window anywhere in the land, with a panorama over the vast remotenesses of Westmorland unfolding as the trains drifted down the hillsides from its high point at Stainmore summit. In the rankings of the Great Railway Views of Europe, this was one, in the parlance of modern travel, to 'See Before You Died'.

But sadly this is a tale that must be related mostly in the past tense, since the superlatives of the Stainmore railway are no more. Shut even before Beeching in 1962, it is the biggest single loss in the history of the railways of northern England. I'm reflecting on this with a blizzard whistling round my ears on the windswept Podgill Viaduct near Kirkby Stephen in Cumbria – dramatic in every sense. If you ever want a tribute to the audacity of Victorian civil engineering, then this is it: a magnificent structure 155 yards long and 84 feet high across Rigg Beck in the Howgill Fells, with its eleven slender limestone arches providing an elegant silver-grey contrast to the dazzling green of the surrounding hillsides. Although the rails have long been ripped up, the old trackbed is still there, and the mighty stones of the viaduct remain, staunch in their defiance of more than a century of lashing by the cruellest elements the Pennines can provide.

Today there are fewer and fewer people who remember

the days when the trains came this way. But it's not too long ago that I could have been toasting my feet on the heater in a warm train compartment as I sped eastwards to Stainmore, a heady 1,370 feet above sea level, where the hilltops blend with the sky. Tragic today then that there are no longer any services – not even a ghost of a rumble of a carriage or a peep of a whistle. All we have left in these high Pennine fells are the memories. Shhh! Is that the sound of one of the Durham miners' trains bearing the north-east's sons of toil on hard-earned holidays in Blackpool or Morecambe? Or just a little J21 locomotive, doughty work-horse of the North Eastern Railway, struggling up the gradient with a heavy coke train? Sadly it is nothing but the wind whooping on the fells, as if to mock the grandeur that once was here.

And the weather is ever present. No English main line railway faced such extremes as this, the harshest route south of Scotland, with snowdrifts closing the line regularly each winter. But still the goods had to get through, as this was a vital artery connecting the coal and coke fields of County Durham with the great ironworks on the west coast at Barrow, Whitehaven and Workington. In winter it was reckoned that when it was raining on the coast, then there would likely be snow somewhere on the line up in the Pennines. And when there was snow on the line anywhere, there would almost certainly be a raging blizzard on Stainmore.

No wonder it bred a hardy strain of railwaymen willing to work in such grim and dangerous conditions, frequently having to be rescued from snowdrifts and forced to deal with the slippery wheels of long, unbraked freight trains. There was an extra frisson to the potential for danger in that the engineer of the line was Thomas Bouch, responsible for the ill-fated Tay Bridge, which collapsed on a dreadful winter's night in 1879 just as a train was passing over it.

Bouch had got the job on this most challenging of railways because his brother William was the locomotive superinten- dent of the pioneering Stockton & Darlington Railway, but this in no way diminishes his achievements here in this most barren of places, and his structures across the Pennines proved safe and durable to the end. The great Podgill, Merrygill, Redgategill and Smardale Gill viaducts still stand defiant in the landscape like monuments from the Neolithic age. The grandest of Bouch's structures – and the one that would rehabilitate his reputation today if it had not been demolished in the barbaric anti-railway age of the 1960s – was the Belah Viaduct. Nearly 200 feet high and 1,040 feet long, it was built on 15 piers – a 16-arch gossamer structure of impossibly slim girders. There was nothing like it in Britain, and possibly nothing like it anywhere outside the fecund imaginations of the animators of Disney or Dreamworks movies.

To understand the origins of the grandly named South Durham & Lancashire Union Railway – sweeping through the remotest of landscapes over the roof of England from Darlington on the east coast main line to Tebay and Penrith, south of Carlisle on the West Coast Main Line – I've hiked ankle-deep in mud across sleet-swept sheep pastures to reach Kirkby Stephen, one of the last surviving outposts of the line. OK, I'm freezing and soaked through, but what right have I to complain? These are the terrible conditions that generations of men put up with every day of their working lives to keep the trains running.

I'm clearly made of less hardy stock, since I've already turned back once as a blizzard swept along the footpath into this austere little agricultural town, where the Stainmore line was once the main carrier of people and goods. Such was the blind ambition to get there first as the Victorian railways rolled out across the land, that stations are often distant from the communities they purported to serve. Kirkby Stephen suffered especially badly, as its Stainmore line station, near the town centre, was shut in the 1960s, leaving passengers to trek from the alternative on the Settle & Carlisle line up the hill, from where I've just arrived puffing and out of breath.

Still, even though the trains don't run to the centre of town any more, there are signs of rail-borne life as I make my way off the fells through squidgy fields and into a soulless industrial estate. The sound of hammering and the sight of a few rusty diesels in some sidings lead me into the former Kirkby Stephen East station of the Stainmore line. Inside, it's a cosy shrine to the history of what once was and, if the present custodian has his way, what might again be. Here is former Newcastle University lecturer Mike Thompson, expertly wielding a spanner in the old booking hall and dreaming of the days when the trains will return. He shows me the paintwork in the station offices, newly restored in authentic railway colours with Farrow & Ball fastidiousness. How painstaking can you get?

So devoted is Thompson that, although his home is on the other side of the Pennines at Sedgefield in County Durham, he lives in a caravan on the site. He's joined as often as possible by his equally train-mad wife, a hospital consultant in Hartlepool, and supported by the station cats, Quaker and Oates. 'Look at this,' he says, proudly showing off a teak LNER carriage he is restoring from the heyday of the railway. 'So far, it's cost me £180,000. And these lovely luggage rack brackets. Beautiful. Four thousand pounds! See this engine,' he says, pointing to a little Peckett industrial saddle tank, 'that's mine;' gesturing to a diesel shunter next to it, 'and that's my wife's'.

As the sleet hammers on the old station roof, Thompson explains how, after the railway's closure in 1962, the station became a bobbin factory and a woodworking shop, until he bought it ('rather like something in the Amazon jungle') with some chums, hoping to get the trains back running again. The railway here only lasted a hundred years, he tells me – it arrived late and left early. Contrary to popular belief, the north of England was not a crucible for the early development of railways everywhere. Sure, the pioneering Stockton & Darlington, and Liverpool & Manchester led the way, concentrating on getting goods to and from the sea as quickly and cheaply as possible. But here it was a different tale. Who would want to promote a railway in these wild Pennine moorlands – 2,800 square miles with little industry and containing infinitely more sheep than potential passengers?

But by the mid-nineteenth century, with the first flush of the railway boom over, hungry entrepreneurs were seeking out less obvious markets, and it was in November 1856 that a group of hard-headed industrialists got together and passed a resolution declaring that it 'was expedient that a Railway be formed to connect the extensive Coal and Ironstone fields in the East part of the Island with the important Shipping Ports and Manufacturies on the West side of the Island'. By 1857 Bouch had accepted the job of engineer for the line, agreeing to supervise its entire construction. The Tay Bridge fiasco was in the future, and optimism was all around.

The proposition was simple. Durham produced large quantities of coal and coke, with thousands of beehive ovens that had spare capacity for coke making. The western side of Cumberland and Westmorland was rich in iron ore, with blast furnaces on the doorstep. Here was the perfect opportunity to sell coal and coke for use in the ironworks, and the Stainmore line would be perfect for moving the fuel in one direction and the ore the opposite way. Even better, the iron ore in Cleveland to the east was much improved by mixing it with the purer ores on the west coast.

Since there were no rival railways in this desolate territory, the building of the Stainmore line raced ahead, with the Duke of Cleveland, the local estate owner, cutting the first sod at Kirkby Stephen on 25 August 1857. 'On the day of the sod-cutting ceremony,' reported the *Westmorland Gazette* joyously,

all the shops in Kirkby Stephen were closed and the town enjoyed a general holiday. Triumphal arches and flags were everywhere and the bells of the parish church rang forth a peal. The Duke arrived at the King's Arms Hotel at 11.30 a.m. and a procession led by a navvy with a wheelbarrow and spade was formed. The barrow was of 'polished mahogany with handsome mouldings, polished brass nobs and felloe'. Whether the navvy who bore the barrow on his shoulders was a real son of the soil or embankment and the cutting, we are not prepared to say, but he looked stalwart and sturdy and sunburned enough.

There were more ceremonies later in the year when the foundation stones of the three main viaducts at Tees, Deepdale and Belah were embedded. The line was opened for freight traffic on 4 July 1861 and for passengers on 8 August that year.

Meanwhile an Act of Parliament was pushed through for the connecting Eden Valley Railway, which branched off from Kirkby Stephen, connecting with the West Coast Main Line to Scotland at Penrith. The first sod here was cut by Lord Brougham on 28 July 1857, and was followed by a procession containing sixteen banners, including those urging 'May Westmorland Flourish', 'Peaceful & Plenty' and 'Religious and Civil Liberty'. At 2.30 p.m. a large company sat down to a lavish dinner in a tent behind the King's Head

Hotel and a ball was held in the hotel later in the day. The line opened for minerals on 10 April 1862 and for passengers two months later, with both lines becoming part of the expanded Stockton & Darlington Railway.

Despite the tricky landscape, there were relatively few of the landslips or other tribulations experienced by engineers on other difficult lines, although there was the usual drunkenness, rowdyism and pilfering among the navvies, who earned just three shillings a day for their dirty and dangerous work – leading to the appointment of a constable (first class) to watch over the works. The policeman was to be appointed by the Westmorland and Cumberland force and paid monthly, the amount to be claimed quarterly from the railway company. The chief constable had suggested there should be four officers altogether, but the stingy railway company would only pay for one, even though his wages were a mere £1. 1s. od. a week plus 1s. 5d. boot allowance and 1s. a month for oil. He was also allowed a greatcoat, cape and badge, plus two pairs of 'trowsers' [*sic*], and his duties did not include the 'preservation of game' – which meant he might enjoy the occasional pheasant with his family!

But not all was conflict. There was a delicious note of harmony too between the 'invaders' and the local population. The Eden Valley contractor Joseph Lawton, from Newcastle, married a local girl, Arabella Fairer from Warcop, and after the wedding at the local church threw a grand party, where the workers on the line caroused with the locals and a good time was had by all.

The promoters of the railway, despite (or perhaps because of) their Quaker background, were especially cheese-paring when it came to its civil engineering structures, spending as little as possible. Although Bouch slightly overran his budget, his economy was exemplary, with the main line over Stainmore costing a quarter of the price per mile of the average cost of a British railway at the time. The risk was considerable, since Bouch had no experience of building iron bridges, but as it turned out his two Pennine iron viaducts at Belah and Deepdale proved to be marvels of their age. The reasons for using iron trestles were the need for speed and the height. Material excavated from the east side of each of these two deep valleys was urgently needed for embankments on the west side, and the best way to get it across was to build an iron viaduct.

The prosaic language of civil engineering fails to convey the poetry and mystique that always surrounded Belah. The inauguration ceremony in this bleak depopulated landscape at the start of construction on 25 November 1857 verged on the lyrical, as Henry Pease, deputy chairman of the railway company and a local MP, laid the foundation stone. The proceedings, as described by the *Durham Chronicle*, were poetic indeed.

The morning was clear and frosty, the hills of Stainmore were covered with snow and the scenery around the steep valley of the River Belah was exceeding wild and imposing. Mr J. Whitewell of Kendal addressed the audience. He said they had met amidst sublime scenery which surrounded them to see the immense gap over which Mr Bouch, the engineer proposed to leap, an effort, the magnitude of which had astonished everyone in the district. These engineers must be bold fellows to undertake this monster leap, but bold and vast as the project was, he believed . . . it would be accomplished.

The contractors, Gilkes, Wilson and Company, took just forty-three days to reach the central pier, using no modern equipment, methods of communication or even scaffolding. Each of the piers was made of twelve-inch cast-iron columns arranged in two parallel lines of three each and braced to each other by cross girders at five-foot intervals. The fifteen piers were set sixty feet apart, and looked for all they were worth like a prize-winning entry to a *Meccano* magazine competition. It may have been terrifying to construct – or even to look at – yet there was not a single accident during the entire process of construction.

The awe with which the new structure was regarded is evident from the description of it in a Westmorland directory a few years later.

The Belah Viaduct, over which the N. E. Railway is conveyed, is one of the most imposing triumphs of engineering skill in the British Isles. No adequate idea of the wonderful height of the viaduct can be formed unless a person walks underneath it and then views it at a short distance. Seen in a clear moonlight, when the snow is on the ground or a fleecy cloud of mist partly envelops it, and one of the long trains happens to be passing, the whole appears to be more like the work of enchantment than a very solid reality.

No wonder there were tears in the eyes of the demolition men ordered to tear it down in 1963, just a year after the last train ran – working at the behest of the Tory transport minister Ernest Marples, who sanctioned the line's closure. These hardened veterans of the scrapyard deemed it a tragedy that such a wonder of Victorian engineering should be destroyed.

But let's not get depressed. Why not head back to the mid-1950s to take a journey west from Darlington, turning the clock back to the days, within living memory, when the line was enjoying an Indian summer – metaphorical, of course, since the chill Pennine winds mean it's never quite summer here. The forbidding landscape and poor roads meant that lorries had not yet stolen all the freight, and heavy thirty-wagon trains double-headed by brand new British Railways 4MT tender locomotives ruled the roost. Joining our passenger train at Darlington Bank Top station, the coaches would most likely be superannuated and worn hand-me-downs, displaced from the main line. But even they would have a new 2MT tank engine on the front, fresh out of the works. By 1958 brand-new diesel multiple units had taken over all passenger services, but it was a feature of the railways in the 1950s and 1960s that the arrival of new forms of motive power was nearly always a harbinger of closure.

Looking up at the hands on the magnificent red-brick clock tower of Darlington station, we are bang on time. Reaching the Stainmore line proper at the junction in the little market town of Barnard Castle, we cross the Tees twice – the second time over the massive stone-piered steel-topped Tees Viaduct, 132 feet high and 732 feet long. Ever climbing, with the bark of the engine exhaust bouncing off the surrounding ravine, Lartington West signal box warns that we shall soon be on the mighty curving iron viaduct, 161 feet over Deepdale Beck – a taste of the similar but even more dramatic Belah Viaduct yet to come.

We pause at Bowes, where the local academy inspired Dickens to create his fictional Dotheboys Hall in *Nicholas Nickleby*, in which that most monstrous of schoolteachers, Wackford Squeers, reigned supreme. Monstrous too is the hard, forbidding trek from here towards Stainmore summit, passing from Durham into Westmorland. No wonder the railway cottages to be seen from the train were called God's Bridge. Let's hope the weather forecast is propitious as we climb ever higher, or we may find ourselves embedded in the snow, a frequent event in many winters.

In the arctic conditions of 1947 the Penrith to Darlington train on the morning of 3 February became stuck in the snow on the 1:59 climb to Stainmore summit. Fortunately there was a banking engine at the back, which retrieved the passengers, including a honeymoon couple and a woman with a baby, ferrying them back aboard the last carriage to Kirkby Stephen amid much joshing of the honeymooners. After a week, teams trying to rescue the train were three miles further apart than when they started. A freezing fortnight later, even army flamethrowers could not release the train. 'It was hissing in the wind,' as one joker put it. At the beginning of March they tried again, with two Rolls-Royce jet engines mounted on a truck, but still the drifts proved immovable. Explosives helped to break up the ice, but then it froze again immediately. Meanwhile the snow restarted, and the digging had to begin again. It wasn't until two months after the fateful train had set off from Kirkby Stephen that the locomotive was finally released from its icy prison.

But even amid the bleakness of Stainmore there were joys to be had. One of the signalmen told Peter Walton in his book *The Stainmore and Eden Valley Railways,*

I spent the happiest days of my life in the isolated Stainmore cabin. As an aspiring young signalman I became acquainted with the beauty of a sunrise on a summer morning, the call of the grouse in the heather . . . or the simple majesty of a sunset over the valley. I treasure most of all the brilliance of the Northern Lights seen during the night shift when it *did* seem as if the stars could be picked out of their velvet background. When one of the coloured searchlights of the aurora shot across the sky, things began to happen in the cabin. Bells used to jingle, block indicators danced . . . and the phone circuit would crackle like a demented Geiger counter.

The freight trains would have needed a banking engine here, but with our three coaches and just a handful of passengers, we are bowling up to the summits and then spinning down the 1:59 descent through the still-treeless landscape to Bleath Gill. Rescue teams were permanently on standby to extract stranded trains, their efforts celebrated in a 1955 British Transport Films documentary, *Snowdrift at Bleath Gill* – a demonstration of the laborious technique of digging cross-trenches in drifted snow, before charging the drifts with a locomotive at full tilt.

Filmed in an industrial world that had scarcely changed for half a century, this is a portrait of a labour force and a way of life that had almost entirely vanished by the 1960s. Wiry men in greasy overalls fight the elements without regard for the mantras of health and safety or the modern conveniences of phones or computers. Stephenson and Brunel would have recognised the primitive methods used to free the stranded locomotive. When a steam engine becomes snowbound, it is hot and thaws much of the snow around it – which then turns to ice. To clear it, paraffin-soaked rags are set alight around the running gear until the ice melts. Meanwhile the locomotive itself seems to be ablaze. All this drama is accompanied in the film by the soundtrack of the lovely lilting accents of the northern Pennines, as the men get on with their job.

We're picking up speed through Barras now, with its substantial stone station, once the highest main line station in England until Dent opened on the Settle & Carlisle in 1877. Next is the big dipper of the Belah Viaduct, with the loneliest signal box on the line. Belah box was another bleak outpost, employing three men and open around the clock. The fire was always burning even in summer. Passing trains dropped off lumps of coal together with cans of water to supplement supplies from a nearby well. One of the signalmen was a dab hand at catching rabbits, and peewits' eggs were regarded as the most delicious of delicacies. Another signalman, George Bishop, who worked the box from 1901 to 1905, was a cricketing enthusiast and had an arrangement with a guard to deliver his evening paper so he could follow the Test match scores. But one day the wind blew the paper out of his hands and down into the valley below, so he climbed hundreds of feet down the viaduct, triumphantly finding it, to learn that the great England batsman R. E. Forster was 287 not out, a world record Test score.

Thank goodness we are now back in the tranquil pastures and gentle woodland of the Eden and Lune Valleys, past Kirkby Stephen. At Penrith or Tebay we may change for Blackpool, Morecambe or the Lake District. There was one passenger train which appeared in no timetable yet ran regularly once a fortnight for thirty years. This was the Durham Miners' Convalescent Train, which carried injured and sick miners from the coalfields to recuperate in the magnificent Gothic Conishead Priory, near Ulverston, which had been converted into a convalescent home. The sight of the glorious fells along the Stainmore line for the sick men as they headed for recuperation was said to be a restorative in itself.

The first whispers of closure came early, and long before Dr Beeching had darkened the railway scene. Local freight services from stations along the line started to go in 1952, although the line remained busy with through freights and excursions from the industrial towns of the north-east to the Lancashire seaside resorts. In the late 1950s the new diesel multiple-unit trains cheered up the passengers and made easy work of the Stainmore gradients, and hope rose as painters moved in to refurbish the girders of the Belah Viaduct.

But then the bombshell dropped. First the early-morning

and late trains were axed. Then, on 2 December 1959, the closure notices went up, reinforcing the adage of the period: 'If they paint your station, you can be sure it's going to be closed.' (The cost of refurbishment was often used as an excuse for shutting targeted railways in the 1960s.) Other dirty tricks were deployed, including holding official meetings for objectors a long distance away, so many of the non-car-owning population were unable to attend. Books were cooked to make the line appear unviable in as many ways as possible, including putting an expensive new roof on the engine shed at Kirkby Stephen, even though the end of steam was just months away.

So convinced was a local quarry owner – one Watson Sayer – that the line had a viable future that he offered to buy it with all its assets. Predictably British Railways turned him down. The last passenger service ran on 20 January 1962, the frequency having dwindled to just three trains each way daily. The remaining freights were diverted via Newcastle and Carlisle. The final obsequies were performed by a steam special, the Stainmore Limited, with 400 passengers on board and double-headed by two British Railways Standard locomotives, Nos 76049 and 77003 – their mixed-traffic livery shone up to the finish of a ripe blackberry. This was a mixed blessing for some who had turned out to mourn, since the last surviving J21, stalwart of the line for half a century and which had been booked to work the train, had to stand down from its one moment of glory.

Two boys from Newcastle Royal Grammar School, dressed in black, laid a wreath. One mourner arrived on a penny-farthing and others on elderly bicycles – symbolising the general view that transport progress had been set back a century. The melancholy notes of 'Auld Lang Syne' were played on bagpipes, tears were shed, final photographs were taken, and the Stainmore line ceased to be. As one former railwayman surveying the scene after closure remarked, 'We were not looking at some remote branch line killed by road transport, but an ex-main line entirely wiped out.'

Today, while the trains haven't run over the entire route for more than half a century and the weeds now stand higher than ever, there are few greater pleasures in these high places than to stride on foot along the surviving route of the railway. Here is one of the last areas of England where infrastructure has been allowed peacefully to fade back into the landscape, untroubled by developers seeking to make a quick buck. The mightiest of the stone viaducts remain, as well as the remains of various signal boxes and platelayers' huts. You can still see the stone buttresses for the old Belah Viaduct, protruding like rotten teeth from the hillside. At Barras the former platforms can be detected amid the undergrowth, and the stationmaster's house is now a private residence.

The site of Stainmore has been lovingly marked by a reproduction of the original sign, itself now preserved in the National Railway Museum. Its curved profile, dwarfing anyone who stands alongside it, is punched out of the metal like a stencil and reads: STAINMORE SUMMIT. HEIGHT 1,370 FEET. Most haunting of all is the skeleton of Belah signal box, now a shelter for sheep but which also performs a kind of religious role for the band of enthusiasts who troop up through the louring clouds to pay homage to the memories of Stainmore. Apart from Mike Thompson's shrine at Kirkby Stephen, only a couple of miles of track survive – near Appleby in the west and now operated by the private Eden Valley Railway Company – a tiny fragment that lived on after the closure in 1962, first to serve Hartley Quarry at Kirkby Stephen and then a rarely used army camp at Warcop, finally shutting in 1989.

But if you want to summon up the moody atmosphere of the old railway, then you must walk across the three great viaducts at the western end of the line, which have been linked together by a footpath. Unlike my previous wind-lashed excursion to the railway, the sun is shining today, with all the newness of early spring, and it's not difficult to summon up the drama of a heavy train loaded with pig iron or limestone, slogging its way over the 552-foot-long Smardale Gill Viaduct. Let's imagine that on the front is one of the supremely handsome 4-4-0 locomotives designed by William Bouch, Thomas's brother, for the opening of the line – very advanced for its day, with large windows and the first fully enclosed cab on any British engine, necessary as a protection against the weather. Plumes of steam rise into the blue Westmorland sky as the engine pants ever harder over the Scandal Valley (what an inappropriate name! 'Innocent' seems a far better word to sum up this unspoilt landscape). The only thing to interrupt the reverie is the appearance of a plaque on one of the abutments proclaiming that the viaduct has been restored with financial help from the (very modern) Virgin Trains.

But no Pendolinos will ever run here. The only sound is the crunch of gravel beneath my feet. At Podgill Viaduct, with its nine thirty-foot-span arches, it is a vertiginous eighty-four-foot drop to the glistening Ladthwaite Beck below. Peering down from the 366-foot Merrygill Viaduct, the view is dizzying as I contemplate precipitously the narrow valley of Hartley Beck. The satanic-looking Hartley Quarry behind the trees, which supplied so much traffic to the railway in its heyday, still functions amid a grey haze of dust, producing aggregate for road building.

Don't be confused by the BEWARE sign looming up ahead. This is not a warning of approaching trains, but an exhortation to protect the area's rare red squirrels, part of the wildlife that flourishes as the railway continues its reversion to nature – including brilliant-coloured macaws, which swoop and dive around my head. Theirs is an unlikely Pennine existence, hailing from a conservation centre nearby. Scrambling down between the arches of the Podgill Viaduct to the Ladthwaite Beck, I see nestling against the warmth of the limestone a rare Scotch Argus butterfly, flapping the bold brown 'eyes' on its wings as if to advertise that this is its last breeding ground in England. I tiptoe away with an elated feeling that the old Stainmore railway has a new and enduring purpose in life.

There are still dreamers who believe it will be revived, and not just Mike Thompson, toiling away on his restoration projects amid the rain and the rust at Kirkby Stephen East. Further along the old line the Eden Valley Railway Company is hoping to extend its railway track for another few miles. Whether an old British Railways diesel multiple unit in Network South East livery or sundry other British Railways 1960s-era relics operated by volunteers can recreate the glory that once was remains to be seen. But the rest of the route across the high hills to the east seems doomed – thankfully perhaps – to remain a memory of the days when brave people did dirty and cold work without complaint, when you could take a train to remote places for the price of a cheap ticket, when communities pulled together to value their local railway stations as an essential expression of social solidarity. Even so, it is apparent to anyone who has stood in the cutting wind, watching the sheep huddled together from the cold in the remains of Belah signal box, that the ghosts of the old railway are still there, stalking the gills and the moors.

The saddest spectre of all – that of the unfortunate Thomas Bouch – had no inkling of the lasting achievement of his creation across the Pennines. Although it was destroyed physically by a pusillanimous breed of modern politicians, the line will always live on in legend. By October 1881 Bouch was dead 'of a broken heart', as the *Illustrated London News* put it. Even his death did not deter some of the more merciless North British Railway shareholders, who hounded his widow for compensation long after the Tay Bridge disaster. And the prestigious publication *The Engineer*, which had been supportive during Bouch's lifetime, turned on him savagely when he died. Referring to the 'ill-advised and ill-conceived piece of business' of the Tay Bridge, it commented tartly that it was 'a little surprising . . . that he ever got much bridge work entrusted to him again'. Poor Bouch, it must be said, was as much a victim of the Tay Bridge disaster as the passengers and train crew who perished in the icy waters of the river that night.

These days Bouch is most often recalled in the embarrassing doggerel of the poet William McGonagall, who wrote, 'It must have been an awful sight,/ To witness in the dusky moonlight/ While the Storm Fiend did laugh and angry did bray,/ Along the Railway Bridge of the Silv'ry Tay.'

Yet the engineer's triumphs on the Stainmore line tell an opposite story. In 1859 John Close, a writer from Kirkby Stephen – nicknamed Poet Close by *Punch* magazine, to which he was a prolific contributor – composed a poem of twenty-nine quatrains entitled *Beelah* [sic] *Viaduct, Wonder of the Age*, and dedicated to its engineer, with the first lines running, 'Oh Bouch! What a prolific brain is thine/ To scheme at first this strange gigantic plan.'

But the final note for posterity is enshrined in yet more verse found in papers buried under the central pier of the Belah viaduct in 1963 as the demolition crews moved in after more than a hundred years of faultless service. They were placed there on 6 September 1859, and – while not exactly material for Poets' Corner — do a far better job than McGonagall in repositioning the unfortunate Thomas Bouch to his rightful place in the civil engineering hall of fame.

'The erection of this gigantic and beautiful Iron Structure — the Belah viaduct — was commenced on the 19th day of July in the year of our Lord 1859 . . . One of its highest piers of 200 feet, we raise as our Ebenezer.' It goes on:

In future ages these lines will tell
Who built this structure o'er the dell.
Gilkes Wilson with his eighty men
Raised Belah's viaduct o'er the glen . . .
And thousands wonder at the glorious sight,
When trains will run aloft both day and night;
For ages past, no human tongue could tell
Of such a structure o'er thy monstrous gill.
Time will roll on and mortals may increase
When those who see it now, we hope will rest in peace.

Chapter Five

The glamour that ran out of steam

The Flying Scotsman, the Cornish Riviera, the
Coronation Scot – such speed, such luxury! In days gone
by almost every main line had its named expresses. These
glamorous trains are a fast-receding memory in the
corporate world of today's franchised railways.

It's either outrageously late or impossibly early, depending
on your point of view. Tiptoeing in the moonlight along
the cobbles of Edinburgh's Old Town to Waverley station, I
dodge the last drunks weaving their way home like the cast
from one of Ian Rankin's Rebus novels. As for me, I'm
bleary-eyed from a 4.30 a.m. alarm call, dashing to catch the
first thing that moves out of Scotland's capital city each day.

Even the newly minted tram service to the airport is not up and about yet as I cross a deserted Princes Street to book my ticket for the 5.40 a.m. train to London King's Cross.

With electric motors whirring, the coaches of this IC225 train are already waiting for me at the end of Platform 11. But this is no ordinary service. Though the carriages of the 05.40 may be trying their best to look indistinguishable from the corporate-liveried East Coast electrics that plough up and down the line to London all day, there's a treat for passengers with the energy to walk to the front at this unearthly hour. Resplendent in red with a large blue saltire, is a locomotive with the famous curved nameplate on the front, and painted on the side in foot-high letters are some of the most magical words in the lore of the railways: FLYING SCOTSMAN.

If the train could speak, it might add, 'Yes, and I'm the oldest named train in the world in continuous service and the fastest train from Scotland to London this morning, taking just four hours from city to city – even faster than those fancy tilting Pendolinos over on the Euston line.' But it's a bit early in the day for triumphalism.

This morning's Flying Scotsman is the direct descendant of the famous Scotch Express of 1862, which would imperiously leave London's King's Cross and Edinburgh's Waverley stations simultaneously at 10 a.m., taking ten and a half hours for the journey, including a half-hour stop for lunch at York. It acquired its name officially in the 1920s, when the west and east coast routes to Scotland abandoned their agreement not to compete on journey times, and the London & North Eastern Railway launched a non-stop service over the 393 miles between London and Edinburgh. The inaugural non-stopper, on 1 May 1928, was hauled by A3 Class No. 4472 *Flying Scotsman* and broke the record for the longest non-stop rail journey on the planet, though the journey still took nearly twice as long as the schedule of my train today.

(I must heed the niceties for rail buffs here, and point out that the train and the locomotive, though frequently confused, are not the same thing. The *Flying Scotsman* loco-motive is part of the British national collection; the Flying Scotsman train is what I'm on today. Can a locomotive be a train? Well that's another story, although I'm sure doctrinal theses are already being written on the subject.)

Over the years the Scotsman was in the vanguard of almost every increment of modernisation on the railway. From the outset, passengers could pay a shilling to listen to the radio over headphones before strolling to the onboard barber's shop for a trim or to the cocktail bar for a pre-lunch G & T. Corridor tenders were provided for the locomotives, so that the crew could be changed midway to keep up the speed. The train was one of the few namers to keep going during the war, and the Flying Scotsman brand was promoted throughout the British Railways era as the premier named train on the network. Its centenary in 1962 was marked by a special train launched with a ceremonial send-off by the Lord Mayor of London, inaugurating a speeded-up six-hour service between the English and Scottish capitals operated by the new Deltic diesel locomotives, the most powerful things on the tracks.

On privatisation in 1994, the entire east coast route was named after it by the incumbent franchise holder, the Great North Eastern Railway, which dubbed it the Route of the Flying Scotsman – a legend borne on every carriage. More recently the train was given a makeover by its last operator, East Coast, which decked out the locomotive and driving trailer with purple highlights and gave an extra tweak to the accelerator, with the aim of bringing back a 'touch of glamour and romance' while restoring the rivalry with its old foe, the west coast route. (Though a foe no longer, since Virgin, the west coast franchise holder, has taken over running the east coast line, too.)

But we have to admit this morning that it is not quite the train it was. There is no handsome Stirling Single on the front, or Ivatt Atlantic. Nor a brilliantly polished apple-green Gresley Pacific named after the nimblest racehorses of the day. There is no thundering Deltic diesel bearing the name of a mighty regiment. There's not even a name-board on the front. But at least it is still with us. Trains such as this are rare survivors indeed on our modern railway network. Long gone is the Coronation Scot, stirring hearts at Euston with its streamlined crimson and gold Coronation Class locomotives. Memories are fading now of the exotic Golden Arrow train to Paris, with an air-smoothed Merchant Navy at the head of a rake of Pullmans – uniformed stewards in starched jackets ready to fulfil the passenger's every whim. No more grilled kippers and steaming silver pots of coffee at breakfast on the Brighton Belle. Once upon a time there were more than 130 named trains steaming up and down the land. Now just five of our modern priva-tised rail companies feature named trains in their timetables. We have lost something indefinably precious about train travel in Britain today.

But a whiff of that magic can still be discerned in first class aboard this morning's Scotsman. Can there be an experience more sybaritic than being served a freshly cooked breakfast with a glorious panorama through the carriage window of a silvery morning sun rising over the North Sea as the train speeds across the border at Berwick. Paul, the steward, is at my elbow, uttering the magic words, 'Would you like the full English, sir?' But there's another ingredient, less palpable. Study the mood of all these early-rising execu-tives, suit jackets neatly hooked above seats as they blink into their Acers, Dells and Toshibas. Although no one would dare utter the words – and certainly not in the icy social *froideur* of a British dawn – they're almost certainly thinking how much of a cut above the ordinary commuter they are. The trains, the food and the seats may be identikit. There are no white tablecloths, no embossed menus, no deference from epauletted chief stewards. But aren't we smart to have chosen the Scotsman! No wonder some of the named expresses of the past were known as club trains.

What is it about named express trains that confers such stardust? An article in *The Times* in 1938 to mark the centenary of the London Midland & Scottish Railway got to the heart of it: 'Sentimentality, snobbishness, romanticism, call the weakness by what name you please, will always make the passenger prefer to travel by a train with a name, rather than the 9.15. Though 'few of us except boys small enough to travel on half a ticket, bother our heads much about the engine which draws us'.

That master of the art of railway travel Paul Theroux understood this only too well, even aboard a relatively minor service through the backcountry of Mexico. 'The Jarocho Express,' he writes, 'was one of those trains – rarer now than they used to be – which you board feeling exhausted and disembark from feeling like a million dollars.' Even as far back as 1862 – the Scotsman's inaugural year – a manual called *The Railway Travellers' Handybook* guided discerning passengers to the best trains. Its author heaped praise on the 'engine selected for the express train, the carriages the most secure and the *employés* the most intelligent and trustworthy the management can select . . . The extraordinary momentum which is attained enables the train to dash through interposing obstacles communicating scarcely any shock to the passengers.'

But speed was only part of it. In fact, 'Express' attached to a title was sometimes the opposite of what it seemed. You were mightily mistaken if you thought that boarding the Cambrian Coast Express at Paddington would get you to anywhere in Wales in a hurry. Slogging up to Talerddig summit in Montgomeryshire on a winter's day, the speed dropped to 20 mph. Instead, the word was an invitation into a world not necessarily of speed, but of luxury, exclusivity and glamour. At their best, the named expresses imbued their cosseted passengers with a sense of privilege and superiority. Only if you were lucky did you get the bonus of some extra miles per hour.

There is no better account of the magic of such trains than the 1947 description by the railway historian C. Hamilton Ellis of the Scotch Express leaving St Pancras in the heyday of the Victorian railway. 'Imagine, then, St Pancras on an early summer night of 1876,' enthuses Ellis.

It really is an admirable thing, this new Midland 'Scotch Express'. There stands the superb line of carriages; a twelve-wheel composite, some six wheelers – even these very superior of their kind – and a Pullman sleeping car for Edinburgh. What a Pullman at that. The name *Castalia* glistens in an oval-framed scroll on each side, amid a welter of panels gorgeous in gold-leaf on a dark brown base . . . terribly new and unblemished, she furnishes sleeping accommodation for the best people.

He continues in an almost orgasmic tone:

She scintillates with silverplate and gilding, her handsome bronze kerosene lamps in a coloured clerestory, shedding a warm radiance over rich panels and sleek plush. There in a little while, stately gentlemen will be cautiously extracting themselves from broadcloth and starch, fine ladies and lovely girls will be shedding stiff linen and whalebone as delicately as possible within the uneasy privacy of their green-curtained berths – save for the plutocrats who have booked the single private compartment at the end. Here, under the vast dim parabola of the roof, we see only the dignity, the elegance, the last word in travelling comfort. At the head, superbly in tandem, are two of Matthew Kirtley's latest and finest express engines, deep emerald green and so clean that they reflect the station and signal lamps as if theirs were a vitreous rather than a ferrous quality.

Nearly a century later the journey seemed just as glamorous when I took one of that train's successors, the Thames–Clyde Express, on my first long-distance journey away from home as a teenage boy without my parents. In those days this was one of only two named expresses to run over the rugged Settle & Carlisle line, one of the most scenic railways in the world. Never mind that the word express could not have been more inaccurate, with the journey from St Pancras to Glasgow St Enoch taking a tardy nine hours and forty minutes. There, simmering on the front, complete with THAMES–CLYDE EXPRESS headboard, was one of the most impossibly exciting locomotives any young trainspotter could encounter. I still have its details inscribed in boyish scrawl in my notebook: 'Royal Scot' class No. 46110 *Grenadier Guardsman* from Kentish Town shed. V. clean! Shed code 14B.'

Such first journeys, filled as they are with a heady mix of anticipation and trepidation, are heightened experiences for most of us, let alone a child on the verge of adolescence. For me on that day in 1962 the sight from the carriage window of the high Pennine fells bathed in evening gold and stretching as far as the eye could see was an epiphany. But it was, necessarily, a moment frozen in time. At the end of the 1975 timetable the Thames–Clyde Express would be obliterated, along with so many named trains of that era, as the commissars at British Railways headquarters in

London's Marylebone Road deemed that they no longer fitted in with the image of the modern railway.

As my Scotsman today sighs to a halt at the buffers in King's Cross after 153 years of service, we must mourn all the other named expresses that have departed for the final time. What a tragedy to have dispensed with the Irish Mail from Euston to Holyhead, which was honoured with its title in 1848 – the first named train in the world, even before the Flying Scotsman. This was the year the Chester & Holyhead Railway opened, and fast trains took over from the elderly horse-drawn stagecoaches that had long ferried the mail up and down the road to Telford, now the A5. More than a century of tradition was put in the bin when the train was killed off by the bean counters of British Railways' London Midland Region in 1985. Still, we must be grateful that the original had set a trend for naming trains that became all the rage as the twentieth century dawned. Here was a new age, and the burgeoning publicity departments of the railway companies were keen to present a new image of trains as the fastest and most luxurious form of travel on earth.

The Great Western was a pioneer in naming its own Cornish Riviera Express in 1904. Then, the Paddington to Plymouth leg of the trip to Penzance was the fastest non-stop railway journey in the world, and the company offered three guineas as a prize for the best name chosen by a reader of the *Railway Magazine*. As the 1930s got under way, railways around the world vied to brand their fastest trains. In the lead was the Cheltenham Flyer (the unofficial name of the Cheltenham Spa Express), which in 1932 was claimed by the Great Western to be the fastest train in the world. Not to be outdone, the LNER introduced its streamlined Silver Jubilee from London to Edinburgh in 1935, followed by its sister the Coronation in 1937. Meanwhile LMS struck back with its own streamliner, the Coronation Scot of 1938. Such beauty, such power, such speed! And all were celebrated in a host of associated promotional paraphernalia – advertisements, publicity leaflets and 'window-gazer' guides. The Irish Mail even had special luggage labels, proclaiming it 'The oldest named train in the world'.

Most of the 'namers' were stopped in their tracks in the dark days of World War II, as austerity put an end to such fripperies. With bombs and blackouts all around, there were in any case no trains on the network that could be remotely described as expresses. Only the Flying Scotsman, the Night Scotsman and the Aberdonian limped on through wartime – all with drastic speed restrictions. But the glory days of Britain's great named express trains were yet to unfold as the nationalised British Railways set out to rekindle the excitement of rail travel when the nation emerged from austerity and headed into the never-had-it-so-good days of the 1950s and 1960s.

In this brief period – before the arrival of the Ford Popular and cheap air charters to Torremolinos – a galaxy of great trains flourished: from the Brighton Belle, the Bristolian and the Caledonian to the Ulster Express and the White Rose. Special headboards were cast from aluminium and steel and adorned with brightly painted badges, shields, crests, flags and symbols. The carriages often bore roof boards proclaiming their route, and some, such as the Caledonian from Euston to Glasgow, even carried their name on an elaborately painted tailboard on the gangway of the final coach. How exciting to watch it vanishing into the distance trailing a plume of steam. There were boat trains such as the Cunarder, fine dining trains such as the Tees-Tyne Pullman and the Harrogate Sunday Pullman, trains with regal names such as the Elizabethan from King's Cross to Edinburgh, and trains with the most workaday of names, such as the Trans-Pennine and the Hull Executive. (Whoever named this one must have been blissfully unaware of John Betjeman's famous lampooning poem 'Executive' – 'No cuffs than mine are cleaner . . . I use the firm's Cortina.')

Even some freight trains pulled by the early diesels were elevated with titles, such as the King's Cross Freighter and the Lea Valley Enterprise, though it's hard to see how such labels bestowed the least bit of glamour. The most famous of these was the Condor – a fast freight between London and Glasgow – although its name did not derive from anything so exciting as the giant South American vulture. Rather, it was a prosaic abbreviation of 'containers door-to-door'.

But by the late 1960s the times were a-changing. The age of main-line steam was coming to an end. The very last named train hauled by steam on British Railways was, appropriately enough, another Irish boat train – the 06.15 Belfast Boat Express from Heysham Harbour to Manchester Victoria on 4 May 1968. And with its departure much of the romance that adhered to the railways vanished, literally, in a puff of smoke. The old headboards, often greasy and battered from the steam age, were still sometimes stuck on to the front of the shiny new diesels and electrics. But they looked increasingly incongruous, since there often wasn't a proper place to put them, shaped as they were for the cylindrical smokeboxes of steam locomotives. There seemed even less point when a new generation of multiple-unit trains came along. The front and the back of the train looked identical – as were most of the services on the timetable throughout the day. And why interrupt the sleek lines of these multi-million-pound pieces of technology with a clunky piece of greasy metal, so redolent, it seemed, of the bad old days?

The most famous chronicler of named expresses, the late Cecil J. Allen, whose bible of named trains, *The Titled Trains of Great Britain*, ran into several editions from 1946 onwards, remarked in the fifth edition of 1967 that 'with the gradual disappearance of steam power, much of the romance that attached to the famous named trains of the past disappeared also'. In the space of thirty years the number of titled trains he recorded had grown from 70 to more than 120, but by the mid-1960s 69 of these services were no longer running. Allen commented,

> It is remarkable that at the present time, when all principal trains in countries like France and Germany bear titles, British railway authorities are setting their face against the practice, and steadily removing train names rather than adding to them. The excuse offered is that the higher speeds of today make it possible for the same sets of coaches to be used on three or four long-distance runs on the one day, so that the continued use of names would involve fitting or removing carriage nameboards to a troublesome extent; moreover the tendency is towards standard schedules of equipment rather than to the running of expresses of exceptional speed or luxury. But one cannot help feeling that public attraction as well as romance are being lost in this way.

Most of today's passengers would almost certainly agree with him. What a wealth of heritage was callously thrown away in almost every sphere of the railway's operations. Tragic above all was the loss of the named Anglo-Scottish expresses. First introduced by the London & North Western Railway and the Caledonian Railway in 1862, the Royal Scot – running non-stop from Euston to Glasgow and leaving simultaneously from both stations at 10 a.m. – was one of the most famous trains in the world. From the 1930s onwards, it would always be hauled by one of Sir William Stanier's powerful Coronation or Princess Class locomotives, and even in the 1950s was still celebrated as one of the world's grandest trains.

The text on the back of its restaurant car wine list in 1957, which you could peruse over your aperitif, rhapsodised:

The Royal Scot is the lineal descendant of the first train which, in February 1848, linked the Thames with the Clyde, travelling by the West Coast route, the first all-rail route between London and Glasgow. Today The Royal Scot still holds a leading place in the list of British named trains. Throughout the years, the comfort and amenities of the train have been steadily improved, to culminate in the smooth-riding, all-steel carriages of the latest British Railways design.

A few years later none of this seemed to matter, and the name was binned in 1973.

Over at King's Cross the same fate befell other famous Scottish trains, such as the Talisman and the Elizabethan. The Talisman was the heir to the pre-war streamlined morning express to Edinburgh – the Coronation – and was always hauled by the most immaculate locomotives the King's Cross shed could provide. The name even lasted into the era of the HST diesel trains, before finally expiring in 1991. The Elizabethan, named for the coronation of Queen Elizabeth II in 1953, was the most heavily loaded fast train in Britain at 420 tons. It last ran under steam in September 1961, although the headboard was still carried for a time by the Deltic diesels that took over the line in 1962.

Equally sad was the loss of the holiday trains. The most famous, the Atlantic Coast Express, was axed in the 1960s despite a noble history bearing generations of families with their buckets and spades to the resorts of Devon and Cornwall. The ACE, as it was known, dated back to 1926, and in its heyday carried more through portions to more destinations than any other named train in Britain. Even as late as the summer of 1963 there were five departures from Waterloo: 10.15 a.m. with through coaches to Ilfracombe and Torrington; 10.35 a.m. through to Padstow and Bude; 10.45 a.m. with sections to Seaton and Lyme Regis; more at 11 a.m. to Torrington and Ilfracombe and yet another departure at 11.15 through to Plymouth, Padstow and Bude. Despite such demand, it was abruptly and painfully axed on 5 September 1964. We may perhaps be thankful that today's First Great Western franchise has revived the title, but this is affixed to a train on a different route, running from Paddington via Reading to Newquay. True fans regard it as an outrage and a heresy that the pride and joy of the Southern Railway should be hijacked by its old rivals at the Great Western.

The previous year had seen the end too for that other famous seaside express, the Scarborough Flyer. Unlike the ACE, this one really did go fast. Launched in 1927 and running only in the summer months, the service was boosted in 1935 with its timing cut to three hours between King's Cross and York, making it one of the fastest trains of the day. There was an added bonus for schoolboy trainspotters in that it was regularly hauled by the cream of the LNER's locomotive fleet. Imagine the double thrill of setting off for a fortnight at the seaside with *Mallard* or *Flying Scotsman* on the front of the train. There was mourning indeed when the last service ran on 8 September 1963. Today the North Yorkshire resort has no through trains to the capital of any kind.

The end of the titled trains, to which so many regions of Britain lent their name, meant that the British seaside would never be the same again. No more would genteel folk take afternoon tea aboard the Pullman cars of the Bournemouth Belle on their way to select private hotels on the Dorset coast with 'H&C water and interior-sprung mattresses in all rooms'. The era of luxury was terminated on 9 July 1967, when commuter-style electric trains took over the line. Gone too was the Southern Region's all-Pullman Devon Belle, with its famous observation car at the rear. Hopeful travellers from the north were no better off; the celebrated Devonian from Bradford to Paignton was pulled in 1975.

Never more would you be able to buy tickets for the holiday trains of East Anglia, steaming out of Liverpool Street to Hunstanton, Lowestoft, Yarmouth and Cromer with their marvellous regional names – the Fenman, the Broadsman and the Easterling. No longer would Glaswegians escape to the fresh air of St Andrews aboard the Fife Coast Express. The legendary Pines Express, which bore the toiling masses from the factories and mills of Liverpool and Manchester across the Mendip Hills for a refreshing fortnight on the south coast came to an abrupt end when the Somerset & Dorset line, which provided a direct route avoiding London, was closed.

In fact, almost every social tribe of Britain was diminished as the lights went out one by one on the great named trains. No more excited emigrants to far-flung corners of the world on the Ocean Liner Express to Southampton, nor hiking boots and crampons on the Lakes Express from Euston to Windermere. Hard-nosed West Midlands businessmen would miss sealing their deals after a trip up to the smoke on the Midlander or the Inter-City. Doing business in Manchester would never be the same after the demise of the Palatine or in Liverpool without the Merseyside Express or in Hull minus the Hull Pullman.

How much less glamorous continental travel would be with the loss of the Golden Arrow and the Hook Continental, with its onward connections to Amsterdam and beyond. The Isle of Man would never be the same without the Manxman, nor Belfast and Dublin without the Shamrock. How dull to have to travel to Butlin's without a reserved seat on the

Butlin's Express dashing to Skegness on a train headed by one of the LNER's famous Football Class locomotives.

Some of these grand old trains didn't give up without a struggle. Passengers, led by actor Lord Olivier, fought back when British Railways started to run down the Brighton Belle, the world's first all-electric Pullman train, at the end of the 1960s. The famous thespian's protest received media coverage across the world. But to no avail: the train was withdrawn entirely on 30 April 1972.

But recently – whisper it not too loudly – the fashion has been reviving. First Great Western, East Coast and East Midlands Trains were all still running a modest stable of namers in 2014. Even Abellio – a subsidiary of the Dutch state rail company – operated a solitary named train on its London to Norwich route. New ones even occasionally enter the constellation, such as the Sheffield Continental – so named because it connects with the Eurostar to Paris at St Pancras International. Thankfully there is still some spirit of poetry and romance in the press and publicity offices of some of our hard-nosed private railway companies.

But there is no escaping the fact that, no matter how romantic the name, the bearers are all anonymous trains in standard formation. Apart from the Flying Scotsman, with its adman's vinyls plastered across the locomotive, they do not carry headboards, mostly making do with a bit of card or paper affixed to a window and some small print in a timetable. They go mostly unrecognised by their passengers, unless you happen to be a nostalgist or an anorak.

Today's Cornish Riviera Express still departs daily from Paddington for Penzance, but is operated by a diesel HST packed full of tight aircraft-style seating to cater for Home Counties commuters. It is a poor thing compared with its predecessor, which in its 1930s heyday would have included the Great Western's sumptuous Centenary coaches and been hauled by one of the monarchs of the locomotive fleet – a mighty Great Western Railway King Class locomotive resplendent with burnished copper and brass and immaculate Brunswick-green paintwork. But at least today's train has the virtue of going faster, reaching Penzance half an hour quicker than in the 1950s.

In fact, for all their ordinariness, most of today's titled trains are nippier than their predecessors. Today's West Riding, an identikit Inter City 225 leaving King's Cross at 06.30, may not offer much glamour compared with its 1937 predecessor – one of the most exciting streamlined trains in the world, with its dedicated articulated dining coaches pulled by a speed-record-breaking garter-blue A4 class Pacific – but the timing to Leeds then was 2 hours 43 minutes, compared to less than two and a half hours today. So let's be thankful for the ones we have got – at least they remind us of the heritage and allow us to bring back the spirit of the glamour of the railways, albeit vicariously.

Could we see yet more return? So far, all the various operators of the line have stuck resolutely behind the Flying Scotsman, and who could deny that a few hearts continued to flutter as my modern train rushed non-stop through Berwick, Durham and York. The east coast has a clutch of other long-distance namers, including the Highland Chieftain to Inverness and the Northern Lights to Aberdeen. First Great Western still flies the flag of its heritage in the west, running eighteen named trains, including such evocative titles from the past as the Cathedrals Express and the Merchant Venturer. The humbly titled East Midlands Trains at St Pancras has attached some glamour to itself by perpetuating the Master Cutler and the Robin Hood. The East Anglian, to Norwich – in continuous service since its inauguration as a streamliner in 1937 – makes a daily appearance at Liverpool Street, showing there is some poetry in the hearts of its Dutch operators.

Over at Euston on the west coast main line the mood has been more utilitarian. Not so long ago the Red Rose would depart proudly to Liverpool or the Comet to Manchester. The Royal Highlander would set off in full pomp to Inverness and the Lakes Express bear off a train full of folk to tread in Wordsworth's footsteps at Buttermere and Keswick. Scarcely an hour would go by without a named train letting off steam in one of Euston's platforms. These days you can spend an entire day watching the destination board flash and not encounter a single named train, although there is a night service that runs under the corporate title Caledonian Sleeper, which is informally known to its fans as the Deerstalker Express.

Can it be that Virgin Trains boss Richard Branson – that master of modern branding – has suffered a lapse of creativity? Surely in his ever-imaginative PR world there might be room to recreate the romance of the named trains we have lost? When I put the question to the Virgin west coast press office, they scratched their heads. Ever charming, they said, 'We'll have to put this one to the marketing team.' And eventually the answer came back: 'The Virgin brand is well understood by customers and Virgin believes that consistent brand messaging should apply across all its services. It has therefore chosen not to name any of its train services.'

That's the end of that then. But never say never. Back in 1961, when the Euston Arch was brutally hacked down, whoever would have thought it would rise again? Yet a reconstruction of the arch has now been incorporated in the blueprint for a new Euston, where it is expected to be a totemic symbol of the new £50 billion HS2, scheduled to open in 2026. Memo to Sir Richard and all the other grandees with a stake in the heroic new Euston. What a marvellous marketing ploy it would be to name a train with a suitably romantic title to match. Get ready to book your tickets for the Coronation Scot 2 . . .

Chapter Six
The train that got ahead of its time

Scousers knew it as the Docker's Umbrella. In its heyday
the Liverpool Overhead Railway was a state-of-the-art
urban transit system; now it is just a memory on
Merseyside. But its vision is emulated round the world.

I'm whizzing in almost celestial fashion over the roof-tops of one of the busiest and buzziest cities on the
planet. Below are the teeming streets of Bangkok, eleven
million population and growing fast. But the noise,
tangled traffic, choked alleyways, stench, simmering heat
and melting pot of humanity that is the Thai capital
could be a world away, since I'm ensconced coolly aboard

the Skytrain, the world's busiest and most modern elevated urban railway.

Effortlessly and silently, the fast silver and blue air-conditioned electric trains whisk more than 600,000 passengers daily high above the streets along a fifty-five-kilometre network of tracks. Since the line opened in 1999 it has become possible to cross this gigantic metropolis in minutes, liberated from the hooting, parping tangle of cars, buses, scooters and rickshaws in the streets below. This may be the Third World, but sailing along aboard my train, I'm happy to be in Parallel World.

Cut to another mighty commercial city on the other side of the globe, and I'm trudging through the backstreets of Liverpool fringing the brown waters of the Mersey in search of another great urban elevated railway, one now vanished into the recesses of time. Like the Skytrain, the Liverpool Overhead Railway was a marvel of its age. The Ovee or Docker's Umbrella, as it was known, was the world's first electric elevated railway and the first rail system to use that underrated wonder of modern transport, the escalator.

The Liverpool Overhead Railway was an international pioneer in other ways too, deploying Britain's first automatic semaphore signals and then the first electric coloured lights, a technology that controls most modern trains today. In its heyday, at the end of World War I, the short six-and-a-half-mile route was carrying around twenty-two million passengers a year. The rattle of the trains, with their austere brown wooden carriages suspended on girders sixteen feet above the street, was the definitive background soundtrack to one of the world's great port cities, which in its day was a mighty rival to New York. It is hard to imagine the shock to Merseyside when it was shut down in 1956. We had not yet encountered Dr Beeching, but it indisputably ranks as one of the most traumatic British railway line closures of all time.

Few railway systems have been so completely obliterated as this great transport artery of the once-second city of the British empire, with all signs of it almost entirely purged. Which is why I'm standing at a cold bus stop on Lime Street waiting for the number 82 to Toxteth, hoping I might find the vestiges of the terminus in the docklands streets where the line once began. No Maggie Mays or drunken sailors on today's Lime Street, with its boarded-up shops, just a gaggle of Chinese university students passing by on their way to the halls of residence fronting Lime Street station – a sign of changing times. The mood is also downbeat when I alight on Park Road, once the beating heart of the South Docks.

In Liverpool's commercial heyday these terraced streets would have been bustling; now even the ghosts seem to have packed up and gone home. The Queen's Head pub on the corner of the appropriately Dickensian Dorrit Street is derelict. The Royal Oak, which would once have resonated with the optimism and zest for life of Scouse working-class culture, is boarded up. More poignant still is the grand art deco Gaumont Cinema. With its 1,500 seats and cavernous interior, this great dream factory once had the most modern projection system in the world. Now it is home to roosting pigeons, and water trickles down its once-splendid frontage. Sad that it is now not even in demand in its most recent incarnation as a bingo hall.

But what's this? Few might recognise it now, but on the corner of Kedlesdon Street, with its tiny terraced houses, buried deep below the ground under the derelict offices of an abandoned engineering works called Roscoe, are the remains of the Dingle terminus, virtually all that survives of the Ovee. After slumbering for half a century, it announced its presence in dramatic fashion in 2012 when the tunnel wall collapsed causing the houses above to be evacuated.

Of course there have been other great elevated railways

of the world. New York had its own, especially the famous Manhattan Railway and its Second, Third, Sixth and Ninth Avenue lines. The Boston Elevated Railway, with its distinctive orange trains, was part of the lifeblood of the city until much of it was closed in the 1980s. The 113-mile Chicago El or L lives on today as the third-busiest metro system in the US after New York and Washington, with 231 million passengers a year. But the Liverpool Overhead was in a class of its own – the first, the most revolutionary and, in the hearts of the people of this most heart-on-the-sleeve of cities, probably the most loved by the citizens who used it.

The Docker's Umbrella was not just another railway, it was a landmark and an institution embedded deep in the heart of all Scousers, as much cherished in its own day as the Beatles would be later – and John, Paul, George and Ringo knew it well as boys. When closure suddenly stole up on 30 December 1956 – because the cost of essential repairs had mounted to more than £2 million – disbelieving crowds lined the route, many in tears, scarcely comprehending what was happening. 'Why had nobody foreseen this?' the cry went up. But there were other priorities in a city which had only recently emerged from the terrible ravages of World War II and whose commercial fortunes were on the brink of calamity.

The outpourings of nostalgia were all the more extravagant since the railway was linked in the minds of many Merseysiders with Liverpool's one-time greatness as a port, which in the post-war world was starting to slip away with the rise of air travel, containerisation and the beginning of the tilt southwards in the economy of the nation. What a contrast to seventy years before, when the railway was first built. Liverpool's docks were among the wonders of the world. Even by the eighteenth century the trade in manufactures, sugar and slaves had already created immense riches for the city's merchants.

Cotton was integral to the fabulous enrichment of the city, arriving in ships' holds on the third leg of their triangular run: Lancashire's wool and linen to west Africa, slaves in their thousands across to the Atlantic to the West Indies and American colonies, raw cotton, tobacco and rum back to Lancashire. Liverpool's role in the world cotton trade was without rival, making it one of the richest non-capital cities on the planet. It was these profits that helped to finance that other great local transport undertaking – the Liverpool & Manchester Railway, Britain's first fully steam-powered passenger line, in 1830.

As plans were laid for the Liverpool Overhead Railway, the port was in its prime. By the mid-nineteenth century there was an almost insatiable demand for labour in America, where wages were five times those in Europe, and 1,000 ships a year were taking emigrants across the Atlantic. In the peak year of 1852 nearly 300,000 – many from Ireland – said their farewells before heading off to a new life in America. The shipping bonanza did not stop there. Liverpool was also a major outlet for the goods of industrial England, including mineral salts from Cheshire, iron and cloth from Yorkshire, coal from Lancashire, pottery from Staffordshire and engineering products from Birmingham. At first most ships went to America, returning with tar, turpentine, timber, tobacco and of course cotton. But the entire world was soon in the grasp of Liverpool's merchants. The first ship had docked from Calcutta in 1815. The China trade was opened up to Liverpool shipping in 1833, and by 1851, the year of the Australian gold rush, Liverpool shipowners led the world with their super-speedy wool clippers.

But back on the Liverpool waterfront commerce was being strangled by the congestion along the Dock Road, which ran along the Mersey shore from north to south. Buses, lorries, horse-drawn carts and drays tangled with wheezing steam shunters pulling packed goods trains in and out of the docks using the many crossings interrupting the road. One ingenious solution was developed in 1856 by a clever engineer called William Joseph Curtiss, in which specially adapted buses could run on sidings and tracks. With the flip of a lever, the flanges of the wheels would retract and the bus would return to the road, rattling over the granite setts to overtake slow-moving goods trains. Though Heath Robinson would surely have delighted in it, it was hardly efficient, and poor Curtiss abandoned the idea when he was forced to pay tolls to use the tracks. It was obvious something more ambitious had to be done to separate passengers from cargoes.

The need for a passenger railway following the line of Liverpool's docks had been recognised as early as 1852, and in 1878 the Mersey Docks and Harbour Board put forward a parliamentary bill for an elevated line five and a quarter miles long. The Board of Trade objected to the proposed single track with passing places, and the plan had to be amended to provide a double-line railway, which was sanctioned in 1882. But dithering and prevarication were the order of the day until 1888, when a group of local businessmen frustrated with the lack of progress got their own railway together, forming the Liverpool Overhead Railway Company and commissioning two of the greatest engineers of the day to develop a grand plan. Who better to engage than Sir Douglas Fox, famous for the tricky construction of the railway up Mount Snowdon and the Great Central Railway's ambitious London extension, and James Henry Greathead, inventor of the eponymous Greathead Shield, a brilliant device that bored through the London clay to create the tunnels for London's Tube? Within a year these two titans of the civil engineering world were ready, and work got under way in October 1889.

But it wasn't just the infrastructure – with trains hugging the river suspended high on a serpentine steel platform – that was revolutionary. Steam motive power for haulage had to be ruled out for fear that sparks from the ash pans would ignite flammable ships' cargoes. Why not go further, it was argued, and employ that new-fangled technology – electric power? Although hardly revolutionary now, the only similar operations at the time the Overhead was conceived were the Blackpool tramways and Volk's electric railway along the seafront at Brighton. In 1890 the City & South London broke the mould as the world's first major electric railway. But the Overhead became the world's first electric elevated railway and the first to be operated by electric automatic signals.

Construction was finished in January 1893, and the line was formally opened on 6 March by the Marquess of Salisbury, who flicked the switch on the power at the railway's own generating station at Bramley-Moore Dock, with its 'awe-inspiring' range of machinery, including six Lancashire boilers and four steam horizontal engines. Services began at Alexandra Dock in the north, with eleven other stations at Brocklebank, Canada, Sandon, Clarence, Princes, Pier Head, James Street, Custom House, Wapping, Brunswick and Toxteth, most taking their names from adjacent docks.

It was immediately regarded as a wonder of the era, and its reputation quickly spread on the bush telegraph operated by sailors from across the globe, who had never seen a marvel like it. What a delight, in an age when railways were characterised by slowness and filth, to find a mode of transport whose attributes were precisely the opposite – speed, cleanliness and an absence of noise. But with only poorly paid dock workers as a source of revenue, ticket sales outside working hours could not deliver the revenue needed for a thriving railway. So the line was extended to entice passengers from the more affluent residential areas in the north and south of the city. There were to be new termini – at Seaforth Sands, a stretch of beach along the Mersey where it was possible for people from the city terraces to paddle on the muddy edges of the Mersey and pretend to be at the seaside – and the quaintly named Dingle in the south. The last section involved building a new station at Herculaneum Dock and boring a half-mile tunnel through sandstone rock to the new terminus, bringing the route length up to six and a half miles. The first passengers at Dingle station were flummoxed at having to descend a flight of steps underground to board what was billed as an overhead railway, but this was soon accepted as one of the oddities of one of Britain's most individualistic lines.

In 1905 the route was extended further north to the Lancashire & Yorkshire's station at Seaforth and Litherland, allowing passengers to connect to that railway's Liverpool to Southport Line, and for a while through services ran between Southport and Dingle, effectively turning the little Liverpool Overhead into a main line along the Lancashire coast, although these services ceased at the outbreak of the First World War. A further useful connection was made with the L&Y's line to Aintree, enabling the Ovee to take docklands families out of the city to enjoy a flutter on the Grand National.

Technological advances along the little railway continued apace. In 1901 the first railway escalator and only the second in the country (the first was at Charles Harrod's London department store in 1898) was installed at Seaforth Sands station. Advertised as a 'Reno system moving staircase' it took its name from the American inventor Jesse Reno, who had created a novelty ride at Coney Island in 1895 – though perhaps 'staircase' was too dignified a term since passengers had to clamber onto a moving belt with rubber ridges at a twenty-five-degree angle. Sadly this primitive Lancashire version of the escalator had to be withdrawn five years later after a rash of claims from ladies who had caught their camisoles in the mechanism, ripping off some expensive lace in the process.

When the electrically operated semaphore signals were replaced in 1921 by Westinghouse coloured light signals, these once again set the pace as the first such examples in the country. Even the hinged doors on the carriages were balanced in such a way that they would jerk shut when the train set off. A visiting New Yorker observed that the Overhead had the finest automatic doors he had ever seen. But never mind the technology; the view from on high along the Mersey was one of the most memorable to be had in any world city. You might be a docker travelling on a humble workman's ticket or a tourist freshly disembarked from America, enticed by a series of posters for which the Overhead was famous – elaborate prints showing panoramic vistas of docks lined with the vessels of the great shipping companies of the world. 'See the wonderful docks and gigantic liners,' they proclaimed. 'Book the round trip (13 miles). Trains every few minutes.'

And wonderful it was. The young Herman Melville, author of *Moby Dick*, wrote in 1849, 'The sight of these mighty docks filled my young mind with wonder and delight . . . In Liverpool, I beheld long Chinese walls of masonry; vast piers of stone; and a succession of granite-rimmed docks. The extent and solidity of these structures seemed equal to what I had read of the old Pyramids of Egypt.' For the modest price of the fare, which in the 1930s was as little as 2d. for a trip along the entire length of the line, you were a privileged passenger in an unfolding diorama of the history of world shipping.

As your train clicketty-clacked high above the wharves, you might glimpse the scarlet funnels of the great Cunard liners, which had pioneered from Liverpool in 1840 the world's first scheduled transatlantic service, taking just fourteen days to Boston. Here too might be seen over the years the ships of the White Star, another of Liverpool's great lines. The company's *Oceanic* opened up a new era for steamships in the 1870s, with its waterproof, fireproof bulkheads, though her sister the *Titanic*, which notoriously hit an iceberg in 1912 with the loss of more than 1,500 lives, proved to be less resilient! (Although *Titanic* bore the name of Liverpool on her stern, she never actually visited the city.)

Watch out for the ships of the local Brocklebank family, founders of the oldest shipping line in the world, as well as those of Blue Funnel, established by the Liverpool Nonconformist entrepreneur Alfred Holt, who started out as an apprentice on the Liverpool & Manchester Railway. Blue Funnel's fast coal-fired ships put paid to the era of sail. Other great local firms whose vessels you might spot on this journey included the Bibby Line, founded in 1807, Clan Line, Pacific Steam Navigation, and Lamport & Holt, who developed the first mosquito-proof ship.

You were unlikely to miss the yellow funnels and white hulls of the ships of the Liverpool-based Elder Dempster line, which controlled 500 vessels in its 150-year history, dominating the west Africa trade. Elder Dempster almost single-handedly as a company invented the banana as a favourite fruit for the British, giving them away to Liverpool street traders in an early version of free advertising. Celebrity-watchers should keep their eyes skinned, since that most glamorous of transatlantic lines, Canadian Pacific, might have one of its famous Empress liners arriving in port, heading imperiously along the river, with the firm's trademark red and white chequered flag ready to discharge its payload of North American socialites heading for the boat train to London.

The demise of the Liverpool Overhead Railway heralded the end of the liners too. As a young journalist on the *Liverpool Echo* I was sent to report on the very last arrival of a regular transatlantic passenger service in the city on 23 November 1971, when the *Empress of Canada* steamed in from Montreal. I remember dock workers standing in silence as she moved gracefully up the Mersey. 'It was almost the like the Cenotaph on Remembrance Day,' recalled the master, Captain W. E. Williams. True, the city has a new cruise terminal on the waterfront, where some of the world's largest ships can tie up, but most Merseysiders would agree it's a poor substitute for the great days of old.

But let's not be sad, since there was never much time for regret in the bustling heyday of the Ovee. Hard to recapture it now, but here was a tough but magical city teeming with life and activity, dominated by its mighty river and an intense sense of urgency as arrivals and departures came almost endlessly along its miles of docks and wharves. In the city streets uphill from the Mersey were the stern Victorian offices of the merchants, brokers and shipowners, with their polished brass plates and pompous-sounding names. Add to this the beating of hooves, the gongs of trams, the whistles of the trains and the singing from the Dock Road pubs thronged with exhausted but mostly cheerful men sinking pints of Higson's, Bent's and Walker's bitter. These might be the very same ones identified in Liverpool dockers' slang in journalist Frank Shaw's entertaining book *My Liverpool*. Here was Dulux (always gets it in one coat), London Fog (he never lifts) and the Chemist. Helping his chums to stolen bounty off the dockside, he shouts merrily, 'Here's more f' yer [morphia].'

Standing imperiously at the centre of it all, with the Overhead rumbling past just yards away, are the famous Three Graces at the heart of the waterfront – the Royal Liver Building, topped with its two mythical liver birds, the Cunard Building and the Mersey Docks and Harbour Board Building. The image of the Overhead's trains superimposed on this waterfront panorama resonated throughout the empire. It's no exaggeration to say that no railway on the planet was the starting point for more exotic destinations than the Liverpool Overhead Railway, since generations of sailors travelled on its trains to access their ships to faraway places. In its day it was the Piccadilly Line to Heathrow, the Heathrow Express and the Gatwick Express rolled into one.

So climb aboard for a journey along the line, but don't expect luxury. With austere wooden seats, except in first class, these are among the plainest carriages in Britain. And don't even think of the Skytrain. (These days we must defer increasingly to Asia for sophistication in metro systems; after all, the Hong Kong Metro, in the shape of MTR, jointly runs today's London Overground.) Let's instead locate ourselves in the period just after World War II, one of the busiest times for the Overhead, while the docks were still in their prime and before the decline set in. Even at this time, however, the trains – despite their electric operation – had a slightly fusty air of the past about them. But the entrance to Dingle station is cheerful enough, with its cinema-like foyer and a notice by the ticket office proclaiming the cheapness and value of the tickets compared with the city's buses and trams.

Soon there's a rumble from the tunnel ahead and the headlight of an approaching train illuminates the tangle of tracks. With a sigh of air brakes, it pulls into the island platform and all is bustle as doors are slammed, wooden-framed carriage windows rattle and the familiar *gudder-gudder* sound so characteristic of old electric trains starts to resonate. The driver moves smartly from one end of the train to the other and clunks his brass controller key firmly onto its mount in the cab.

Blinking in the darkness after the Toxteth sunshine outside, the train interior with its dim lights seems gloomy beyond belief. But we have chosen a perch on the left side of the carriage, where we shall soon find ourselves among the most privileged passengers anywhere on Britain's rail network.

There's a frantic wave of his flag from the guard, and the train begins to move, the wheels hammering and squealing over the points as we roll off into the tunnel, motors humming and the grimy tunnel bricks brilliantly illuminated by the lightning flashes from the conductor rail.

Half a mile on, we're out in the sunshine and up in the air suspended on the solid girder work, which lacks the baroque flourishes of, say, the Métropolitain in Paris or the L in Chicago but has the virtue of appearing modern in this early post-war period when anything antiquated-looking is facing the wrecker's ball. All along the broad sweep of the Mersey is a panorama which is both the hell and heaven of the Industrial Revolution at a glance. Here are dockside cranes soaring skywards, glinting acres of sidings, steam and smoke pouring into the sky, cathedral-like warehouses and an unimaginable tonnage of shipping lined up beside the quays, while the Mersey ferries buzz like water beetles over the river. One might appropriate the famous description of the New York High Line written by Adam Gopnik of the *New Yorker*: 'It does not offer a god's-eye view of the city exactly, but something rarer, the view of a lesser angel, of a cupid in a renaissance painting, of the *putti* looking down on a renaissance manger.'

We're picking up speed now through the South Docks (who would know from this busy scene that commercial shipping would be all but extinct here by the 1970s), but despite our altitude we're far safer than on most British main lines of the period, since the track contains a stopping device that applies the brakes should a train overshoot a signal. We're through Herculaneum, Toxteth and Brunswick. (In later years the stations dropped the 'Dock', and souvenir hunters snapped up tickets from Pier Head to Canada for just a few pence to impress their friends!) Billows of steam issue from the shunting engines nipping in and out of dock entrances below us. These were both the sustenance and downfall of the Ovee, since the steam and sulphur rotted away the girders to the point where they eventually became irreparable.

The wheels are squealing now as we approach the central area, and towering above us is Giles Gilbert Scott's mighty Anglican cathedral — a 'symphony in sandstone' as it was once described. The frame of this, the largest church building in Britain, though yet to be completed, dominates the surrounding terraces, which are humble but when the sun glints off the rows of shiny slate roofs just as exalted in their own way. This is the heart of Liverpool's famous Sailor Town. Every ingredient in the commercial life of a busy port is here. Shipping offices, chandlers, sail makers, wheel-wrights, tobacconists, greasy-spoon snack bars, pawnbrokers, off-licences, brothels — almost every aspect of human aspi-ration and degradation is to be found here, as well as, of course, on every corner the regulation public house.

The docks get smaller and older as we rattle through Wapping, Custom House and James Street, and tempting though it is to swivel your view seawards, the better view is on the other side of the carriage, incorporating the throng of Merseyside humanity that oils the wheels of this great city. John Gahan puts it colourfully in his book about the Ovee, *Seventeen Stations to Dingle*: 'Behind glass windows large and small one sees clerks at their desks in the mostly old and gloomy offices, girls in blue overalls at benches in a clothing manufacturers, men queueing up at lunchtime in the cocoa rooms for pint mugs of tea and inch-thick sand-wiches. Groups of seafaring men, including bands of Coolies who walk along in single file, mingle with the men of Merseyside in the cosmopolitan port . . .'

But look out too for the towering brick walls and elegant colonnades of the early-Victorian warehouses, including Jesse Hartley's Albert Dock from 1846, which would eventually become Grade 1 listed and help to rescue Liverpool from the doldrums as a tourist attraction by becoming the northern home of the Tate Gallery. Not many vessels are tied up today, since this is one of the oldest city docks and already mostly obsolete. But no time for sentiment, as the brakes start to grind for arrival at Pier Head station, the busiest on the line, with connections to the famous 'ferries 'cross the Mersey' to Birkenhead, Wallasey and New Brighton.

You might 'lern yerself some Scouse' here as the train fills up. Gahan points out (and as a Scouser himself, he is not being patronising) that Liverpudlians like 'to talk freely and for all to hear'. So you might be greeted by 'Ullowhack' or 'Whereareyerworkinlads?' You may also, if you are lucky, learn the art of striking a match on the sole of your boot or opening a beer bottle with your teeth. Curious, you may think, that the train itself is curiously quiet compared with the loud chatter on board. This is thanks to another Ovee innovation – flange lubricators set in the track, which automatically smear the rails with grease, eliminating the squealing as the trains pass, so as not to rattle the grand and sober offices of the Liverpool merchants hereby.

Heading north again along the Mersey there are no such constraints. The train's motors build up to their characteristic whine as we pick up speed. Here are the city's busiest docks, through Canada, Brocklebank, Alexandra and Gladstone. When the doors open here, you will find on the air the unmistakable salty whiff of the Atlantic. Gladstone Dock was the haunt of the great international liners, which would disembark their passengers here. In less busy times it was possible, for a modest price, to buy a permit from the Overhead booking office to take a tour of these behemoths before they departed, and to live out momentarily the glamour of being a transatlantic passenger for the price of just a few pence. Don't be surprised to find a buzz of international conversation as the train doors open, or people asking in strange accents, 'Is this place really England?'

And so on to the end of the line, where you might want to park your deckchair on the beach at Seaforth Sands, knot your handkerchief and focus your binoculars on the giant ships queuing up for their berths. Or you might change at Seaforth and Litherland onto a main line train, and head to Southport, where the sands would provide sunbathing with a little more class.

But no such whimsy for most Liverpudlians, bent on getting home in the rush hour. 'The carriages are tightly packed,' writes Gahan,

with home-going overalled men in peaked caps or battered trilbies until there was scarcely room to breathe, and at each station along the line, the platforms are thronged with prospective passengers up to six deep. As soon as the train comes to a halt the doors are flung open and they pile in, and woe betide anyone trying to alight. Courtesy is an absent virtue but everyone is cheerful and much banter is exchanged between various groups of men. Sometimes several will commence to sing and others will join in until the atmosphere becomes positively sociable, with an occasional good-humoured admonition to 'shut up' from colleagues reading their copies of the *Liverpool Echo*.

Sometimes itinerant salvationists would work the carriages, hoping to save the occasional soul; not much hope here – Liverpool's dockers were never interested overmuch in God-botherers or do-gooders. The no-smoking notices were routinely disregarded, and the air in the carriages was usually thick with tobacco smoke. The fug on board is superbly recreated in a vignette of the railways in Terence Davies's famously nostalgic film set in Liverpool in the 1940s and 1950s, *Distant Voices, Still Lives*, one of the most widely admired British films of the post-war era.

But it wasn't to last. One slushy, grey, miserable day in February 1955 the headlines in the evening papers delivered a bombshell – the Docker's Umbrella would have to close. There was disbelief throughout the city. One former engineer proclaimed, 'If they stop the railway for one day, there will be anarchy on the docks!' But the cold facts were irrefutable. Sixty years of weather had left the ironwork in such a fragile state that most of it would have to be renewed. Combined with this, the economic tide had turned. Liverpool's importance as a world port was beginning to diminish, leading to cuts in the workforce, growing numbers of redundant warehouses and a shrinking economy. The cost of renovation was too much for the privately financed railway.

Even so, it had carried nine million passengers in the previous year – not surprising since fares were so competitive. A poster in 1955 advertised, 'Save time, save money. The Overhead is still the cheapest transport in the city.' And it certainly was – a weekly season ticket from Dingle to Pier Head cost just four shillings. In 1956 an eleventh-hour bid was made to save the railway, as the Mersey Docks & Harbour Board met to discuss the impact the closure would have on the working of the docks. Local councillors and trade unionists joined in the outcry. But it fell on deaf ears. The then transport minister, Harold Watkinson, ruled that there would be no government bailout, arguing that buses could do the job at a cheaper price. With a heavy heart the shareholders agreed to the closure and the winding-up of the Liverpool Overhead Railway Company.

That autumn sombre members of staff pasted up closure notices on all the stations, and it was a grim winter's night indeed on 30 December when the service finally ended. The last trains left simultaneously at 10.03 p.m. – from Seaforth and Litherland in the north, in the charge of Driver Sutcliffe Fawcett, and Dingle in the south, with Driver Jack Mackey at the controls. Both final services were packed to the doors, and hundreds more tore themselves away from warm firesides to be able to tell their grandchildren that they had witnessed the line's passing. There were bangs from the fog detonators placed along the track (probably the first time for years they had been used, since the line had automatic signalling), and flashes from the arcing conductor rails lit up the Three Graces. Sirens from ships all along the waterfront wailed a tribute through the cold night air. At one station staff wept as they passed the station cat through a train window to a passenger who had offered to adopt it.

As the final up train pulled in at Dingle, the crowds were reluctant to depart as a rumour did the rounds that the closure might be temporary. But the station inspector was already on the phone to Seaforth to check that the last down train had arrived. When he was satisfied, he pulled over the main switch for the final time, cutting the electric current and snuffing out the signal lights. The Liverpool Overhead Railway was well and truly dead. The anguish sounded even in the ranks of management. No less a figure than H. Maxwell Ruston, the company's general manager, declared, 'The time will come when Merseysiders must rue the day when they permitted the City Fathers to throttle the lifeblood of this unique undertaking.'

There is something intensely melancholy about any train consigned to spending its final days in a museum. But at least there is an entire gallery devoted to one of the former carriages of the Liverpool Overhead Railway in the new Museum of Liverpool on the waterfront. But for all its gloss and polish, it is more coffin-like than most. Sure, this last surviving car is immaculately restored, brass burnished and the panelling fragrant with beeswax. Even the SPITTING PROHIBITED sign has been lovingly polished. The memorabilia on the surrounding walls is beautifully curated, with yarns from former employees about their working lives. But the essence of the Docker's Umbrella – the clangs and clanks, the shouts and banter from the dockers, the smoke and steam from the ships, the general melee of dockside life – can never be replicated. Nor, as any Liverpudlian would tell you, could the human essence of this great port city ever be bottled and sanitised.

We weren't to know it half a century ago when the city seemed doomed to decline, but the spirit of commercial Liverpool would rise from the dead once again. Here just by the museum in the new Liverpool One shopping mall, on the edge of the waterfront where the docks once rotted into dereliction, I'm being jostled by crowds of shoppers just yards from where the Ovee trains would have rattled by. With its department stores, shops and cinemas, it's now the biggest open-air retail centre in Britain. Imagine being whisked along to buy some of the vast range of designer goodies at the fashionable John Lewis store by an elevated train.

There are still folk around who remember the line today. The veteran BBC Radio Merseyside presenter Billy Butler recalls:

I used to get the LOR on the way to work. I remember seeing all the ships when you looked out of the window. It was a bus to me – a functional train ride to work. When I worked on the docks, I recall seeing the *Empress of Canada* – we all went to see that. In hindsight it's easy to say we should have kept it, but it would now be an excellent tourist attraction. My biggest worry was always that King Kong, from the film, would sweep down and pick me up in the carriage. That still haunts me.

But, King Kong or not, the sad truth is that the Liverpool Overhead Railway will never return. Even so, what better way to revive its memory than some verses composed by a local enthusiast? Not Betjeman. Or even Roger McGough. But for now we can but dream and forgive the errors of the past.

> From Seaforth Sands to Dingle, a lengthy metal span,
> Traversed the land of docks and quays,
> Through which the trains once ran.
> The Overhead, our railway, known to one and all,
> Served the docks and river front, a wondrous place withall
> To work in early morning, or coming home at night,
> The crowds flocked to the stations, every train packed tight.
> They gazed upon the shipping a wondrous sight to all,
> For ships of every nation made this a port of call.
> Since the railway vanished, with no vestigial trace,
> This great dock-land of Liverpool is a less inviting place.

Chapter Seven

On the Slow, Mouldy and Jolting –
the railway that time forgot

The charms of the old Stratford-upon-Avon & Midland
Junction Railway, meandering through the rural heart of
England, were legendary. But don't try to get anywhere in
a hurry on this, one of the slowest trains in the land.

Head on out past the queues at Shakespeare's birthplace
in Henley Street. Don't get seduced by the lure of
tonight's performance at the Shakespeare Memorial Theatre,
even though the latest heart-throb off the TV might be
playing. No dallying, please, to feed the Avon swans. We're

heading north-west out of town, leaving behind the Hathaway Tea Rooms and the Cymbeline Hotel and keeping going till the half-timbered fantasy of tourist Stratford-upon-Avon gives way to the dreary borderlands of West Midlands suburbia. And onwards still, to where the pavements start to peter out into truly mean streets (even lovely towns like Stratford have them) and I am standing on the so-called Seven Meadows Road, whose bucolic name belies the reality of this thunderous A4390 dual carriageway, where I hug the grass verge to avoid being crushed by the massive HGVs sweeping by.

But the long hike has been worth it. Here it is – buried beneath the roadside couch grasses and buddleia I can just discern the platform edge of the station that was once the nerve centre of the old Stratford-upon-Avon & Midland Junction Railway. Who could imagine that this was once the main line of one of the most obscure yet romantic railways in the land? Feeling my way through the tangle of brushwood, I can just discern too a rusting set of buffer stops, overgrown by saplings, like some inexplicable totem from a prehistoric era. Rooting around in the weeds below, I find some of the original ballast. I rub a piece in my hand. It is still stained with the soot and grease from the days when the trains once passed by here. The rains of decades have steadfastly failed to wash away the still-powerful presence of this iconic railway.

Turn round now and close your eyes and imagine the busy life of the station that once stood here. A polished black locomotive, with the initials SMJ painted on its tender, is hissing impatiently, and behind it the rake of six rather elderly coaches in freshly polished brown and cream livery is so clean you can smell the beeswax. A small crowd of passengers has just alighted after a journey down from London, and with the help of porters, smartly dressed in green corduroy trousers and blue jackets with silver buttons, is making its way through the booking hall to the horse-drawn wagonettes that will take them on a sightseeing trip around the town. They might perhaps take tea at the Shakespeare Hotel or a jaunt on the Avon aboard the steam launches *Titania* or *Ariel*.

This genteel Edwardian moment is long before Shakespeare got a full commercial makeover, and farmers, tradesmen, cows, sheep and pigs vastly outnumber tourists in Stratford. But thanks to the railway company's prototype marketing men, no one alighting here could possibly mistake where they were. Almost everything in sight, from the posters on the platform to the notices in the booking hall to the labels on their luggage, proclaims that passengers are on THE SHAKE-SPEARE ROUTE. Even the map in the booking hall shows Stratford plonked at the centre of the British railway universe, with a large circle across the West Midlands — even bigger than that denoting London — signifying the town. With such a persuasive association with Britain's greatest play-wright, you might imagine this to be the grandest of railways — bestriding its world, in the poet's words, 'like a Colossus' — but the truth is infinitely less heroic.

Not for nothing was the Stratford-upon-Avon & Midland Junction Railway known to its passengers as the Slow, Mouldy and Jolting, and to those who were victims of its mostly unreliable trains, the Save Me, Jesus. Booking your ticket along the Shakespeare Route at Stratford, some jested, could at best be a Shakespearean comedy, but if you were trying to get anywhere in a hurry it was more a tragedy, with a sparse service, late trains and frequently missed connections. This most remote of railways rambled for fifty-five miles from nowhere in particular to nowhere even more in particular through some of the most deserted countryside of the English Midlands. It was perhaps the worst among the worst cases of the hopeless railway lines of Britain, yet despite its brief functioning life of around half a century, it has attracted a more powerful following down the years than many a scenic branch or high-speed main line. This backwater, with neither comfort nor charm, reliability nor speed, was the Eddie the Eagle of railways – a heroic British failure on wheels.

Stratford was the Crewe of this meandering enterprise, which ran from Blisworth, a hamlet in Northamptonshire famous for little except its tunnel on the Grand Union Canal, to Broom Junction – just a platform and a few houses on the Midland Railway between Evesham and Redditch. Apart from Stratford, the only place of any consequence on the line was the sleepy town of Towcester, whose claim to fame was its racecourse and a church with the biggest peal of bells in Britain. From here a branch wandered through the empty countryside to Banbury.

The trains may have been empty, but the names of the wayside stations were delicious. 'Wappenham, Helmdon and Farthinghoe – all stations to Banbury,' the Towcester porter would once have cried. Indeed, there can hardly have been a railway in the land with a more poetic collection of station, signal-box and junction names – all invoking the soul of a vanished rural England. Here passengers could alight at Fenny Compton, Moreton Pinkney and Salcey Forest stations – the latter having no road access at all. Clattering wagons would be shunted into sidings along rusty tracks at obscure Aston-le-Walls and Burton Dassett, while the signalman at the wonderfully titled Cockley Brake Junction would lean on his elbows, pull his levers and dispatch the (very) occasional train on its way. All dead and gone, with scarcely a trace remaining. Well, not quite. But we'll come to that later.

The origins of the Stratford-upon-Avon & Midland Junction Railway, as with so many speculative railways of the period, derive from the cobbling-together of various bits

of track built more in hope than economic reality during
the great Victorian mania of the mid-nineteenth century,
when railways were promoted in the most unlikely places.
Jack Simmons in his classic history *The Railways of Britain*
talks about an 'element of lunacy in the business', and *Punch*
in 1846 ridiculed the companies that were floated and found
subscribers fool enough to back them. Its spoof 'John
O'Groats and Land's End Junction, with branches to Ben
Lomond and Battersea' was scarcely less foolhardy than some
that were promoted in actuality, including, sadly, our very
own Stratford-upon-Avon & Midland Junction. Even so, the
directors were unshaken in their faith that one day the various
bits would amount to an empire that would ultimately bring
them riches. It never happened. For the poor old SMJ, an
empire gained through a succession of half-cock amalgamations and the odd bankruptcy was destined sadly to be an
empire that would eventually be lost.

The story of the line, wrote its historian J. M. Dunn,

in places as elusive as the line itself, is a curious example
of the survival of the unfit. Traffic obstinately refused
to flow east and west along its single track; the main
lines disdained, after some cautious experiments, to use
the connections it afforded; and yet, in spite of financial straits for which embarrassment would be too mild
a word, it survived. That fact alone made it noteworthy
to the railway historian; so too did the remarkable
collection of locomotives, including even a Fairlie
double-boiler machine in the railway middle ages – that
at different times dragged its vehicles across the
Warwickshire plain.

So it's worth bearing with the Byzantine tale of the line's
construction, complex though it is. If the slow, difficult

birth of the SMJ seems hard to comprehend now in hindsight, just imagine trying to sell the idea to the small landowners, provincial businessmen and other sundry burghers whose support was needed to make it work. The first part of the railway dates from 1847, only seventeen years after the pioneering Liverpool to Manchester Railway, so it wasn't a latecomer entering the market after all the best schemes had been cherry-picked. This was the year that parliamentary powers were granted for a railway between Northampton and Banbury, although no track came into use until 1866.

However, the ambitions of the straggle of lines that became the SMJ were far bigger than moving a few crates of chickens around rural Northamptonshire. Here, as the directors saw it, was a chance to stoke the fires of the Industrial Revolution by moving iron ore from the local mines to the furnaces of South Wales. The Welsh ironworks had to import haematite on unreliable coasters over choppy seas around the coast from Furness in Cumbria. But, like almost everything associated with the SMJ, the opportunity was spotted too late, and high-grade ore was already arriving from Spain. Never again, except briefly during the two world wars and just before it closed, would the Slow, Mouldy and Jolting fulfil its original function – and this became the eventual story of its life (and slow death).

The main line of the SMJ originated with the authorisation of the East & West Junction Railway on 23 June 1864. This was to connect the Northampton & Banbury line with the Great Western Railway at Stratford-upon-Avon via a junction at Towcester, a distance of just over thirty-three miles. The first sod was cut by Lady Palmerston at Towcester on 3 August 1864, using an elegant silver spade to shovel the earth into a mahogany wheelbarrow. In a grim omen of what was to turn out to be a cash-starved future, the initial capital of £300,000 quickly ran out and another £300,000 had to be raised to complete the line. Plans to extend the route eastwards to connect with the Great Northern Railway at Hitchin were swiftly quashed when that railway's accountants sensibly refused to stump up the money for what they perceived to be a total loser.

Still, by 1871 track had been laid over more than two thirds of the route as far as the Warwickshire village of Kineton, and on 1 July 1873 the first trains made their tentative way between there and Stratford, where the railway had built its own spanking new station — well, that's how the directors liked to view it. The *Stratford Herald* announced it in rather modest terms as 'a small but substantially erected brick building standing on land formerly known as Church Farm'. Naturally all the dignitaries of the surrounding area wanted to be seen on the first train, which would, they hoped, propel their communities into the modern world after slumbering in a life virtually unchanged since medieval times. According to the newspaper, the 'ladies and gentlemen' alighted at Kineton station; banners and garlands were festooned around the platforms and the church bells pealed out. Messrs Crampton and Sons, the contractors for the line, headed by T. R. Crampton 'well-known locomotive engineer', entertained the guests to 'a most recherché luncheon to celebrate the completion of the line'.

Colonel Yelland, the government's inspector, offered his compliments on the 'completeness of the permanent way', and the *Herald* went on to report that the contractors 'by their courteous conduct and rare business requirement, won for themselves the respect and esteem of all those who in the course of business were brought into contact with them'. But joy was neither unrestrained nor universal. There was less good news in the local press about the navvies — itinerant workers, many from an Irish background — who had laboured to build the line. Like many railway construction workers across the land at this time, these hard-living men had spread anxiety in sedate local communities with their high-spirited behaviour, mostly occasioned by long working hours and being away from their families for long periods. Strong drink, which brought generous profits to local publicans, played not a little part.

High jinks and worse on the part of the navvies led to 'alarm' among the local magistrates, who appointed special constables 'occasioned by the behaviour and reasonable apprehension of the persons who have been for some months past and are now being employed upon a certain railway in said parish of Ettington, called the East & West Junction Railway'. The magistrates charged for the wages of five constables, but the railway sensibly refused to pay up without evidence of lawlessness. So the local justices posted their list of allegations in April 1872. The tally ran to:

One case of assault of a violent nature upon a female.
One charge of feloniously and violently assaulting a gamekeeper with intent to do him grievous bodily harm.
One case of burglary.
Five cases of felony.
Two cases of malicious injury to property.
Several cases of drunkenness in the borough.

The most audacious accusation was against Joseph Lee, a subcontractor for the railway, who was accused of 'exercising his worldly calling on Sunday December 10 1872, the same not being a work of necessity or charity'. All Lee had been doing was shoring up a collapsing culvert, and his case was dismissed. Peace reigned henceforth.

Unfortunately, financial stability didn't. The directors promoted another line westwards, to be called the Evesham, Redditch & Stratford-upon-Avon Railway, to meet the

Midland Railway at isolated Broom Junction. But the mean-minded spirits of the Great Western would not permit an easy connection into their own tracks at Stratford, so another had to be found elsewhere. Meanwhile receipts on the original line were dismal, and in 1874 the directors tried to raise money with some fresh debentures. But the company's credit was shot and it fell into the hands of the receiver. All passenger traffic was suspended on 31 July 1877 and none was carried for the next eight years.

But never underestimate the optimism of the Victorian railway speculator. Despite much of their property being in hock, the directors rolled the Monopoly dice yet again with a view to extending eastwards, this time to a couple of even more lonely junctions — at Roade in Northamptonshire, on the London & North Western line to the north, and to Olney in Buckinghamshire, connecting ultimately with the main line of the Midland Railway — creating a third company to share the crumbs on this meagre route, the snappily named Easton Neston Mineral & Towcester, Roade & Olney Junction Railway. Reckoning correctly that ENMTR&OJR might be too much of a mouthful, the name was soon changed to the (hardly more memorable) Stratford-upon-Avon, Towcester & Midland Junction Railway.

Predictably another set of financial disasters followed, including the bankruptcy of one of the line's main contractors. It wasn't until 1891 that the full route from Olney to the west started to function, with a contract for coal trains from the goods depot at London's St Pancras to run all the way west to Bristol. But the curse of the East & West was to strike again. The Midland Railway engines proved too heavy for the track, and by 1898 the entire ramshackle concern had collapsed into bankruptcy.

Luckily, the line's ruinous finances and calamitous operations proved to be its saviour, since nobody in the land was foolish enough to make a bid for it. Not surprising, since by this time the track was overgrown with weeds and half the locomotive stock was broken down and out of use. In desperation, a bill was passed in Parliament bundling all the bits and pieces into one company – and so on 1 January 1909 the mighty Stratford-upon-Avon & Midland Junction Railway was born.

Its new chairman, the dynamic Harry Willmott, who had for fifteen years been the London goods manager of the Great Eastern Railway, set about a programme of reform – an uphill task (literally, since the cheaply built line was full of nasty gradients and sharp curves). The total population served by the fourteen stations between Broom and Blisworth was only 18,000. All the stations were villages except for Towcester (2,775) and Stratford (8,500) – and here the rival GWR cherry-picked the best passengers for its direct line to London. The railway was so short of cash that it sold the grass clippings from its embankments as hay to local farmers to pay for uniforms, while one of its directors admitted to a staff dinner that their line was 'the worst-paying per mile of any railway in the United Kingdom'. Latterly, it was claimed that the railway's receipts were directly dependent on the quantity of produce grown on its allotments and embankments.

But Harry, who installed his son Russell as traffic manager at the tender age of twenty-nine, was undeterred. His newly formed company boldly adopted the telegraphic address of Regularity, Stratford-upon-Avon – completely failing to see the irony. Special coaches were attached to London trains, first via Blisworth into Euston and then after 1902, by way of a connection with the newly built Great Central Railway, into London's Marylebone – nine and a half miles shorter than the established Great Western route into Paddington. The Shakespeare Route was shamelessly plugged everywhere, with a special scarlet promotion wraparound for the time-table. But 'fortune's fickle wheel' — to use the Shakespearean parlance that the railway was so fond of — intervened once again when the railway's special Shakespeare Festival in 1910 had to be cancelled midway because of the death of King Edward VII. The traffic manager had to report a loss of £500 — a disastrously large sum in those days, which the railway could ill afford.

Despite chairman Harry's new broom, the management of the railway was highly eccentric, with Willmott Senior living a hundred miles away in Guildford. At ten o'clock prompt each morning he would ring his son for a brief chat. In return, Russell sent a memo each evening reporting on the events of the day. Sometimes these would be returned with sardonic comments scrawled in the margins. One such comment read, 'Fish make brains . . . eat a bloody whale!' The hapless Russell, meanwhile, doubled up as part-time engineer and locomotive superintendent, a job he retained even after he moved on to take the job of general manager of the Isle of Wight Central Railway. Staff dreaded his visits. He always travelled on the London train on Monday mornings, connecting with the 08.35 from Blisworth. He would ride on the locomotive, ticking off staff for letting the safety valves blow and wasting coal. He also had a habit of riding up and down the track on a platelayers' trolley.

But the Willmotts were not entirely barmy; in fact they saw themselves as progress personified. In this spirit they pioneered a contraption called a Rail-o-phone. The device allowed communication between a moving train and a fixed point, and was inaugurated on 20 April 1911 by the mayor of Stratford (aboard a train) and Marie Corelli, a famous novelist of the day (in the town). We may not recall much about her now, but at that time her novels — which outsold Kipling, Wells and Conan Doyle put together — made her

Britain's most-read fiction author as well as Stratford's most notable celebrity resident. Later it was claimed that the Rail-o-phone could actually bring trains to a halt by pressing a device in a signal box. An experiment was arranged whereby two trains would race towards each other on a single track and the Rail-o-phone would avert a collision. It may not have been as daring as it sounded, since the *Stratford Herald* reported, 'A liberal margin for safety was allowed, so there were no thrills.' Unsurprisingly, the Rail-o-phone was never heard of again.

Later, in the 1930s, LMS managers used the SMJ as a test bed for another avant-garde if even more Heath Robinson machine, known as the Ro-Railer. This was a single-deck bus built by Karrier Motors of Huddersfield, fitted with both flanged steel wheels and rubber tyres, allowing it in theory to work equally well on road and rail. It started off as a train from Blisworth and ran over the rails as far as Stratford goods yard, where it pulled into the cattle dock and the rail wheels were raised, allowing the tyres to take the weight of the vehicle. From there the bus pottered merrily around the streets of Stratford, taking passengers to the new and luxurious Welcombe Hotel, recently opened by the London Midland & Scottish Railway. At least that was the theory. But far from impressing its upmarket passengers, the Ro-Railer proved to be hard riding, noisy and smelly, and to vibrate horribly. The wheel-change mechanism, which boasted a five-minute switchover time, was in reality prone to frequent breakdowns.

To be fair, the normal motive power along the line was even less reliable – mostly a jumble sale of clapped-out machines acquired as cheaply as possible from remnant auctions. The East & West Junction Railway's first locomotive – an o-6-o saddle tank, built by Manning Wardle in 1866 – is shown in the official pictures of the inaugural train in 1871 with no cab and a section of stovepipe perched on top of the chimney to take the fumes away from the carriages. The next engines, numbered 1 to 6, were acquired on hire purchase from Beyer Peacock in Manchester, but the SMJ reneged on the payments and they were repossessed before being sold on to the Lancashire & Yorkshire Railway. Their replacements included a couple of second-hand French loco-motives — a 2-4-0 named *Ceres* and an 0-6-0 called *Savoie*. The first could only manage a boiler pressure of eighty pounds and was scrapped, while the second had such a rotten tender that the locomotive had to be rebuilt as a tank engine.

The company went bargain hunting again and bought a couple of highly unusual Fairlie double-boiler locomotives which had been destined for a railway in Mexico. One of these was the first in the UK to have the Walschaerts valve gear — a means of transferring power to the wheels that became standard for all modern steam locomotives. (The Fairlie type can be seen in operation even today on the preserved Ffestiniog Railway in Wales.) But the railway was hardly in the business of technical innovation and, in any case, the locomotives had to be sold off after traffic was suspended in 1877. Various elderly contraptions subsequently came and went in what was to become a permanent bring-and-buy sale. In 1903 the line acquired its first and only express engine, a handsome 2-4-0 from Beyer Peacock, but this must have been a mistake, since the company ran no express passenger trains — nor was it ever likely to, given the state of the track. Not for nothing was the locomotive given the inauspicious number 13, since the directors had once again missed the boat of progress, it being the last locomo-tive of this obsolete type ever to be built for a British railway. Other disastrous purchases included a locomotive from which a wheel dropped off and another whose water tank was too small for the train to get from one end of the line to the other.

It was no wonder the trains broke down so often. In his history of the line Arthur Jordan, a one-time employee, reports that the engine staff, who had mostly left school at twelve and worked on farms before becoming railwaymen, had little technical knowledge. There was no equipment to coal the trains, and each knob of coal had to be thrown up individually by hand into the tender. Working conditions were primitive, and Jordan describes how 'I have seen those labourers at their meal break with only bread and jam to eat, and although desperately thirsty in hot weather, unable to afford the cheapest beer. There were no washbasins, only the use of hot water from an engine and soft soap, to which sand might be added if grease proved difficult to remove.' None of the engines was fitted with seats, and the crew was forced to stand for all the eight back-breaking hours of their shifts.

Still, the engine liveries were nice and the paintwork always seemed to gleam. The shed overseer – one Inspector Matthews – was fond of removing his white breast-pocket handkerchief and wiping it along a locomotive's coupling rod. If it picked up even a smidgeon of grease, the cleaner would get a sound ticking-off. At first the locomotives were painted in 'crimson lake' with panels lined out in black and edged both sides in yellow. When No. 13 arrived, it was turned out in a lovely dark blue – and once the SMJ had taken over full control, the engines were painted black with green and yellow lining and gold lettering. But none of them was destined to last long. Of the thirteen engines that passed into the ownership of the London, Midland and Scottish Railway when it absorbed the SMJ in 1923, all had been sent to the scrapyard by 1930.

Not that any of the locomotives ever had to work very

hard since the railway never had much of a service – certainly not for passengers. The best that could be mustered for most of its life were three trains each way a day between Blisworth and Stratford, and four between Blisworth and Broom. So slow and unreliable were the trains that if one ran to time it was regarded as something of a miracle. But one day the impossible happened and one of the morning trains rolled into the station on time to the second. Moved by this unusual circumstance, a passenger is said to have gone up to the driver to pay a personal tribute. 'Sir,' he said, 'I've been travelling on this line for many years and this is the first time I've known this train to be on time. I tender you my heartiest congratulations. Have a cigar!' Regretfully and solemnly, the driver pushed away the proffered gift. 'As a conscientious person and an honest man I can't take it. The fact is we were due in at this time yesterday morning.'

Perhaps there never was such a thing as a heyday for the beleaguered SMJ, but if there was, it would have been in the period between 1890 and 1923. So let's take a fictitious journey along the main line, aided by the memories of Arthur Jordan, who started his working life in the booking office at Stratford, where his mother also worked as the manageress of the station refreshment room.

Boarding at Blisworth, you might have already heard many of the derogatory nicknames summing up the reputation of the line – not just Slow, Mouldy and Jolting, but Slow, Mournful Journey and, in the case of the original East & West Junction, the Erratic and Wandering. You certainly won't be expecting much comfort from the carriages. If you were particularly unlucky, you might find yourself in the company's four-wheel coach. This ran from 1850 to 1909, when it was the oldest vehicle in existence in Britain to employ the Westinghouse brake system. Until 1900 lighting was by oil lamps dropped into 'pots' in the carriage, but it wasn't until 1910 that the train had any heating, relying on foot warmers placed in the compartments by porters. Arriving from Euston, we must hope we haven't missed our connection, since there is a four-hour gap between trains. No wonder the Blisworth Station Hotel across the way (still to be seen from the main line today as the Walnut Tree Hotel) is doing a roaring trade.

Chuffing away onto the single track, we pass a bleak landscape of iron-ore quarries before arriving at Towcester. In later years you might be jostled by 8,000 or so passengers travelling to the local racecourse. Founded in 1928 in the grounds of Easton Neston Hall, the races drew punters to the track's sharp bends and uphill finish, which would provide thrills and very often spills. Thrillingly too, a special through train would sometimes come all the way from St Pancras. Heading westwards through Blakesley, you might spot a wisp of steam over a hedge and perform a double-take as a miniature steam locomotive passes by in a field. But this fifteen-inch-gauge line was no toy – it was used to transport coal and other supplies to the local Blakesley Hall.

Bizarrely, one of the most authentic-looking 'steam' loco-motives on the line actually had an internal combustion engine concealed inside it. This 4-4-4 'tank engine', called *Blacolvesley*, still survives and holds the record as the oldest internal combustion railway locomotive in the world. And so we roll on through sometimes-rickety tracks to Moreton Pinkney, where if you listen carefully you might pick up an American drawl from sightseers on their way to nearby Sulgrave Hall, ancient home of George Washington's family.

Look out for a big junction coming up, linking in with the Great Central line to Marylebone opened in 1899 and the last main line built in Britain. Thank goodness for the GC, for without the connections here to London the SMJ might have expired even earlier than it did. The spot was famous too for the occasion in March 1916 when a train pulled by SMJ No. 3 was buried overnight in a snowdrift that piled up, according to the locals, as high as the twenty-fifth rung on the signal-box ladder. Without food, passengers stayed warm by drinking coffee made with hot water drained from the locomotive boiler. One passenger claimed it was superior to that served in the station buffet at Stratford.

Indeed 'Make Do and Mend' should have been the inscription on the heraldic arms of the Stratford-upon-Avon & Midland Junction. At the next calling point, Byfield, a donkey was used to pump water for the locomotives, trotting round in a circle harnessed to a pole. Staff keen to speed up the train would commandeer a horse from a field, which would double the donkey's productivity. But then the railway had a soft spot for horses. The directors removed barbed wire from the trackside so that the steeds of the many local hunts would not get injured. They also issued keys to the trackside farm gates to the hunt masters so they could tally-ho across the neighbouring fields without obstruction

But pause a minute. We are entering Warwickshire already, running parallel with the Great Western main line to London at Fenny Compton — twenty-two miles along the route from where we started. No great friend to the SMJ, the Great Western offered a connection here, but the SMJ trains had to reverse from their separate station. As it happens there's no one waiting or alighting on the platform today, so we're already steaming onwards to the Civil War battle site of Edge Hill, where for a short period the Edge Hill Light Railway, an even more tragic lost cause than the SMJ, had a connection. We don't need to travel down the Edge Hill Railway now, since we shall meet its eccentric owner and chief engineer, Colonel Holman Stephens — 'patron saint of lost railways' — in Chapter 14 of this book.

Kineton station was legendary for many years for winning

first prize in the SMJ station garden competition, but this is small beer compared to tiny Ettington's lofty place in the SMJ pantheon. At this next station along the line keen-eyed passengers might get a glimpse of the shimmering water of two lakes set in manicured parkland. Remodelled by Robert Adam and set in grounds landscaped by Capability Brown, this is Compton Verney, the palatial seat of Lord Willoughby de Broke, one of the line's senior directors, famous for his lavish staff parties.

In the years running up to World War I special trains would convey the workers to Ettington station, from where they were required to walk two miles to milord's seat. A silver band played, group photographs were taken and a meat tea was served on the lawn. But beforehand the workers were ushered to attend divine service in the family chapel, surrounded by monuments to the Willoughby de Broke family. The singing of 'Onward Christian Soldiers' followed by 'O God Our Help in Ages Past' was particularly appropriate, given that the railway was even at this stage struggling to stave off its own death. The sermon, preached by the aptly named Reverend Liveing, drew comparisons between steam engines and men. Which, asked the vicar, was the quicker to run out of puff?

Not that the staff were always ready to doff their caps. One of the more bloody-minded drivers, Dick Paget, who was famous for wearing farmer's breeches aboard his engine, one day spotted Lord Willoughby handing a tip to the guard. The train was then late as a result of picking up a horsebox and missed its London connection. Lord Willoughby demanded of the driver why the lost time could not have been made up. 'Ah,' replied the cheeky Paget, 'you greased the wrong end of the train for that, my lord!'

Yawning Yettington was the nickname for the area around the station before the railway arrived. But no opportunity for snoozing now, since with a roar and a rare burst of speed a banana train flashes by with a couple of panting engines, double-headed on the front, on its way to London from Avonmouth docks with one of the few profitable loads the railway ever carried. No one was ever sure whether the 'banana line' nickname was a compliment or an insult (as in banana republic). As for our own train, progress continues snail-like until at last here is a glimpse of the spire of Holy Trinity church and the turrets of the Shakespeare Memorial Theatre, which burned down in 1926. When news of the blaze spread, the Stratford stationmaster fired up the company's ancient Merryweather fire appliance. Fortunately it wasn't needed.

Now, just a short rumble over the six-arch viaduct across the Avon and we're wheezing into the platform at Stratford. Don't look too closely at your watch, though. It took 94 minutes to cover the 70 miles on the main line down from London, but another 83 minutes for the 38 miles to Stratford. The best thing might be to retire to the refreshment room – known as the Shant after the places during the construction of the line where the navvies would sing their shanties – and to ponder over a bottle of the local Flowers Ale why the Bard's name, which generally guaranteed the commercial success of even the most modest Stratford product, failed so dismally when applied to the Shakespeare Route.

Throughout most of the life of the line the trains plodded on, mostly undisturbed by the outside world, and there were few brushes with fame. The SMJ touched the hem of royalty only briefly, when in 1909 Princess Marie of Schleswig-Holstein paid a visit to Stratford. The arrival of the American ambassador, William Reid, in the same year went off with more of a bang, since the local newspaper reported the discharging of some sixty or seventy detonators along the line, while the locomotive carried British and American flags on the front with a headboard reading HARVARD. The ambassador had come to open Harvard House in the town, with its connection to John Harvard, founder of Harvard College.

There was probably never a time in the SMJ's history when rot couldn't be said to be setting in, but the decline certainly accelerated when in 1927 a canny entrepreneur spotted a way to circumvent Stratford's moral guardians, who wouldn't allow films to be screened on the Sabbath. The religious scruples of the SMJ didn't allow Sunday trains to run either, but the new Stratford Blue bus service was happy to take punters in their droves to neighbouring Evesham to go to the talkies. Bus competition had arrived. Why bother with train travel on other days when you could be picked up near your front door?

There was a brief renaissance for the railway during World War II, when the line came in handy to transport raw materials and munitions, to divert the occasional troop train and to serve a nearby airfield. There was a minor drama when a Wellington bomber crashed across the tracks, but luckily an approaching goods train was halted in time. But after the war it was back to (little or almost no) business as usual. Passenger services between Stratford-upon-Avon and Broom were withdrawn by the LMS in 1947. And then the axe finally fell on the rest of the line. Its historian J. M. Dunn described how he took a journey in May 1951, when the train 'consisted of one bogie composite coach only, hauled by a Midland 0-6-0 tender engine, and the passengers could have been accommodated in one compartment'.

And so, on 5 April 1952, the grim reaper set the scene for the final journey. The *Stratford Herald* headlined its story MAYOR DRIVES THE BLISWORTH FLYER, and the very last train carried over 200 people – probably as many in total as had travelled in the previous twelve months. As it pulled away from the station, all the engines in Stratford shed blew mournfully on their whistles. A British Railways official blustered that the line would 'still have a bright future' — which nobody quite believed. In fact there was an Indian summer for part of the line, that section westwards from Woodford West. From the early 1950s night-time trains (five in each direction, six days a week) conveyed semi-finished steel products, scrap metal and coal between the Great Central main line and the Western Region at Broom Junction.

After the opening of a new south-facing spur at Stratford in 1960 up to a dozen freights daily in each direction, including fast fitted freights from York to Bristol and South Wales, gave the line some hope for the future. Additionally, since the war regular iron-ore trains had continued to run from Byfield and Blisworth quarries to Woodford yards and Blisworth exchange yard. But like every good thing in the short life of the SMJ, it wasn't to last. Beeching's cynical rundown of the Great Central main line, a serious shortage of signalmen and the slump in production in the Northamptonshire iron quarries saw to that.

As the shadow of final closure fell in 1965 — just before the arrival of the track-lifting trains — the line was to have its final fling. The Queen Mother was visiting Stratford — not Brutus-like to bury the remains of the SMJ but to celebrate the restoration of a local canal. The Royal Train was scheduled to carry her home at the end of the day from the old SMJ station, now in such a state of dereliction that British Railways resurfaced the platform especially for this one distinguished visitor much to the fury of the local rail unions. But then logic has never mattered in the history of this beleaguered railway.

'Such, then,' wrote J. M. Dunn 'was the SMJ. Through many tribulations and under various names the old "East and West", which began its career in 1864 and was "in

Chancery" five years later before a mile of line was opened, struggled and survived. Its allies were no better off than it was itself; and The Shakespeare Route looked better on the map than it could be in fact. All the same, for part of its life the railway was managed with an enthusiasm that deserved a better fate than it received – long life without prosperity.'

The early directors would have been delighted with Dunn's plaudits, but the story doesn't quite end there. Deep in the heart of Warwickshire, near the tiny village of Fenny Compton, a parish of 797 souls, one small rusty section of the SMJ still exists, over which the occasional train gingerly makes its way. This is the very first section ever built, extending a few miles along to the next village of Kineton, whose moment of fame arrived on that heady day in 1864 when Lady Palmerston wielded her silver spade amid 'arches of flowers and evergreens'. It was the line's first and last glorious moment.

Don't try to visit it today unless you are prepared for an encounter with a Ministry of Defence security guard attached to a large dog with slavering jaws. Which is why on this grey, louring winter's afternoon I'm travelling along the old Great Western Railway line that once ran from Birkenhead to Paddington in an attempt to spot the junction with the old tracks to Stratford. With this in mind, I'm glued to the window of the 10.27 Manchester to Bournemouth Voyager service somewhere south of Leamington.

Today's overcrowded services on the Cross Country franchise aboard short, noisy trains may be deemed, I suppose, the modern equivalent of the SMJ. Not the Slow and Mouldy but certainly the Crowded and Comfortless. So crowded today, in fact, that the trolley lady wants to park her contraption next to the window where I am waiting for my glimpse of the final stub of the SMJ to appear. 'Sorry, love,' she says. 'You'll have to move out of the way. It's hell along there in that carriage.'

'But I can't,' I reply. 'I'm waiting to see the last glimpse of Britain's most inefficient railway pass by.'

I think she may have taken this personally. But no time to worry, for here it is — some rusty rails branching off into the distance through some waterlogged fields.

At the end of this line is a place that no ordinary mortals can enter — a railway graveyard full of old rolling stock unwanted by the train companies, securely guarded within a former Ministry of Defence ammunition depot. The contents of this yard are so secret that they consume mega-bytes of Internet trainspotter paranoia. Could it even be that there is a hoard of veteran locomotives buried secretly underground here, concealed from the prying of Google Earth satellites? Who knows? But the smell of death always hovered around the old SMJ, and how appropriate that the last bit of the line should live on as a modern Valhalla.

As always with the Shakespeare Route, there is a ready quote to be plucked from the Bard. What better epitaph for the slowest railway in the land than Falstaff's: 'I were better to be eaten to death with a rust than to be scoured to nothing with perpetual motion'?

Shame the Slow, Mouldy and Jolting's ever-inventive PR men aren't around today. They would probably have pasted it up as a motto on every station.

Chapter Eight
In the company of ghosts on Britain's spookiest service

Could there be anything creepier than a journey aboard a
deserted train that runs just once a day through forgotten
Yorkshire? Yet this zombie of the tracks opens a door
into the mists of early railway history.

It was spooky enough trying to buy a ticket in the first
place. 'A day return to Goole on the direct line, please,' I
ask the booking clerk at Leeds station, which is buzzing on
this busy summer's day. 'It's the one that stops at Hensall,
Snaith and Rawcliffe,' I explain, trying to be helpful when
his gaze goes blank.

There's a pause, and there seems to be a bit of a chill in

the air. 'Are you sure, son? I can sell you a ticket to get there, but don't make any plans to come back in a hurry.' What's wrong? I can feel the hairs bristling on the back of my neck. 'There's only one train a day down the line, and sometimes it doesn't come back.'

There are other worrying omens. Scanning for my 17.16 train on the departure board, I note it's at Platform 17a, the furthest, pokiest platform in the remotest, emptiest corner of this bustling station. And there don't seem to be many other passengers on this ancient Pacer train with its primitive four-wheel carriages, one of the oldest in the network. Everything about the train seems distinctly unwelcoming despite the warmth of this July afternoon. Even the guard, a small wizened man staring into his ticket machine, seems oddly preoccupied.

Perhaps this is because the train is running late. Or maybe there is another more sinister cause, since the 17.16 to Goole has a special status in railway iconography as one of Britain's ghost trains. These ethereal services wend their eerie way around the rail network almost entirely unknown to the travelling public and running mostly empty, since they operate at deliberately inconvenient times, often giving passengers no prospect of getting home again. They are truly 'the trains now departed'.

The Pontefract Line, as it's known – from Leeds to Goole – has a single train in one direction in the morning with a solitary service the other way in the afternoon, returning to Leeds if it's in the mood. Not a schedule for anyone wanting to get anywhere in a hurry – more, perhaps, an itinerary for the living dead. Progress tonight into the East Riding of Yorkshire may be the equivalent of crossing the Lethe into rail purgatory. 'Skeleton service' suddenly has a new meaning.

Yet, zombie of the tracks though it may be, my Goole train and others like it around the country have a very real existence in the minds of the bureaucrats who control

Britain's rail system, since they help maintain the fiction that a railway line is still open for business when in reality it has been abandoned. For the price of an occasional train service with some clapped-out carriages or in some cases even a bus, the train operators are able to duck the long and costly consultation, accompanied by inevitable howls of public protest, that the law stipulates when a railway line is to be closed. This is why ghost trains are sometimes known as parliamentary or parly trains – because they supply the bare minimum of service required by statute without having to bother with a closure process.

In this Alice-in-Wonderland world it is especially desirable if the train staff are as obstructive as possible. As we clatter over the points east out of Leeds, I ask the guard whether the return train from Goole will be running tonight, since I don't want to be stranded. 'Dunno,' he says helpfully. 'But what about this one – surely these coaches will form the return service? 'Not necessarily. This one might go back to Wakefield. And sometimes they're cancelled.' A long pause. 'And sometimes they're not . . .'

But frustrating though it might sometimes be, a journey aboard a ghost train can offer special pleasures, especially when it prowls along a line that is seldom used today. Even the name is a window into a lost world of railway history. Parly services originated in the Railway Act of 1844, which brought in regulated services and higher safety standards after a group of stonemasons were catapulted to their deaths from an overturned third-class carriage.

Travelling conditions for the working classes in the early days of the railways were terrible, and the companies did very little to encourage the poorer classes to take advantage of the new benefits of railway travel. The Stockton & Darlington Railway did not provide third-class facilities until 1835, and then only because it hoped to dissuade people from the dangerous practice of walking along the railway tracks. The Midland Counties Railway was typical of many early companies. Although the railway carried third-class passengers, the carriages were no more than open boxes without seats carrying sixty passengers each. It was assumed that 'no one will go in it who can afford to go in others. The passengers will stand, they are taken as the pigs are.' The Great Western, meanwhile, provided carriages of 'an inferior description' travelling at very low speeds for its third-class patrons, very often without windows in a style foreshadowing that which would be used a century later to transport victims to the Nazi death camps. Both the London & Birmingham and London & South Western Railways thought nothing of mixing their third-class passengers with 'cattle, horses and empty wagons'. The *Illustrated London News* described such carriages as a 'species of shower bath'.

Snobbery also played its part. C.A. Saunders, secretary of the Great Western Railway, claimed on several occasions in the 1840s that the behaviour of third-class passengers caused offence to other rail patrons – a view that reinforced a determination to segregate the classes on both trains and stations. The belief that the 'lower orders' would annoy or even drive away higher-class patrons, or simply vandalise railway property, is a recurring theme in railway history. For example, the chairman of the North Eastern Railway complained that when curtains were provided in third-class carriages, the passengers 'cut them off and probably used them as pocket handkerchiefs'.

Class prejudice wasn't the only influence on railway policy. Underlying the business strategies of most companies were more hard-headed commercial considerations. Just like today, many of the early main-line companies believed that a high-class service was the road to high profits. They didn't want to clog up their trains with large numbers of poor passengers paying low fares. The directors of the Leeds & Selby and the Manchester, Bolton & Bury reported gleefully that increasing fares caused numbers to decline but revenues to increase.

Enter the Railway Regulation Act of 1844, brought in by William Gladstone, president of the Board of Trade. Surprisingly, given the antipathy of the Victorians to any kind of state interference, Gladstone's principal ambition was to regulate the railways, and the original draft of the bill, as presented to Parliament, would have given the government a powerful range of controls over train services, including the idea of eventually nationalising them. However, howls of protest from the railway owners led to the bill being watered down.

But Gladstone's act had at least one positive outcome – in forcing the railway companies to guarantee at least one train per day on every line, running at a minimum speed of 12 mph, stopping at all stations, and with a fare of not more than 1d. a mile. They were also required to offer an increased level of comfort. These trains were labelled 'Parl' or 'Gov' at the head of the timetable.

However, the train companies came up with a clever ruse to duck their responsibilities while sticking to the letter of the law. The parly services were often scheduled at the least convenient hour and operated by the surliest staff to make the service as unattractive as possible. For example, the first train out of Paddington to the West Country was the 6 a.m. parliamentary train. Railway staff cynically dubbed it the Plymouth Cheap. The outcome was that even poor people were often forced onto the more expensive trains at a penny-farthing a mile. The parly trains even got a mention in Gilbert and Sullivan's *The Mikado* in lyrics satirising upper-class attitudes: 'The idiot who, in railway carriages/ Scribbles on window-panes/ We only suffer/ To ride on a buffer/ On Parliamentary trains.'

Today's parliamentary trains operate on a similar principle, with services so unattractive that few people in their right mind would want to use them unless they had to. Certainly the Leeds to Goole service seems desperately unloved, as is the landscape it passes through. Yet this local network of railways was once at the centre of the beating heart of industrial Britain. Journeying by train from Leeds City station today, it is hard to imagine anyone battling to lay claim to this drab railway hinterland through post-industrial West Yorkshire, yet so vicious was the rivalry between the North Midland Railway and the Great Northern Railway to get their trains to the promised land of Leeds in the 1840s that it led to the notorious Methley Junction Incident – one of the nastiest episodes in the railway mania that gripped Britain at the time.

When the GNR refused to yield to the Midland's demand not to build its own line to Leeds, the Midland threatened unsuccessfully to stop its trains and levy a toll on every passenger. On the eve of the opening GNR officials, suspicious that the Midland might be up to something dastardly, sent a light engine along the track and found the points had been removed at Methley, a junction just outside the city. The perpetrator was never identified, but what would have been the consequences for the passengers on the first train along the next morning do not bear thinking about.

The only signs of cut-throat competition today are in the shopping arcades of the city's slick new station, where the magnificent restored art deco concourse built by the LMS has been given over to McDonald's, Wetherspoon's and Sainsbury's. Meanwhile, alongside the tracks towards Goole, the weeds grow high. Saplings are already turning into trees along the disused trackbed of the old Central Station Viaduct, curving off into the distance. Post-Beeching closures force our train to reverse at Castleford – in its day a boom town with proud Rugby League triumphs but now with foot-high weeds on the platforms and a shuttered and abandoned signal box. The legacy of the 1960s is a truncated patchwork of lines that no intelligent civil engineer would ever have devised. However, Castleford has a poignant place in the annals of British industrial history as the home of one of the very last steam locomotives in commercial use: an Austerity 0-6-0-saddle tank lived on as a shunter at the Wheldale Colliery until 1982.

Entering Pontefract, line-side slag heaps stand as mournful monuments to the pre-Thatcher years when the coal mines once kept the local furnaces burning. But despite the rundown, the town still has two of its five famous liquorice factories and boasts three separate stations, all with charming Yorkshire names – Monkhill, Tanshelf and Baghill. We clatter past a decrepit Lancashire & Yorkshire Railway signal cabin, marked PRINCE OF WALES COLLIERY, where perhaps a phantom signalman still shunts trucks full to the brim with the black gold that once brought prosperity to this area. Meanwhile, the freight trains still rumble by, these days conveying imported coal and biomass to the vast local power stations at Ferrybridge and Drax. As I passed, in summer 2014, the very last local coal mine that fed the turbines – at Kellingley – was under sentence of closure; doomed to shut irrevocably a year later.

Sadness too at Knottingley, which was once a stop on the main line from York to London, where the fine double-span overall roof has been demolished and the station buildings reduced to bus shelters. Spookily, one of the letters is falling off the sign on the Railway Hotel in the station yard. From here on, as the train rumbles on into remoter countryside, I am the sole passenger. And I start to question whether I am still in the land of the living when we stop at little Hensall station, a time capsule with an enamel sign advertising Wills

Capstan cigarettes, where an ancient railwayman opens equally ancient crossing gates by hand. It is reassuring to know from the latest statistics from the Office of Rail Regulation that the station is used by 184 (human) passengers a year.

Darkness is falling as our ghost train sighs to a halt at Goole station – mausoleum-like with its peeling paint and empty platforms. The antique platform clock reads 18.26, and the words of Flanders and Swann from their famous 1963 song 'Slow Train' couldn't be truer: 'No one departs, no one arrives,/ From Selby to Goole, from St Erth to St Ives.' But it is comforting to know from the destination flashed up on the board that at least we're scheduled to head back in the other direction tonight. Just the driver, the guard – and me.

But who's this? A second passenger is sitting bolt upright in the front coach. With his bushy Victorian beard, could he be the ghost of railways past? Nothing so exotic. He turns out to be Brian, a retired teacher from Halifax, one of the ghosties – the tribe of railway enthusiasts that roams the land, travelling at unearthly hours to 'cop' the ghost trains of Britain. 'There used to be a good service on this line not so long ago,' he tells me, 'but all of a sudden in 2001 the train company Arriva replaced all the services between Leeds, Wakefield, Castleford, Knottingley and Goole with buses. They claimed they were short of drivers and trains. Hmmm. By the time they brought back the Goole train six months later, it was the perfect excuse to turn it into a ghost service. And it's been the same ever since.'

Still, Brian isn't worried, since ghost trains are his hobby, and he tells me he has copped them all. 'And this is my third time on this one – it's one of my favourites,' he says. In fact, some of the parly trains are often so packed with ghosties like Brian that they defeat their purpose – none more so than the most famous of them all, the Stalybridge Flyer. This two-coach diesel railcar is one of the rarest trains in Britain, leaving Stockport at 9.22 a.m. on Fridays only for the short journey around south Manchester. There is no return service, which may be just as well, since many of the ghosties who pack the service each week find themselves waylaid by the legendary real ales and home-made black puddings at Britain's most famous railway buffet on the platform at Stalybridge. An even rarer service runs between Frodsham and Runcorn, near Liverpool, which has only one train a week – on Saturdays in summer.

In fact, the north of England offers ghost-train paradise – or hell if you are unlucky enough to be dependent on them. There are only four services a day between Helsby and Ellesmere Port in Cheshire. And at Styal, between Crewe and Manchester, just three services a day stop while the rest race through, forcing passengers to drive to the next station at Wilmslow. (This appears to be true lunacy, since local campaigners have proved that a stop would not add to overall train times.) There are some stations, such as the historic Gainsborough Central in Lincolnshire, where no passenger trains at all stop on weekdays, yet on Saturday there are three services to Sheffield and three to Cleethorpes. This station reached a low point in 2003 when the annual number of fare-paying passengers boarding trains was officially recorded as just five. A far cry from opening day in 1849, when it was the pride of the Manchester, Sheffield and Lincolnshire Railway and hundreds turned out to admire its fine classical portico – now, like so many grand railway buildings, pulled down in favour of a bus shelter.

On the Ely to Norwich line, Shippea Hill – surreally named since it sits in the middle of Fenland – has a surreal train service to match. On weekdays there is one eastbound train to Norwich, but passengers have to wait till Saturday for the westbound train to Cambridge. Lakenheath, the next station along the line, has a similarly sparse service but is served by different trains. Poor Teesside Airport station, on the Darlington to Middlesbrough line, has an average of just one passenger a week, making even the most obscure Ryanair destination at some godforsaken town in the Baltic appear like Heathrow.

But the most surreal and inaccessible ghost station of all lies, paradoxically, on Britain's busiest railway, the west coast main line between Euston and Glasgow. Each day the weed-covered platforms at Polesworth in Warwickshire can be glimpsed tantalisingly by thousands of passengers speeding on their way north and south. Polesworth, which had six weekday services as recently as the 1980s, now has a single train – the 07.23 to Crewe. Passengers cannot travel in the southbound direction because the footbridge to the up plat-form was removed six years ago and no one has bothered to put it back.

Other ghost trains date back to Beeching days, keeping the rails shiny with occasional services running over obscure curves and junctions. Back in the 1960s, for instance, Beeching butchered the railways around Lancaster, forcing trains across the Pennines on the old Midland route from Leeds to Morecambe to traverse a zigzag route, reversing at Lancaster to access the resort. However, occasionally a ghost train takes the direct line over what's known as Bare Lane Curve. But pssst – don't tell anyone!

There was until recently a journey even more obscure, more recherché, aboard a train that is so ethereal that it was actually a bus. This came about in 2008 after a member of the public complained to the Department for Transport that the axing of the twice-daily service from Brighton to Birmingham via Kensington Olympia left a short section of track without a passenger service. The response was to provide a fifty-seat motor coach, at a cost to the taxpayer of £500 a day, which invariably ran empty. Fortunately sense prevailed, and after numerous shadowy, passenger-less journeys through the streets of west London an exorcism was performed in 2013, and the service was formally put out of its misery.

But perhaps the most evocative journey on any ghost train is along the old Paddington line through the Chilterns that once went to the West Midlands and on to Chester and Birkenhead. To most Great Western devotees the initials GWR have long been synonymous with Brunel's majestic route from London to Bristol and its dramatic extension through to Cornwall and the far west. Yet in its day the Great Western's Birmingham main line was one of its most prestigious routes, until its rundown in the years following Beeching.

This was the last great main line of the steam age, built to the highest engineering standards. After it opened in 1906, the Great Western's publicity rhapsodised, 'It has opened up a district of phenomenal beauty which has somehow or other managed to retain, notwithstanding its nearness to London, most of those old-world characteristics which have vanished from more remote parts of the country. The new line will open up . . . a land asleep since the days of the stagecoach.' Here was once the stamping ground of the Kings and Castles – jewels in the crown of the locomotive fleet – which hauled fast expresses such as the Inter-City, the Cambrian Coast Express and the Shakespeare Express. Even in the 1960s it was chosen as the route of a brand-new sumptuous diesel train, the Birmingham Pullman, in which crisply dressed stewards served the finest railway cuisine of the day at every seat.

It could hardly be more different when I revisit one bright autumn morning half a century later. Waiting for me on Platform 14, a long dark walk from the main Paddington concourse, is the spookiest train in Britain – the 11.36 a.m. ghost to Gerrards Cross in Buckinghamshire. Certainly, this once-grand main line seems on its last legs as the train crunches along a rusted single track past the back end of the industrial estates off the Great West Road.

As the sole passenger, I am privileged to enjoy the bull-dozed remains of the Old Oak Common engine sheds, which once housed the great copper-trimmed giants of Great Western steam. What ghosts still roam here! There's more post-industrial nostalgia as we pass behind the art deco Hoover factory, now converted into a Tesco supermarket. Disused sidings are shrouded with dying buddleia as we rumble by an old-fashioned wooden signal box and even more antiquated semaphore signals sited incongruously near a gigantic modern waste transfer station.

But when I get off at Gerrards Cross I find that I am no longer alone. The ethereal figure at the end of the deserted platform pointing his iPhone at the front of the train is no spectre but Steve, an off-duty train driver, who is, like Brian back in Goole, one of the ghosties who haunt trains like this one. 'Actually,' Steve tells me with the conspiratorial air of a man in the know, 'the train operator Chiltern Railways keeps this route open for crew training.' Training for what? it is tempting to ask. Surely not taking souls into the next world? The average London commuter is in hell already.

'There's always a reason, however obscure,' Steve explains pedantically, 'for every ghost service,' as I find out when I ring up Northern Rail to enquire about the skeleton service on the Knottingley line.

'Surely putting on more trains might encourage more people to use them?' I ask innocently.

'It's out of our hands,' their spokesman tells me. 'We simply follow the service level specified by the Department for Transport. That's what we have to do under the terms of our franchise. And so we do it.'

'The whole situation is completely crazy,' says Barry Doe

of *Rail* magazine, Britain's foremost timetable expert. So why don't the authorities simply put all these sad railway wraiths out of their misery? The problem, Doe says, is that in the old days of nationalisation British Railways were only too happy to put the closure notices up. But since privatisation the railways have been controlled and regulated by the Department for Transport, and no one in government dares to raise the politically sensitive subject of axing train services. 'We're stuck in a limbo world,' says Doe.

When I arrive back in Paddington, after a return journey on the alternative line to London Marylebone and a bus back to Paddington along the Marylebone Road, the early-evening commuters are already besieging the home-bound services on what are, according to the latest statistics, among the top ten most overcrowded trains in Britain. Here is a subject worth pondering. Is it a quaint and charming eccentricity straight out of the world of Gilbert and Sullivan that an empty train leaves this station each day while passengers on other services are transported like cattle in conditions not dissimilar to those that appalled Mr Gladstone 150 years previously?

Or does it simply confirm that the way we run our railways is totally barmy?

Chapter Nine

Goodbye to the toy train

Who could forget the delightful little Lynton &
Barnstaple narrow-gauge railway which once traversed
Exmoor through the Switzerland of England? Certainly
not the legions of enthusiasts who have never recovered
from its closure more than eighty years ago.

Could there be a more revered closed railway in the land
with a meaner, more miserable substitute to replace it?
As I search for my bus, a right old mist is swirling in from
the Atlantic on this early autumn morning, and its chilly
fingers are probing all the recesses of Barnstaple bus station.
At the back end of town, never a place of much charm at
the best of times, it is deserted apart from a couple of

superannuated New Agers swigging the last drops from cans of Stongbow. The assembly of shelters here that calls itself a bus station could single-handedly provide a doctoral thesis on the decline of rural public transport in the twenty-first century.

No integrated interchange for a brave transport future this. The diaspora of north Devon villages dotted around what has been known since Victorian times as the Switzerland of England are served by a raggle-taggle bunch of private coach operators with no coordinated timetable that I can find. Do I want Beacon Bus or Turners Tours, Riders Travel or TT Coaches? 'Is this the Lynton and Barnstaple service?' I ask as a battered yellow and blue single-decker pulls in. It seems an appalling heresy to utter the name of the fabled and much mourned Lynton & Barnstaple Railway in the context of this long-in-the tooth road vehicle. 'Hold on,' says the driver, busily inspecting a dent on the side of his bus. 'I had a bit of a scrape on the way down.'

Once our journey to the small north Devon resorts of Lynton and Lynmouth, twenty miles from here, would have started at Barnstaple Town station on the dreamy banks of the Taw, aboard what many enthusiasts have long regarded as one of the most perfect little railways ever created through some of the most beautiful scenery on God's earth. A smart green locomotive, massive brass dome polished to perfection, with a couple of rich brown and creamy white carriages, would have been waiting for the London connection to roll into the bay across the platform. With one or two exceptions, there cannot ever have been so many superlatives nor so many eulogies for such a tiny train.

Despite its demise eighty years ago, the Lynton & Barnstaple Railway ranks alongside the Darjeeling Himalaya Railway in India and the Ffestiniog Railway in Wales as one of the iconic narrow-gauge railways of the world. Narrow-gauge railways, because of their cheapness to build, were once regarded as the poor relations of full-size trains – operating quarries, mines, paper mills, running humble passenger services off the beaten track. Once there were thousands of them, part of an industrial heritage now forgotten.

But, unlike these, the L&B – conceived at the end of the nineteenth century and running on a switchback course through the most beautiful parts of north Devon into the romantic hills of Exmoor – became a legend in its own short lifetime of thirty-seven years. Here was poetry compared to the prose of most of its peers, and conceived with the vision of a successful media entrepreneur who believed he understood the future of British taste. The track gauge of just 1 foot 11½ inches enabled it to twist and turn precipitously in the hills. Its cargoes were passengers rather than freight. Yet, although frequently referred to as such, it was no toy, being constructed and operated to the exacting standards of a full-grown railway. Its greatest achievement, perhaps, was that its glories ultimately exceeded even those of the beautiful landscape through which it passed.

Central to the appeal of the Lynton & Barnstaple was that romantic Keatsian quality long so attractive to the British sensibility – being doomed to die almost from the outset. From its inception in 1898, nearly everything went wrong. The trackbed cost far more to build through the difficult landscape than anyone reckoned, and the ensuing financial burden coincided with the start of the motor age. By the 1920s, road traffic was starting to eat into its revenues, and as the income dwindled, maintenance suffered. In 1923 it was given a fresh start by the newly formed Southern Railway, who bought a brand-new locomotive and rolling stock. Even this hard-nosed company, whose core business was running London commuter services, could not fail to be seduced by the L&B charm.

But unlike the narrow-gauge railways of Wales, whose heart was in transporting hardware — quarry stone and slate, stuff that could be weighed, measured and costed — the business model of the L&B was more fragile. Even before it had a chance to establish itself, its fickle market of tourists was rapidly turning to the charabanc, with its ability to go where fancy took it along the roads and lanes of Devon. Despite the railway's quaintness, with its Emmet-like locomotives and their long tall funnels, charming small stations and views from the carriage window which surpassed those of almost every other railway of its kind in Europe, it could not survive the Great Depression. On one dismal day at the end of September 1935 more than a thousand people stood in the pouring rain on Barnstaple station to perform the obsequies as the last train rolled in.

Today, as I set off in search of what still remains, the scenery is as glorious as ever, although accessing it involves a long journey through the switchback curves and gear-juddering hills of the A39, rolling around death-defying hairpin bends on the fringes of Exmoor. But after a bone-shaking ride of nearly an hour, there in the drizzle alongside the road I spy the unmistakable cloud of steam from a tiny engine at the head of a couple of wooden carriages waiting to depart in a perfect little station, with cosy stone buildings and a name so bucolic you could hardly make it up. WOODY BAY, says the Southern Railway concrete sign on the platform, still fringed with moss as though nothing has changed in the past eighty years.

As if to complete the sepia atmosphere of time warp, a kettle is boiling in the booking office and the station cat wraps itself around my feet as the ticket clerk pulls an old-style cardboard ticket out of the rack, with his old-world ink-stamping machine at the ready. Could this be a hallu-cination? I wonder as I think of Samuel Taylor Coleridge and his drug-fuelled versifying at Porlock just along the coast. (And no, I didn't take any quinine tablets for the stomach-churning bus trip to get here.) Here, in high definition not virtual reality, is the most famous station on England's most famous narrow-gauge railway – and at 1,000 feet above sea level the highest stop in the entire 365-mile span of the territory of the Southern Railway from Kent to Cornwall. It's as though the clocks have continued to tick on since the last train ran back in 1935.

Authentic though the scene might seem, the works plate on the little green engine – a 0-4-2 T tank called *Isaac* – gives it away. Built by the famous locomotive engineers W. G. Bagnall for a South African platinum mine in 1953, the old L&B was but a memory by then. But no time to ruminate now. Ticket in hand I'm off, jolting along on slatted wooden seats, a heady cocktail of steam and Atlantic spray percolating through the old-fashioned windows, which drop down all the way with a tug on an old-fashioned leather strap – once so beloved of schoolboys with penknives, who would take them home for souvenirs.

After a mile we squeal to a stop, and Driver Pete and Fireman John crank the reverser before running the engine round the train for the return journey to Woody Bay. What? Journey over already? 'We've done very well to get this far,' John tells me, explaining how the preservationists of the present-day Lynton & Barnstaple only started on their mission to rebuild the line in 1979. But so far it's just a resurrected fragment of what was once constructed across these moors to such great hopes and dreams.

The inception of the original line in the 1890s was as eccentric as the brief years between its birth and death. There cannot be many railways that share their heritage with Page 3 of the *Sun*, but the Lynton & Barnstaple owes its conception to the media baron Sir George Newnes, who lived in Lynton and made a fortune from the mass-circulation magazine *Titbits*, direct forerunner of today's tabloid press. Newnes was also publisher of the *Strand Magazine*, in which Arthur Conan Doyle made his debut with the Sherlock Holmes stories, but it was his entry into the sleepy world of north Devon that really shook things up. Until the middle of the nineteenth century the remote twin villages of Lynton and Lynmouth had been in decline, with populations falling and the local herring shoals fished out. But with its spectacular Exmoor location, the Lynton area of north Devon was beginning to develop a tourist industry, even though local transport was so poor that able-bodied passengers aboard the horse-drawn coach services were forced to get out on steep hills and walk – and sometimes even push.

Enter Sir George and Lady Newnes, touring the area on holiday in the 1880s. They fell in love so madly with the area that they bought their own grand house in Lynton. And so powerful was the influence of this metropolitan grandee on the local economy that it was no time before he sponsored a rail link to the outside world. The first sod was dug at the site of Lynton station by Lady Newnes on 17 September 1885, and her husband was in buoyant mood when he gave an interview in 1898 to the *Railway Magazine*, declaiming (in the style of a man who clearly knew how to work the media), 'I believe that Lynton has for some time enjoyed the distinction of being the only place in England extensively visited by tourists, despite the fact that it is twenty miles from any railway station . . . Almost by the time these words are in print, the iron horse – or should I say iron pony – will be journeying every day to the Switzerland of England.'

But not everyone was so bullish. There were plenty of detractors too, even from as far away as Yorkshire, where the *Sheffield Independent* ran an editorial bemoaning the fact that 'the very mountains of England may soon become no better than the hills of the Rhine – many of them adorned with a rack-and-pinion railway, a restaurant and a promenade. Some may rejoice that Lynton was delivered over to the clutches of the steam monster; but there are a select few who will mourn, and mourn with reason.'

These 'select few' weren't the only ones who wished the new railway ill. It was jinxed well before the first ticket was ever issued. The building contract for the line had been awarded to James Nuttall of Manchester, whose £42,100 tender was considerably less than the £48,000 submitted by the local firm Jones Brothers, who had expected to get the job. But this was a disastrous error, and the construction of the line turned out to be a financial shambles, with Nuttall finding he had to hack a hillside railway through rocky outcrops, rather than laying a surface line through the easy-going clay that he had been expecting. Worse, the railway was also forced to overpay for the land, parting with a sum described by Newnes at the opening ceremony as 'daylight robbery'. Work fell behind schedule, and the line opened a year late, with the contractor suing the company for a further £40,000. Although Nuttall got into financial difficulties and the L&B was spared by a court from having to pay, the fledging railway started its working life with a financial albatross around its neck. The dismal reality was that it would never recover.

Still, the quaint little 2-6-2T tank engines, bought from engineers Manning Wardle for £1,050 each, were jolly enough – named *Exe*, *Yeo* and *Taw* after the local rivers. Sixteen carriages were also supplied, including observation cars, specially ordered to Newnes's specification so that the scenery could be enjoyed at its best. So enthusiastic was the motive-power department that another engine – a 2-4-2T tank called *Lyn* – was ordered immediately from the American Baldwin Locomotive Works of Philadelphia. Initially traffic seemed to justify it, with 1,200 passengers a week carried after the opening on 16 May 1898.

In 1903 the L&B played its part in British transport history by providing the first ever feeder service of motor buses to and from a railway station. Two six-horsepower Milnes-Daimler vehicles were provided for connections from the intermediate station of Blackmoor to the seaside resort of Ilfracombe. They were bizarre vehicles with no windscreens, seating twenty people, and there were no doors. The experiment was brought abruptly to an end, however, when one vehicle was pulled over by the police for reaching the terrifying speed of 8 mph! To quote the local newspaper, 'One of these cars was travelling at a little over 8 mph on a bye-road when the police interfered, a prosecution was instituted and a heavy fine was inflicted.' The buses were eventually flogged off to the Great Western for use on its Helston to Lizard service.

But in these early days, while never exactly prosperous, the company managed to make ends meet, with a small excess of income over expenditure every year. In 1909 and 1913 profits topped the £3,000 mark, and the directors managed to squeeze out a 0.5 per cent dividend. Even in the World War I years, pit props provided good business and another 0.5 per cent was paid in 1919. It is while these glory days are still bright, before the sad years of decline and closure, that we might rub the lamp of the railway genie and recreate a journey along the line in its heyday.

Let's imagine the early-morning train at Barnstaple station, where two platforms were sufficient for both the main-line trains and the L&B services. From 1899 onwards there were five services a day. The first one down, at 6.22 a.m., would connect with the overnight train from London, bringing the newspapers and the mail. The first up train – leaving Lynton at 9 a.m. – would convey passengers onto the London train, which eventually became the Atlantic Coast Express, the most superior train on the Southern Railway.

The locomotives were always beautifully kept and must have looked very smart in their original livery. The crews at Pilton sheds, outside Barnstaple, buffed away with pride, working the polish into a fish-scale pattern, while the brass-work – chimney, cap, dome and safety-valve covers – was invariably glittering. The basic colour was a deep green, often referred to as dark emerald or holly green. This was originally offset by a broad black line with a narrower orange line inside. The frames, cylinders and other gear below the tank sides and running plate were painted in a reddish brown, while the buffer beams and headlamps were vermilion. 'A beautiful sight,' as one early passenger put it.

No sooner are we out of Barnstaple, than we're climbing – no better way to get the feel than in the words of the Ward Lock *Red Guide to Lynton and Lynmouth*:

In order to avoid the expense of tunnels, long embank-ments and bridges, the line was made to wind and twist so that its course resembles a mountain torrent. At more than one point the turns are so sharp that even a short train may be on both sections of an 'S' curve simultaneously. Heading north from Snapper Halt, the line crossed and re-crossed the River Yeo, before turning onto the Chelfham Viaduct (pronounced 'Chilham') the line's major engineering feature, with its eight arches, 70 feet high, spanning the Stoke Rivers Valley.

Built of yellow Marland bricks, this still stands today, although in the days of the railway the high parapets frus-tratingly obscured the views of the surrounding scenery.

At Bratton Fleming station you might just catch sight of a stag in full cry as the train climbs ever higher. 'It was a line of little things,' said Frank Box, a photographer whose images have left later generations some of the most charming memories of the line. 'It seemed a marvel how, on a gauge of only 1 ft 11½ inches, a coach seating four a side could be safely poised,' he wrote. 'As one jogged along there was ample time to observe the simple everyday scenes of the countryside; the litter of pigs and the primroses near Snapper; magpies slowly winging their flight from copse to copse; the morning newspaper flung out by the guard as one climbed near the farm at Chumhill; the wild daffodils and some beautiful velvety-coated carthorse foals below Wistlandpound – lovely name.' Other highlights for Box were a 'white-walled homestead perched so prominently above a sensational horseshoe curve; rabbits in their hundreds on a sunny hillside near Parracombe. Then the train would stop suddenly while the driver alighted and tenderly lifted into safety a small lamb which had strayed onto the "two-foot".'

Buried away in the Devon backwoods, it not surprising that the line had its share of eccentricities. On one occasion a party of American tourists chartered a locomotive and brake van so they could view the scenery in appropriate Edwardian style. Naturally they provisioned themselves with a lavish hamper and some fine vintages of the best wine, and when they arrived at Lynton they presented the leftovers to the crew. It turned out to be a merry evening, and as dawn broke the men woke up with sore heads in a quarry some way from the station with the horrible realisation they were booked to drive the managing director to Barnstaple. Worse still, when they got to their engine the fire was out. Some frantic chopping of sleepers got it going, and they managed to start the train. But the pressure was low, and little did the unsuspecting executive realise that the journey was only accomplished by coasting down the gradients under control of the handbrake, operated by a crew with thick heads. Another favourite trick of the staff, when the trains weren't running on Sundays, was to place an inspection trolley on the track at Woody Bay and speed down on it to Lynton using only a piece of wood for a brake.

Drink played its part in many an L&B escapade. The stationmaster at Woody Bay was partial to an evening pint or two, but the general manager had a summer hut in the grounds of the neighbouring hotel, where he liked to spend weekends. To cover himself before popping out for a snifter, the stationmaster would ring along the line and ask if 'Mumble Mumble' was on his way. All the staff knew Mumble Mumble's identity and would tip him off accordingly. But this backfired one night when the stationmaster rang the next station and asked whether Mumble Mumble was on the train. 'This *is* Mumble Mumble,' came the reply.

For better or worse, the local fauna played its part in the operation of the line – frequently delaying the trains but also providing the crews with a ready supply of fresh meat. Chickens would fly squawking from under the wheels of the engines, which had to stop frequently for cattle to be cleared from the line. Then there were obstinate pigs, which would only move with a slap from the fireman's shovel. But a red deer trapped in the fencing wires would provide a rare treat for the crews, and some delicious venison would be on the menu for days.

And so we head on to the terminus at Lynton – where the station, at 700 feet above the sea, was unpopular with the locals, who weren't prepared to huff and puff up the steep hill. There were some who even ascribed to Newnes a nimbyish reluctance to let the railway spoil the ambience of his own mansion, Hollerday House. But there is no doubt that the location of the station, one of the highest buildings in the town, contributed to the line's undoing. Even so, it's hard to disagree with the words of the Southern Railway's official guide – *Devon and Cornish Days*, written by E. P. Leigh-Bennett in the early 1930s: 'In no other train have you ever been taken through such excitingly lovely country. It goes rather slowly with you, for which you are profoundly thankful, because if it rushed along, like its main-line colleagues, you wouldn't be able to feast your eyes on the scenery as you are now doing. Delightful little stations, too. The bumptious little engine gives a falsetto shriek of pride on approaching and leaving all of them. Perfect!'

But perhaps too perfect to last. In 1922 receipts dipped below operating costs for the first time, and the Southern Railway – one of the big four companies formed from the grouping of 1923 – agreed to take it over. Track was relaid and the line generally spruced up, but apart from summer tourist traffic, patrons vanished at an ever-accelerating rate to the roads. By 1935 the accountants up at Waterloo had had enough and the axe fell. Even then, the authorities could not quite let go. As the closure notices went up, the company sent out an oddly sentimental sales pitch for the final summer season. 'Make sure,' it urged, ' of a trip this holiday over the romantic light railway between Barnstaple and Lynton, through the beautiful scenery of the miniature Alps of North Devon, along the edge of Exmoor. The line will be closed on 29 September 1935.'

The very last train was scheduled to leave Lynton at 7.55 p.m., arriving at Barnstaple Town at 9.22 p.m. The train was joined by Lynton Town Council and thirty members of the public. The town band played 'Auld Lang Syne', and to the sound of exploding detonators and prolonged whistling from *Yeo* and *Lew* on the front, the train finally set off. More than a thousand turned out in the pouring rain at Barnstaple to pay their last respects – and after the flashlights had popped, the locos finally backed off into the night, much to the relief of the crews, who were anxious that coal and water supplies were running low. For the L&B's diehard enthusiasts, the eighty years since have been an extended period of mourning.

Even that great north Devon author Henry Williamson, author of *Salar the Salmon* and *Tarka the Otter*, brought along his children for a last farewell. 'Goodbye, little railway,' he wrote in his book *The Children of Shallowford*. 'The children loved you.' The *North Devon Journal* was so moved that it published a poem of its own (to be sung to the tune of 'Jerusalem the Golden'):

> Oh little train to Lynton
> No more we see you glide.
> Among the hills and valleys
> And by the steep hillside.
> The fairest sights in Devon
> Were from your windows seen,
> The moorland's purple heather,
> Blue sea and woodland green.
> And onward like a river
> In motion winding slow
> Through fairylands enchanted,
> Thy course was wont to go.
> Where still the hills and valleys
> In sunshine and in rain
> Will seem to wait for ever,
> The coming of the train.

Alas, it wasn't long before the scrap men arrived. Eager to avoid protests and ensure there was no possibility of a reopening, the Southern ensured that the track was lifted, the station buildings sold off and any reusable equipment put up for auction. Astonishing now, when even the most modest artefacts from the L&B sell at railwayana auctions for sky-high prices, much of it failed to reach its reserve. Locomotives could be had for as little as fourteen pounds, and much of the rolling stock was cut up on site for its scrap value. *Lew,* the only survivor among the locomotives, fetched the massive sum of fifty-two pounds, going on to a new home on a plantation in Brazil. Three coaches survived – one of them spending forty-seven years in a vicarage garden until it was acquired by the National Railway Museum for preservation.

As I arrive back in Barnstaple tonight, the 'Four-Faced Liar' is chiming five (the town-square clock is thus famously maligned because of the habit of all four of its faces telling a different time). Despite the discomforts of the bus, I've made it in double-quick time, compared with the leisurely ninety-eight minutes and fifty-eight seconds it took the final train to steam down from Exmoor. I stroll along to the old station at Barnstaple Town, where *Lyn* or *Exe* or *Lew* or one of their sisters, simmering in the platform after the evening arrival, would have basked in the rays of the setting sun on this balmy evening. Hark, and you can just summon up the rattle of milk churns on the platform and the metallic clunk of porters' barrows loaded with suitcases being wheeled along the stone flags still warm from the day's sunshine. There's a whirr of wires from the old London & South Western wooden signal box (still there, unchanged from 1935, and now doing service as a school office) as the signalman raises the semaphore for the final arrival at 7.26 p.m. from over the hills and far away.

The reality tonight is somewhat different. Dodging the HGVs and following the course of the ring road which has subsumed the railway through Barnstaple, I manage to trace the course of the old line through a car park until it peters out appropriately in a scrapyard. But peering up into the hills, past where proud drivers prepared their steeds in the old engine sheds, much of the route of the old trackbed is tantalisingly still there, snaking ever upwards to where the Chelfham Viaduct timelessly stands sentinel – proud guardian of the line's memories. Will it come back to life again? I think of the words of Driver Pete, a thousand feet back up on Exmoor: 'Our dream is to rebuild the railway all the way from Lynton to Barnstaple. After all, if we intended anything less, we would have to rethink our name.'

On 30 September 1935, the day after the closure, the stationmaster at Barnstaple Town placed a wreath on the buffer stops with a poignant message in the words of Shakespeare: 'Perchance it is not dead but sleepeth.' And why not dream? In the nostalgia-fuelled landscape of railway enthusiasm anything and everything is possible, and sometimes even comes to pass. Talk to the L&B's most passionate present-day enthusiasts and you will even find those who believe that one day *Lew* will be brought home triumphantly from the South American jungle, like some long-lost survivor from a forgotten war.

But we might also sensibly heed the words of one of the modern historians of the line, Chris Leigh: 'Even if the little engines and their coaches could be created and all the obstacles across the right of way removed, no preservationist can turn the clock back. The Lynton & Barnstaple lived and died in the first half of the twentieth century because that was where it belonged. A large part of its charm and character came from the era in which it lived, and the way of life for which it was created, and that most important, mystical ingredient could not be recreated.' We should pay heed, he says, to the 'old adage that distance lends enchantment to the view'.

It is not known whether the great French writer Marcel Proust ever took the little train to Lynton, although he is known to have been fond of reading railway timetables. But his words may provide an epitaph for the old L&B: 'Remembrance of things past is not necessarily the remembrance of things as they were.'

Chapter Ten
Engineering genius in the scrapyard

So many of the fiery marvels of the steam age were lost
for ever, sent prematurely for scrap. Let us mourn them,
including Sir Nigel Gresley's *Cock o' the North*, the *Patriot*,
the mighty *Big Bertha* and the steam engine that thought
it was a diesel.

It's curious how religious imagery has always lent itself so
happily to the railways. The Great Western was known as
God's Wonderful Railway, and grand stations such as St
Pancras are labelled cathedrals of steam. That most famous
of railway clergymen, the Reverend W. Awdry, author of
Thomas the Tank Engine, compared the railway system to the
Church of England: 'Both had their heyday in the mid-

nineteenth century; both own a great deal of Gothic-style architecture, which is expensive to maintain; both are assailed by critics, and both are firmly convinced that they are the best means of getting man to his ultimate destination.'

Now we have the Lazarus locomotives. Nearly half a century since the last of steam on the main line in Britain went for scrap, long-disappeared designs are being miraculously raised from the dead by groups of enthusiasts rebuilding old trains for a new era. And if anybody knows how to bring back 166 tons of steel, brass and copper from the grave, it is Mark Allatt. As he stands here in the former works of the Stockton & Darlington Railway, where the skeleton of a mighty new express steam locomotive is already forming, it is no wonder that many regard him as the closest thing to a modern god of steam engines. This expansive marketing consultant propelled a project to build Britain's first main-line express steam locomotive in modern history, and now he and his team are building another, even grander one, at an estimated cost of £5 million.

The sound of scoffing reverberated throughout the land back in 1990 when a few enthusiasts floated the idea of building *Tornado*, a working example of the London & North Eastern Railway's famous A1 Pacific class, initially by clubbing together nothing more substantial than their beer money. But they reckoned they had a good cause. In the scramble to save the giants of the track as steam came to an end in the 1960s, many emblematic locomotive types were lost, but probably none as distinguished as this class of thoroughbreds, famous for hauling great expresses between London and Scotland. Luckily, their faithful fans never gave up on them, and a coalition of sponsors and train enthusiasts emptied their piggy banks and raised the cash to get a brand-new engine built and operational inside twenty years. Who said good old-fashioned British engineering skills were dead?

The new *Tornado* is a separate breed from some patched-up rust bucket trundling up and down a preserved branch line or a toy train running on some rich man's garden railway. It is a full-size fire-breathing main-line locomotive, built from scratch at a cost of £3 million by British engineers and capable of giving modern trains a run for their money on the fastest main lines. 'Just remember,' says Allatt, '*Tornado* was built as the next locomotive in the class, not as a replica or restoration project.' Better still, *Tornado*, with all its modern electronic kit and conformity to such labyrinthine marvels of bureaucracy as the 2006 Inter-operability of the Conventional Rail System Directive, is even better than the originals of the class without losing any of its pedigree – the latest high-tech Porsche 911, perhaps, compared with the original air-cooled version of 1963. At the time of writing *Tornado* had clocked up 70,000 miles in the seven years since it was built.

Who would have thought that when Class 9F locomotive No. 92220 *Evening Star* rolled off the production line at Swindon in March 1960 – until the *Tornado* the last main-line steam locomotive to be built in the nation that invented the railway – that any more of these antiquated machines with their direct lineage to Stephenson's *Rocket* would be built again? It would not be long before Harold Wilson with his 'white heat of technology' mission statement took over from old-school Sir Alec Douglas-Home as prime minister, and the railways were busy dumping the dirty remnants of the Victorian era and ushering in such futuristic innovations as the double arrow logo and MaxPax coffee, as well as covering almost all their assets with fashionable-at-the-time corporate blue paint.

In eight years time steam on the national network would be as extinct as crank-handled telephones and black and white televisions. Industrial quantities of steam locomotives, some as little as five years old, went for scrap in an undignified orgy of destruction. The romance had gone out of our lives. There could hardly have been a sadder day than 11 August 1968, when thousands of weepy middle-aged men lined the tracks in the north of England as a couple of dilapidated engines (one, Britannia Class *Oliver Cromwell* humiliatingly stripped of its original nameplates) were spruced up to run British Railways' last ever main-line steam train from Liverpool and Manchester to Carlisle and back. The following day the BR politburo issued an edict banning steam on the national tracks for ever, and only the most ardent trainspotter fantasist would have believed that we should see the likes of a shiny new express steam locomotive on the main line again.

But never underestimate the power of British nostalgia and the devotion to the steam engine of the nation that invented it. Historian Roger Lloyd, writing in the 1950s, distils the attraction beautifully:

The slow humming in the distance, swelling fast to a grand fortissimo, and the shriek of the whistle adding to the din as the great engine rushes her train through the station, and the fading into silence until only the tapping of the last pair of wheels over the rail joints is heard — these common sounds and sights owe the thrall in which they hold us all to the fact that a steam engine does something that no other piece of mechanism succeeds in doing. It makes energy visibly and audibly impressive, and it seems to have an endless hold over the human imagination as it does so.

And so, as the last steam locomotives in revenue service ran in 1968, all over the nation railway fans, their enthusiasm undiminished by years of struggling to preserve the branch lines slashed by Beeching in the early 1960s, were regrouping to save the last of steam for the main line. And no matter how perforated by rust, never mind how many parts missing (wheels, cab fittings, rivets, buffers gone – not a problem), many locomotives survived. The scramble to preserve every last steam one was helped by a canny scrap dealer in South Wales called Dai Woodham, St Dai as he became in the iconography of steam preservation. He stayed the execution of the 215 crippled wrecks he had assembled in his weed-infested graveyard, while cutters' torches were busy preparing their less-fortunate sisters in other scrapyards for the smelter.

His actions may not have been entirely motivated by philanthropy, however. The canny Dai stopped cutting up steam locos, as it was quicker, easier and more lucrative to scrap wagons instead, while the steamers were stockpiled against the day when the price of scrap warranted their dismantling. During the 1970s and up to the 1980s, every so often a steam locomotive or two would be broken up when the wagon trade was slack.

One small boy at the time – these days elevated to the official in charge of Britain's locomotive collection at the National Railway Museum in York – told me, 'My parents will confirm that a little boy cried every time he read about that in a magazine.' Anthony Coulls' traumatic boyhood experience is probably not dissimilar to that of many grown men today. As it turned out, the venerable Dai in the end also became nostalgic about the inmates of his scrapyard. Most railway enthusiasts today would agree that the South Wales scrap man deserved his Rolls-Royce in the end.

Whatever the facts, the Baron of the Barry scrapyard now has an assured place in the annals of rail preservation, but the result of his endeavours turned out to be mixed, with a vast oversupply of the types of locomotives that happened to be around at the end of steam, and a dearth of others. Many of the later types were former Southern Railway engines still operating on the main line at the end. On a more pragmatic note, these later Southern types were less appealing to the scrap men, since there was less money to be had from their steel fireboxes, as opposed to the copper linings so beloved of the Great Western. (Some of these wrecks are still waiting to be restored to steam half a century later. And it doesn't seem likely that they will ever be, as rust consumes their innards and the now-elderly men who raised the funds to save them pass on to the great scrapyard in the sky.)

At the same time, only a single locomotive from the London & North Eastern Railway had passed into Woodham's hands. And although the British Transport Commission, charged with retaining for the nation the best of Britain's locomotive types, had done its best to build up a representative collection, some suspected a bias towards certain railways. Sure, the LNER's finest, such as the record-breaking *Mallard* and the fast freight locomotive *Green Arrow*, were saved. But it was left to a private individual, the industrialist Alan Pegler, to preserve that railway's iconic *Flying Scotsman* – even more sacred in the pantheon, some would argue, than *Mallard*. And how come an engine from Richard Maunsell's modest King Arthur class of the Southern Railway – hardly a locomotive to set the pulse racing – was chosen for the national collection over the Eastern Region's mighty A1 Class Pacifics?

The reasons will long be argued, but you only needed to have stood at the end of the platform at King's Cross in the post-war years to appreciate the poetry of the sleek modern A1 engines, designed by Arthur Peppercorn for the cream of the expresses between London and Scotland. Those unconvinced might read off the liturgy of the names. *Hal o' the Wynd* or *Redgauntlet* at the head of the Aberdonian, or *Madge Wildfire* storming north on the Tees-Tyne Pullman. Ah!

Bliss it was to be alive, brandishing your *Ian Allan ABC* for locospotters in the late 1940s and early 1950s, when they reigned.

Enter the A1 Locomotive Trust, the group that built *Tornado* and cleverly tapped into the romantic psyche of a cohort of middle-aged men. All those *Just William* kids, once happy with their duffel bags, spotters' books, enamel badges and Marmite sandwiches – as Nicholas Whitaker, a former trainspotter, describes them in his book *Platform Souls* – have morphed into comfortable baby-boomers. With mortgages paid off, there is time and money to revisit their youth before it's too late.

No wonder Allatt and the group are now confident about performing another Lazarus-like miracle with a project to spirit up a new locomotive from the shades of Sir Nigel Gresley's hallowed and long-lost P2 Class. Born in 1965, Allatt was too young to see the end of steam, although he is proud of a photograph of himself as a babe in arms in front of the *Flying Scotsman*. But his ambitions are messianic: 'What we're doing here is finishing off the last major project of this great designer, who had already done so many wonderful things during the 1930s.' The frames for the locomotive were rolled in the good old-fashioned Scunthorpe steelworks on St George's Day 2014, overseen by Gresley's grandsons – and, with a further dose of patriotism, it has been decided to call the locomotive *Prince of Wales*. Hubris? Standing here in the greasy hall of the old Darlington works, where the lathes once turned to build the trains of the world's first passenger railway, it is clear Allatt's vision is something more.

Though Sir Nigel Gresley's mighty P2s were the most powerful steam passenger locomotives ever built to run on British tracks, their lives were tragically short. Even though there is scarcely anybody alive today who ever saw one, they have acquired cult status among railway enthusiasts, who have always prized rarity above quality. Fortunately the Cock o' the North Class has both in copious quantities. Devastatingly handsome, with smoke deflectors melded into the body of the locomotive, they were built not for speed, despite their sleek looks, but for the heavy sleeping-car expresses on the twisting and heavy gradients of the hundred-mile route between Edinburgh and Aberdeen. Gresley, with a sense of thrift befitting the son of a clergyman, hated the wasteful practice of locomotives having to double-head these 600-ton trains, so he designed a behemoth that could tackle the job on its own.

The iconic status of the P2 partly derives from its unusual 2-8-2 wheel arrangement, known as a Mikado. Although this was the most common wheel arrangement in the world in the twentieth century, with 30,000 such engines built, it was virtually unknown in Britain till *Cock o' the North* came along. The taxonomy of locomotive wheel arrangements gave rise to a curious collection of nicknames, much loved by small-boy trainspotters, who would quiz each other endlessly over their meanings as they poured milky coffee from Aladdin flasks and chewed on Opal Fruits at the end of station platforms.

Only a few ever cracked the code of the system, which was devised by Frederick Whyte, an engineer on the New York Central Railway. The smallest such engines were named after actual locomotives, so a 2-2-0 (the number of front wheels followed by driving wheels followed by trailing wheels) was a Planet, named after Robert Stephenson's famous locomotive for the Liverpool & Manchester Railway. At the other end of the scale was the American Union Pacific Railroad's giant 4-8-8-4 locomotive, known triumphantly to its fans as the Big Boy.

Tempting though it might be to think so, the Mikado

appellation had nothing to do with Gilbert and Sullivan. Literally meaning 'Emperor of Japan', it derived from a batch of locomotives of the 2-8-2 wheel arrangement built by the American Baldwin Company in 1893 for a small Japanese railway. The Pacific, the most famous express locomotive type of all, had a similar derivation, taking its name from a New Zealand locomotive. More baffling were the 2-6-2 Prairie tanks – a favourite workhorse of the Great Western Railway – which provoked many arguments at the end of the platforms at Paddington, since there didn't seem to be many prairies on Dartmoor or along the Cornish Riviera.

All this may seem highly esoteric, but just whisper 'P2' or 'Mikado' to any steam enthusiast in Britain and you will see a dreamy look appear in their eyes. This is because the curious appeal of steam nostalgia has very little to do with the dry qualities of mechanical engineering for its own sake. The writer Bryan Morgan gets close to explaining this when he says, 'There is something clever and useful-seeming about understanding how a locomotive works, something akin to being able to fix up the shelves in the kitchen.' But steam fans, he says, fall into two classes – 'the men who know more about percentage cut-offs, drawbar pulls and fire grate areas than does Crewe's Chief Mechanical Superintendent, and those who profess ignorance of such matters but can still tell at a glance (or without one from the sound alone) just when, where, and by whom any locomotive was built'.

Most of us, I suspect, fall into the second category – especially those who pine for the charismatic locomotives of the past, whose souls rather than their mechanical innards are what matter. 'Locomotives, especially steam ones, have their own beauty,' writes Brian Hollingsworth in his book *The Pleasures of Railways*. 'The faithful talk of a Stanier, a Gresley, a Baldwin, a Churchward or a Chapelon in the same way that art lovers might talk of a Botticelli, a Gauguin, a

Modigliani or a Constable. Paintings are, of course, at a disadvantage compared with locomotives, which are not only three-dimensional but also have movement, as well as producing their own kind of music.'

Perhaps we have no need to try to explain it. As Roger Lloyd writes, 'The connection between the sight of a railway engine' and a 'quite deep feeling of satisfaction is very real for multitudes of people, but it excludes rational analysis.' Herein lies the magic of the P2. First there was their size. The weight of these huge machines made them the most powerful locomotives in Britain aside from a few lumbering articulated freight locomotives, with the engine alone, minus its tender, weighing a mighty 110 tons. Then there was their star quality. No sooner had No. 2001, named *Cock o' the North* (nickname of the fifth Duke of Gordon), emerged from the Doncaster Works in 1934 than it was featured on Pathé News along with the latest fashionable starlets from Hollywood. Even the French – never noted for their admiration of most things British – were impressed. That country's great engineer André Chapelon – whose own locomotives for the Paris–Orleans Railway were reckoned to be the most sophisticated ever built and who had advised Gresley on the P2s – had one of the class shipped to France, where it was put through its paces at the French government's locomotive testing centre at Vitry-sur-Seine and exhibited to some wonderment at Paris's Gare du Nord.

Rarity too played its part. Only eight locomotives with the Mikado wheel arrangement were ever built in Britain, and six were P2s. And of course there were those romantic names. After *Cock o' the North* came *Earl Marischal*, hereditary title of the Keith family, whose castle lay close to the Edinburgh–Aberdeen line near Stonehaven. It was followed by Nos. 2003–6, named *Lord President, Mons Meg, Thane of Fife and Wolf of Badenoch* respectively. So evocative were the names

– perhaps the most romantic ever applied to steam locomotives – that they were transferred to the British Railways Class 87 electric locomotives, the modern greyhounds of the Euston to Glasgow route, when it was electrified in the 1970s.

It was lucky that some of these names lived on, since Gresley's mighty pioneers met an ignominious end – not helped, some would say, by skullduggery within the LNER family. After Gresley's death the P2s were rebuilt by his successor Edward Thompson into more ordinary A2 Pacifics with all the experimental glamour expunged. Thompson was married to the daughter of the North Eastern Railway's chief mechanical engineer, Sir Vincent Raven – who had been overlooked for the LNER top job in favour of Gresley. Supposedly here was a chance for the family to get its own back. Who knows what the truth was? Nevertheless, it was a fact that there was a design fault in the leading pony truck, which meant that the engine was hard on the track. And she was heavy on coal too – having 'a bonny appetite' as the firemen who had to slog away with their shovels put it. But did all the romance have to be engineered out?

An unhappy end awaited other curious pioneers, many now lost without trace. One such was the Great Eastern Railway's *Decapod* – built in 1902 and the most powerful steam locomotive in the world at the time. Designed by the company's locomotive superintendent, James Holden, No. 20 had an enormous boiler with a firebox extending the full width of the locomotive, and the water was carried, not in tanks or a tender, but in a vast chamber beneath the engine. *Decapod* (from the ancient Greek, 'having ten feet') was a pioneer in another sense, becoming the first ten-coupled locomotive in Britain. Even its biggest fans had to admit it was as ugly as sin and one of the most hideous engines ever to put an imprint on British tracks.

Superintendent Holden, who was driven by his Quaker beliefs, was a man full of big ideas. He built the first hostel in London for enginemen, who needed to find a respectable billet after arriving late in the evening with their trains. He was equally keen to improve the lot of commuters into Liverpool Street from the east London suburbs, packed aboard what was at the time the most intensively worked passenger service in Britain. Over many years it became known as the Jazz because of the coloured stripes applied to the sides of the carriages. The superintendent had a personal interest in improving the service, living like many of his customers in Wanstead in the heart of suburban east London. Replacing steam with new electric trains was an obvious option and would have stemmed the loss of passengers to London's newly burgeoning electric tramways. But the directors of the cash-strapped company were chary. Holden's challenge was to discover whether steam locomotives could achieve the same sort of acceleration as electric trains, since steam was the cheaper default option.

Here was an experiment that actually worked. The electrification lobby claimed they could produce a train of 315 tons that could accelerate to 30 mph in 30 seconds. But when put to the test the mighty *Decapod* did better, beating the target with an even bigger train of 335 tons – a full 18 carriages. Unfortunately, the commuters, squashed into their sardine-can trains to Enfield and Chingford, ended up losing doubly. The success of the *Decapod* led to ideas of electrification being shelved for another decade, but the miserly accountants of the GER were not willing to stump up the cash to strengthen the tracks and bridges for powerful new steam engines. Maybe we should not blame them, since this eighty-ton monster weighed a crushing four tons for every foot of its wheelbase. And perhaps we should be glad that these ugly beasts were never allowed to congregate under the cathedral-like glass roof of Liverpool Street – one of the most elegant nineteenth-century stations in the world.

As it turned out, the *Decapod* never ran in service and in 1906 was converted into a 0-8-0 freight engine with a tender. But the railway gods clearly never intended it to be – and the *Decapod* met the fate of other ugly creations with Greek names, such as the *Cyclops*, an odd-looking GWR tank engine with a crane on top, and was consigned to the scrapyard in 1913.

It wasn't until 1919 that another legendary ten-coupled locomotive appeared on British rails. This was the famed *Big Bertha* – a one-off produced by the Midland Railway to push, heave and shove heavy freight trains up the celebrated 1:37 Lickey incline between Bristol and Birmingham. The bank had long presented a huge challenge to locomotive designers. No sooner had suitable locomotives been identified for the job than the load limits went up again as the industrial power of the workshop of the world continued to increase.

Before *Big Bertha* came along, a ragbag of small locomotives had been coupled together to do the banking up the two-mile grade. While it was fine when they were busily wheezing their way up and down, it was very expensive on crews, whose wages had to be paid while the engines were idle between trains. *Big Bertha*, with her distinctive Midland Railway aesthetics designed by chief mechanical engineer Sir Henry Fowler, was far more handsome than the Great Eastern's *Decapod*, and much longer lived, giving faithful service for thirty-five years until retirement in 1956. Special attributes were a raised cab on the tender to protect crews from the elements, since the locomotive spent half its time working in reverse. Also distinctive were its huge raked cylinders for extra power. A giant American-style electric light was fitted to the front of the smokebox in 1921 to permit precision engagement with the rear of trains in the darkness.

The old lady lived on into nationalisation, given the number 58100, which was much coveted by schoolboys with their Ian Allan spotters' books, and all the more desirable since this rare locomotive was rarely observed from the end of any platform. By the time of her withdrawal she had amassed an incredible 838,856 miles, mostly accumulated on her slow four-mile return journeys up and down the Lickey bank. So popular was she with crews that a group of drivers arranged a retirement dinner in her honour. It is tempting to speculate that there might have been fried egg, bacon, sausages and black pudding on the menu, since tons of the stuff had been cooked on a shovel in the locomotive's fire as crews waited their turn to give a helping hand up the bank on a cold morning.

During the last months of her celebrity *Big Bertha* guested on enthusiasts' specials, and was buffed and polished for display at Derby Works open day in 1956. So, it was regarded as a dastardly act when she was quietly cut up at the beginning of April the following year in the erecting shop where she had been built all those decades ago. One of her massive cylinder blocks was saved as a sop to those who had demanded her preservation, but poignantly no museum was willing to take it, and this engineering marvel also found its way to the melting pot.

Romantic though they were, should we really miss all these old steam locomotives that went to the great scrapyard in the sky? Like it or not, it is a dismal fact that there was not very much innovation in the century and a half from the time steam was invented to when it died. This technology may have changed our lives, but it didn't change itself very much. George Stephenson could have driven the *Evening Star* out of the erecting shop at Swindon and felt quite at home with the final incarnation of the product he invented. The diesel generation that came afterwards may not have been far wrong in labelling them kettles since effectively this was what they were – a cab and a firebox with a boiler attached.

But there was one exception – the most innovative, the most experimental, the most controversial and perhaps the ugliest steam locomotive ever built in Britain. Had Oliver Bulleid's Leader Class been a technical success, perhaps we should have steam locomotives buzzing around the network today. As it was, this astonishing machine – with twin cabs and a body like a diesel on chain-driven bogies – was such a spectacular failure that it effectively put the cap on steam innovation for ever.

Not that Bulleid didn't have a superb engineering pedigree. He had learned at the knee of Nigel Gresley on the LNER before joining the Southern and designing the 'air-smoothed' Merchant Navy and West Country Classes in the 1940s. Nicknamed spamcans, these visually exciting engines, designed in the *moderne* style, were to become the mainstay of steam on the British main line as steam drew to close in the mid-1960s, although flaws in their revolutionary engineering led to some being rebuilt and having their streamlined casings removed.

Bulleid's brilliance was never in doubt. But, as his biographer Eric Bannister put it, he was 'rather eccentric and had some strange ideas'. Indeed he seemed to have a new one every week, and of these, his colleagues reckoned, one a year would be brilliant. Still, he loved steam with a passion, and with these two designs under his belt set out to design the coal-fired locomotive that would secure a future for this beloved technology as the diesel era encroached from the US. It was to be the ultimate maid-of-all-work engine, sleek, modern-looking, with no tender or visible water tank and drivable from both ends. The result was No. 36001, the first of the Leader Class, which rolled off the production line at the Brighton Works on 21 June 1949.

Commuters gasped at its revolutionary appearance, since this impressive machine – which would not look out of place even on today's railways – seemed finally to sweep the steam age into the past. It was spectacular indeed but, it turned out, one of the worst failures in a century and a half of steam locomotion. The flaws appeared almost as soon as it was out of the works, when it could not engage reverse gear to make its way back in. On one of its first test runs it became apparent that the water tank was too high for the water crane, and it had to be refilled humiliatingly with a hose from a station porter's office.

The faults piled up remorselessly. The power steam bogies, using sleeve valves (a metal sleeve within the piston, which was supposed to expel the exhaust more efficiently), and the chain drive (replacing conventional valve gear) did not work properly. The reverser continued to jam, and the boiler frequently ran out of steam. Far from being a working environment befitting the modern era, crew conditions were appalling. Driver and fireman were separated, with the stoking done in an enclosed firing cab, where temperatures could reach intolerable levels. Condensation meant that it was often like a Turkish bath, and crews had to wear sacking round their legs to protect themselves from the heat. At one end of the locomotive the smokebox protruded into the driver's cab, producing baking conditions. It was alleged that hot ash had spilled onto the wooden floor on one occasion, threatening to set it ablaze.

But was it really so bad as its detractors claimed? An intriguing tale did the rounds that *Leader*'s failure was due to a dastardly plot by crews, who had secretly sprinkled sand into the sleeve valves. The men were paid a daily rate for the test runs, and – hey presto! – if the locomotive failed they could knock off early. But in the end it didn't matter. By 1950, Robert Riddles, chief mechanical engineer of the newly formed British Railways, had had enough. He ordered *Leader* to be scrapped and construction of the remaining four on order to be halted.

So embarrassing was the failure that cancellation was kept quiet until the *Sunday Dispatch*, a mass-circulation national newspaper, ran a splash on 18 January 1953, headlined RAIL-WAY'S BIGGEST FIASCO. The report went on: 'Three huge railway engines, which cost altogether about £500,000 to build, now lie rusting and useless in sheds and sidings – silent and hidden evidence of the biggest fiasco produced by Britain's nationalised railways. The situation comes to light as a result of *Sunday Dispatch* inquiries prompted by threatened increases in fares and allegations of mismanagement on the railways.' Although the newspaper had no exclusive new information, the reverberations of the story meant that *Leader* was buried for good.

British railway history is littered with many such brilliant oddities that seemed a good idea at the time but on second thoughts were entirely hopeless. A cavalcade of monsters and hybrids has paraded through British locomotive history. Cecil Paget of the Midland Railway designed a locomotive driven by eight cylinders compared with the usual two to four, while the North British Reid-Ramsey locomotive of 1910 attempted to use a ship's condensing steam turbine to drive an electric motor. Another, the Kitson-Still locomotive of the 1920s, aimed to combine the fuel-saving capabilities of the internal combustion engine with the high-starting torque of the steam engine. The result was one of the most hideous-looking machines ever to appear on the railways. It ended up bankrupting Kitson and Company. In his book *Prototype Locomotives* Robert Tufnell likens these bizarre creations to Noël Coward's song 'I Wonder What Happened to Him': 'Similar thoughts may have occurred to students of locomotive design regarding the fate of some unusual locomotives, descriptions of which have appeared in the technical press or in papers given to engineering institutions, before they disappeared from sight.'

Most bizarre of all perhaps in this freak show of oddities were the Siamese-twin locomotives of County Kerry. Back in 1888 the residents of Ballybunion in the west of Ireland, birthplace of Lord Kitchener, thought it about time they were connected to the Irish railway system. Enter a French railway engineer called Charles Lartigue, who had been impressed by camels in the Algerian desert and their ability to carry heavy loads in panniers on their backs. Here, he thought, was the revolution in land transport that the world was waiting for. Instead of trains running on two rails fixed to sleepers, why not have a single rail at waist height supported on trestles? The locomotives and carriages would sit astride the track just like camels' panniers.

The locals saw an opportunity for international fame and applied to Parliament to build what would be the world's first steam passenger monorail. Costing £30,000, the nine-mile line opened on 1 March 1888. Unfortunately what seemed a brilliant idea in the North African desert, where conventional tracks were a problem because of drifting sand, wasn't quite so practical in the bogs of the west of Ireland. One of the main problems was that everything had to be duplicated to prevent the trains from toppling over. For example, the locomotives, sitting astride the tracks, had to have two boilers, with the consequent doubling of maintenance. If Farmer O'Reilly wanted to take a cow to market, he had to balance it with another one – or find two pigs of the same weight. With tracks at waist height, level crossings were impossible. And workable points were a logistical nightmare. Even so, Britain's most eccentrically engineered trains continued to run for another thirty-six years, and such was their fame that a short replica runs as a tourist attraction today.

Many other pioneering designs went to the great scrapyard in the sky, leaving subsequent generations to pine over their loss. 'The problem is that people have always had different criteria about what to save,' says Anthony Coulls, senior curator at the National Railway Museum in York – the man who watches over the national collection. 'Should it be engineering history? Or social history? People have sometimes opted for novelty or big names. Sometimes it's a matter of who shouts the loudest. Yet it seems incredible now that the Great Western binned two of its most historic locomotives, the broad-gauge *North Star* and *Lord of the Isles*, just because there wasn't enough space at Swindon Works to keep them.'

Even in the modern British Railways era – after saving historic locomotives for the nation became more systematic – some decisions were made that would never be taken now. 'Looking back it's unthinkable that *Flying Scotsman* should not have been saved for the nation when it was withdrawn in the 1960s,' says Coulls. For him, with his curator's hat on, perhaps the most important loss of all was a representative of the Salamanca Class – the world's first commercially successful steam locomotives, built by Matthew Murray for the Middleton Railway in 1812, predating even *Puffing Billy* and *Rocket*. The last survivor was sent for scrap in the 1850s.

Coulls' personal list of regrets includes *The Bug*, a tiny locomotive that drew the personal saloon of Dugald Drummond, the London & South Western Railway's locomotive superintendent, along with the modern-era express engines of the London & North Western Railway. Some of its finest products – a Precursor, a Claughton and a

George V Class – were all scrapped in the 1940s. Others might nominate *The Great Bear*, the only Pacific ever built for the Great Western Railway, and Gresley's *Hush-Hush* experimental locomotive, the unique 4-6-4 10000, which was scrapped in 1959.

'The benefit of hindsight is all very well,' says Coulls. 'Now people are asking why more first-generation diesel locomotives weren't saved in the 1950s and 1960s. But at the time they were dismissed as smelly boxes on wheels.' Meanwhile, more Lazarus locomotives are in the pipeline in projects around the country to resurrect the lost souls of steam. Here is an eclectic band of projects with various degrees of appeal, including resurrecting an LMS express Patriot Class, to be called *The Unknown Warrior*, and a handsome London, Brighton & South Coast Atlantic named *Beachy Head*. It's easy to understand the fund-raising appeal of a Great Western Railway Saint to be called *Lady of Legend*, but do we really need another British Railways Standard tank engine from the 1950s?

Surely it is madness to embark on all these rebuildings when there are scores of unrestored or ailing locomotives shunted into sidings at the back of preserved railways all around the country, mouldering away for lack of care. Writing about *Tornado*, the design critic Jonathan Glancey has perhaps the best explanation of the appeal of building afresh: 'It is not simply that [*Tornado*] is a particularly fine example of an express passenger locomotive, but that she is brand new. This is not in itself a virtue, yet *Tornado*'s very existence is a kind of modern miracle and one, perhaps, that could only happen in Britain.'

It is the emotional appeal that captivates Glancey.

Not so very deep down, many people in an ostensibly digital age have a hankering for beautiful machinery, for things well crafted and honestly made; for machines not made far away by cheap and even child labour in distant lands, but by ordinary decent people in the very towns that, famous for their engineering and productive prowess until recent decades, have lost what had seemed their right to craft magnificent machines that everyone involved in their making could rightly be proud of.

But there is yet something else even less tangible. 'By saving these locomotives, we're pulling railway enthusiasm back from the precipice,' says Mark Allatt. 'What we're doing with these brand-new engines is to kill off the idea of railway fan as anorak stone dead. A new generation of enthusiasts is coming forward. And now,' he enthuses, 'we've got Steampunk.' This is a subgenre of science fiction or fantasy based on the steam age with its devotees sometimes even dressing the part too. 'It's a renaissance,' enthuses Allatt. 'Even girls have got interested.'

Chapter Eleven
Last call for the dining car

Crisp tablecloths, silver service and six-course gourmet meals. The railway restaurant car was once the acme of civilised travel. Now, in a world ruled by the soggy bacon roll it is all but vanished. But not quite . . .

I'm about to enjoy the 'Golden Age of Travel'. I know this because it says so on my ticket for this morning's day trip out of London's Victoria station. I am settled in an armchair aboard a 1930s art deco Pullman car called *Audrey*, contemplating a table setting for luncheon which is at least as swank as you could find in any of London's finest dining establishments. We're not talking the Victoria station hotel here –

decent enough maybe for a second-division plc boss to wine and dine (and perhaps have a cuddle with) his PA on the way home to East Grinstead. Think instead of true class – the Grill Room at the Dorchester, maybe, or the Ritz. On the starched white tablecloth in front of me is a dazzling array of silver cutlery, crystal glassware and fresh flowers. And, ah . . . here is the first glass of champagne bubbling silkily into my glass from a steward so discreet that he has gone before I notice.

I'd arrived in London aboard an early-morning train from Sheffield experiencing what we may call without being too unkind 'the utility age of travel'. East Midlands Trains is one of the last British train franchises (apart from Virgin, East Coast and First Great Western) to have staff routinely serve a hot breakfast (or any kind of food) to its passengers. But today, according to the train manager, the 'kitchen is down' so we are entitled to a 'breakfast bacon baguette', which is included in the price of my Business Anytime Plus first-class ticket. I didn't see any rabbis or imams (or even bosses cuddling their secretaries), but even I – hungry as I was – found it hard to stuff what seemed like a wodge of warm cotton wool wrapped around a small piece of pork fat down my throat.

Thank goodness for *Audrey*. 'You'll love *Audrey*, says the lady on Victoria's Platform 2 who takes my ticket for the British Pullman – a four-hour canter around the Surrey Hills aboard the historic carriages of the Venice-Simplon Orient Express, which earn useful revenue pottering around the Home Counties on their days off from normal duties on the luxury trains to Paris, Venice and Istanbul.

And indeed I do love her – every umber and cream and polished brass inch of her frame – and I'm besotted with the perfection of her jazz-age marquetry. *Audrey* is infused with the spirit of dining on trains. She made her debut in

1933, spending forty years with the Brighton Belle, the world's first all-electric Pullman train, and is the direct descendant of the world's first dining car, pioneered by George Mortimer Pullman in the United States in 1868, which was so classy that it was named *Delmonico* after the famous New York restaurant. *Audrey* has another, more British, claim to fame, having reputedly been the Queen Mother's favourite dining carriage. The Duke of Edinburgh is apparently partial to her too – at least it says so in the booklet on my table.

What Prince Philip's flirtation with *Audrey* has to do with the Golden Age of Travel, none of the eighty-two passengers on board, celebrating birthdays, engagements, lottery wins and ruby weddings, probably knows. But by the time we stagger back onto the platform at Victoria four hours later – after a *grande bouffe* of 'Grilled line-caught tuna Niçoise' followed by 'Cauliflower and leek soup with chive crème fraiche', 'Woodland mushroom and basil-stuffed breast of corn-fed chicken', a plate-load of British cheeses and 'Blackcurrant and white chocolate mousse with honeycomb and almond crumble' – we are certain that this really was The Way to Go.

Even the old-school train staff appear to have been delivered in a time capsule from central casting. But Alan, my steward – all white gloves and starched jacket – is the real thing, his inscrutable ruddy face the hallmark of the railway stewards of old – something perhaps to do with years of proximity to hot stoves and scalding plates. 'I've been serving on trains for thirty-six years,' he tells me. 'I started in 1988 on the restaurant cars out of King's Cross, but sadly they're now gone for ever.'

Here is a chap who knows effortlessly how to avoid a ripple while conveying a bowl of steaming soup along the carriage of a moving train, but he is also a living link with one of the vanishing experiences of modern travel: the soothing clink of cutlery on china, the starched tablecloths, a smartly uniformed steward at your elbow serving dinner in the restaurant car as the scenery of our green and pleasant land flashes by through the window. For more than a century the time-honoured words 'Last call for the dining car' have summoned hungry passengers for sittings at lunch or dinner on trains across the land.

Now cuisine on trains – where it exists at all – is rarely more exalted than a microwaved burger or a 'cheese toastie', and the announcement you are most likely to hear is 'The onboard shop is closing at Watford.' For many of us this is a tragedy. As the railway historian Bryan Morgan wrote, 'Diners are much-loved things, for we never quite outgrow our childhood amazement at the idea of refreshment on wheels. The moving sunlit countryside; the strange cries from the hell-hole of the galley; the stewards trying to steer a steady course – all these impart a glow . . .'

Given that Britain pioneered the railways, it took us a long time to get round to putting dining cars on trains. This was partly because early trains had no corridors, but also because of the technical sophistication in the age of coal needed to produce a hot meal on the move. Instead passengers were encouraged to order luncheon baskets at stations, which went by names such as The Democrat or The Aristocrat, depending on the quality of the contents and how much you could afford. The Midland Railway produced 'hot baskets', typically containing a steak or a chop with vegetables, cheese, bread and half a bottle of claret or stout. Orders could be telegraphed ahead, and small boys called nippers called out the passengers' names as the trains came in and delivered the food directly to their carriages.

British railway dining proper began on 1 November 1879, when a Pullman car called *Prince of Wales* with a fully equipped kitchen was attached to the Leeds expresses of the Great

Northern Railway. Passengers reclined in velvet armchairs and rang electric bells, summoning waiters bearing trays of roast meats, fish, puddings and fruit, with crystal decanters of wine. The food was cooked over an open fire at the end of the coach, and despite teething problems, such as soot blowing onto the food whenever the train went through a tunnel, the idea quickly caught on.

Many commentators enthused about the experience. Describing a return journey from Euston to Manchester in 1903, the *Manchester Evening Chronicle* reported, 'The waiter who appears with soup says we are doing sixty miles an hour, although it is difficult to realise it. In the best West End restaurant style, fish, joint, poultry, sweets, cheese, coffee and liqueurs are produced in a magic kind of way from an absurdly small room at the end of the carriage . . .' Value for money was a key ingredient. A review of British dining cars in *Transport* magazine around the same time commented, 'In every respect – the selection of food, its quality and cooking and the charge made for it – the Midland Railway have left nothing to be desired. The Midland wine list is very extensive and the prices asked are very reasonable indeed.' A chop or steak with fried potatoes, bread, butter, tea or coffee could be had for half a crown – around ten pounds in today's money.

Queen Victoria was not so enthused, however. Though an early fan of rail travel, she insisted that her train ran at no more than 40 mph and that it stopped at selected stations whenever she wanted to eat. Even so, Her Majesty enjoyed a cup of tea on the move, and her personal carriage had tea-making equipment installed as early as 1869. Surprisingly the mighty Great Western Railway was late on the scene, not launching dining cars until 1890. This was because Brunel had rashly signed a lease giving exclusive catering rights to the owners of the station buffet at Swindon. But he regretted this decision later, complaining that the coffee tasted like roasted corn, and wrote to the manager in 1842, 'I have long ceased making complaints at Swindon. I avoid taking anything there when I can help it.'

By 1914 there wasn't a single main-line railway except the Highland Railway in the north of Scotland that didn't have scheduled dining car services. Lunch aboard would often have been a five-course affair, with staples such as grilled turbot, roast sirloin, salmon with sauce hollandaise, bread-and-butter pudding, apple tart and crème caramel. The early waiters were aristocrats of their trade, doing apprenticeships in special sealed-off dining cars where they were trained to walk, Monty-Python-style, along a white line wearing a blindfold while the train moved at speed.

Each route around the country had its own culinary specialities. The Lancashire & Yorkshire Railway introduced special 'tea cars' for shorter journeys. On the Metropolitan Railway (now the Metropolitan Line of the Tube) commuting stockbrokers could have both kippers and champagne aboard a special Pullman car to and from the London suburbs. The old Great Eastern Railway, which was the first to provide restaurant cars for third-class passengers, ran evening dining cars to almost every minor town in East Anglia, including midnight 'supper trains' to Essex seaside resorts

On the Cornish Riviera Express in its pre-war heyday a steward from the luncheon car might walk the length of the train, slide open compartment doors and, perhaps tinkling a bell, announce that lunch in the restaurant car was imminent. The price was three shillings. George Behrend in his famous book on the GWR *Gone With Regret* rhapsodises about the white napery and 'silverine cutlery, all emblazoned with the company crest'.

Immaculate service aboard was taken for granted. In the *Cornish Riviera Mystery*, a 1939 thriller about a murder in the dining car, two of the characters are asked by the waiter, 'Usual lunch, Gentlemen?' The conversation goes:

'What is the usual lunch?'

'Tomato soup, sole and fried potatoes, apple tart and cream.'

'I think that will do, don't you?'

But the finest-ever combination of fine dining, comfort and speed came with the great London to Scotland stream-liners of the 1930s. Aboard the Silver Jubilee from King's Cross to Edinburgh in 1938 the luncheon menu offered four courses including soup, grilled lemon sole tartare, roast mutton with redcurrant jelly, braised steak and cold pickled pork, followed by date pudding or charlotte russe. The first-class restaurant cars on the Flying Scotsman were advertised as being 'in Louis XIV style with low-backed loose armchairs blending with painted wall panels in stone picked out with blue mouldings'. In his book *Belles and Whistles*, Andrew Martin describes the special Flying Scotsman cocktail served on board – incorporating whisky, vermouth, bitters and sugar – which could apparently have 'felled a horse'.

In the 1940s the Southern Railway designed unique 'tavern cars' complete with fake brickwork and mock-Tudor beams to create an olde-worlde atmosphere, although they were unpopular with passengers because they had no windows. Many a commuter missed their station after a noggin or two on the way home from the office. Most famous of all was the Brighton line, renowned for its grilled kippers – much loved by the actor Lord Olivier, who campaigned to save them when British Rail tried to drop them from the menu. In the train's final days at the end of the 1960s a kipper for breakfast cost the equivalent of just eleven pence, and grilled steak, chips and peas for lunch a mere ninety-five pence. All served amid the magnificent art deco marquetry of jazz-age carriages with lovely names such as *Doris* and *Vera*. My new girlfriend *Audrey* ran on this train too.

Romantic – and sexy. Many of us were lured by Alfred Hitchcock into the idea of dinner in the diner after watching Cary Grant and Eva Marie Saint in the dining-car seduction scene of *North by Northwest* (1959), surely one of the most erotic encounters in cinema history. No sooner has the lady ordered the trout from the menu of America's most luxurious train, the 20th Century Limited, than Hollywood's most famous schmoozer is lining her up for activities that might be more appropriate in the sleeping car.

This didn't mean one couldn't encounter some horrid culinary experiences. At the start of the twentieth century a reviewer of the food on the London & North Western Railway complained that the boiled haddock in parsley sauce 'was full of bones, small and watery', while the vegetables were an 'insult to the gastric juices'. And, from more modern times, we may remember Michael Caine, playing gangster Jack Carter, who guzzles a bowl of British Rail soup without relish in the opening scenes of the film *Get Carter* aboard a 1970s service to Newcastle. And while the ubiquity of the curling British Railways sandwich may have been overstated, it was not unknown for restaurant staff to stir gravy browning into the coffee. During World War II unsuspecting American servicemen were routinely tricked with watered-down beer.

Even so, who could disagree with the railway commentator Geoffrey Kitchenside, who waxed lyrical in 1979:

There has always been a magic about dining on trains. Eating on a train can be one of life's most enjoyable experiences, with good food well served and a constantly changing panorama as the scenery unfolds before you. Breakfast with dawn breaking over a misty river valley transcends even the finest paintings in the best-known art galleries, while no seascape on canvas could match luncheon on the Cornish Riviera Express as it ran beside the beach between Dawlish and Teignmouth, while dinner on the Midday Scot climbing over the southern uplands of Scotland in the falling light evoked far-greater memories than any sun-sinking-slowly-in-the-west travelogue.

But by this time the writing was on the wall for railway dining. The demise had come steadily, almost before we had noticed. The grandest named trains with their Pullman cars had faded from the timetables in the post-war years. The Devon Belle went in 1954, followed by the Kentish Belle in 1958. The Queen of Scots disappeared in 1964, and the White Rose and Bournemouth Belle soon after in 1967.

But the idea of dining on trains clung on as railway managers tried to adapt it to modern times. In the 1960s BR reinvented train dining with its new luxury diesel multiple-unit Blue Pullmans to Manchester, Birmingham and South Wales, although the ride meant you might end up with a bowl of consommé in your lap. Then there were 'griddle cars', which kept freshly cooked food going on many secondary lines. I recall eating the Tartan Platter during this period – Aberdeen Angus entrecôte, with fried egg and grilled tomato with roll and butter – on a slow train rolling on a Sunday evening along the Highland main line from Perth to Inverness. Even at the end of the 1970s the unjustly maligned Travellers Fare was offering 'home-made' steak and kidney pie with mushrooms as standard on restaurant cars. In his book *Dining at Speed* Chris de Winter Hebron says that even at this time chefs were allowed to make their own pastry for the pies on board if they so chose.

Even at the close of the nationalised era in 1994 there were 249 trains a day with dining cars open to both first- and standard-class passengers. Hard to believe now, but at the beginning of the era of privatisation there were more than eighty a day alone on the east coast line to Scotland – all operated by the Great North Eastern Railway, the original franchise holder. But sadly most of today's private train companies see dining on trains as an anachronism in the modern corporate world and have now purged them almost entirely, substituting what is known in the jargon as an 'at-seat offer' for first-class passengers, where a limited range of mostly pre-prepared food is served on weekdays only. The claim that it is free is disingenuous, since it is priced into the cost of the fare. You cannot opt out of it – nor can you realistically opt in while travelling. Standard-class passengers are barred, unless willing to take out a mortgage for the eye-watering cost of an on-the-day upgrade.

Britain's very last regular service of all-day restaurant cars open to every passenger ran on the evening of 20 May 2011, appropriately along the old Great Northern Railway route out of King's Cross where the pioneer dining car had first run 132 years previously. It was with a mixture of euphoria and sadness that I booked my ticket for the very final train of the evening, the 19.00 from London to Edinburgh. Looking back at my notebook – handwriting squiggly from the jolting of the train – I wrote at the time,

The aroma emanating from the galley in coach No. 11998 is a signal for euphoria and sadness. The reason? Chef Stephen Naisby is loading a batch of sizzling rib-eye steaks on the grill aboard the last ever restaurant service on the East Coast Main Line, bringing to an end a great era of railway history.

The fare served up by Crew Leader Alistair Barclay and his team is as splendid as on that very first day. My freshly cooked Smoked Haddock Arnold Bennett Crêpe is crisp, and the huge rib-eye of steak, topped with fried onions flavoured with Madeira wine, is cooked to a tee. And this is no special valedictory repast, cooked for the occasion. It's all from the standard East Coast Autumn–Winter menu that will be replaced this week by a trolley service of at-seat inclusive snacks, available to first class passengers only.

As if in tribute, the evening sun shines as the train flashes through the eastern counties on its way north, and Crew Leader Barclay, along with members of his team of eight, race through the coach balancing steaming plates and silver-service salvers. Many of the passengers are regulars saying goodbye. Also on board are a group of railway industry grandees, attired in full evening wear – as one of them put it, 'to carry out the mourning suitably dressed . . .'

Just to prove that memories of fine train dining in relatively recent times were not all rose-tinted, it was after I had recounted my journey in an interview on BBC Radio 4 the next morning that I received a letter from a Mrs P. Billingsley of Southport, whose father had been a chef on Pullman trains in the late 1940s and 1950s. 'As a child, I remember my mother starching his "whites" – which of course included his tall chef's hat,' she wrote. She enclosed one of his luncheon menus, which included 'Honey Dew Melon, Dover Sole Colbert, Roast Saddle of Southdown Lamb, Jersey New Potatoes, Lincolnshire Minted Green Peas, Evesham Apple Pie and Devonshire Cream' and added, 'How this was produced in that tiny galley, I do not know. But the clients were obviously satisfied. He kept an autograph book that grateful celebrities had signed for him, including Edward, Duke of Windsor, Charles Boyer, Princess Marina, James Mason and Winston Churchill.'

Today a decent meal on a train is a rare experience. Indeed, many long-distance trains have no catering at all. In the course of writing this book I have endured famished journeys from Euston to Crewe, Birmingham to Marylebone, Charing Cross to Dover and the length and the breadth of Wales with not even the whiff of a packet of crisps or peanuts. Recently 'first-class' lunch on a Glasgow–Exeter train consisted of an egg and cress sandwich and a banana. No fine china or glassware, just a mug of the sort you might find in a transport caff and a plastic place mat. No wonder some train companies offer as much free booze as you can drink. This is presumably to get you to forget the awfulness of the food.

There are rare pockets of excellence, such as Virgin, whose first-class breakfasts are full English and always freshly cooked, with a nice northern touch of a slice of black pudding. East Coast offer a quite decent vegetarian breakfast of red pepper and spinach frittata, mushrooms, grilled tomato and a potato cake. By contrast, on some train operators a first-class ticket entitles you to not much more than a cup of tea and a slice of desiccated fruit cake – if you are lucky. On some days I have consumed so much free coffee that I feel I am travelling faster than the train.

It's a far cry from even quite recent times when entire trains such as the Harrogate Sunday Pullman and the Cambridge Buffet Express had names dedicated to the idea of eating and drinking on board. Back in 1869, just before Britain's first dining car took to the rails, the novelist Anthony Trollope wrote that the 'real disgrace of England is the railway sandwich'. He described it as a 'whited sepulchre, fair enough outside, but so meagre, poor, and spiritless within, such a thing of shreds and parings, such a dab of food, telling us that the poor bone whence it was scraped had been made utterly bare before it was sent into the kitchen for the soup pot'.

In the austerity of the present is it inevitable that we should have to steel our stomachs for Trollope's railway sandwich once more? The long-serving *Rail* magazine commentator Barry Doe, who has consistently campaigned against the scrapping of restaurant cars, says, 'The trouble is that the accountants who run the railways see trains merely as aeroplanes without wings. What they fail to spot is the marketing opportunity of a dining experience that we British regard as very special. On long train journeys operators have a captive audience, and much as they seem not to believe it, passengers do eat. Shame on them for not understanding this!'

But amid the microwaved burgers from the buffet and the tinned-tuna sandwiches from the trolley there is one company that still hasn't quite given up on traditional dining. Predictably this is First Great Western, which alone among the national train operators has kept the core identity of the days when it really was great – retaining the old title in its corporate branding and even painting one of its diesel engines classic Brunswick green and naming some after the legendary Castle Class steam locomotives of old. And they have stayed loyal to the idea of the traditional dining car, where any passenger, no matter their status, can roll up and take a seat. There have latterly been only ten of them a day, operating to South Wales and the West Country. Naturally, they are a bit of a secret – scarcely advertised and with an atmosphere that has something of the mystique of a London gentlemen's club.

There are only seventeen seats in the Pullman car of the 12.06 Paddington to Penzance today and every one is full. Were it not for the white tablecloths and china monogrammed with 'Pullman' and the Great Western Railway crest, this would be just another anonymous HST train carriage, but in some ways it is even more agreeable than the great trains of yore. Instead of coaches with female names and snooty male stewards as in the stuffy days of old, there is a team of buzzing woman stewards in smart black trousers and shirts with red scarves. How much nicer that the efficient Jane, Jenny and Carla are human beings rather than carriages.

By Slough I am tucking into a proper cheese soufflé, a rarity in a restaurant these days let alone on a train; curiously the last time I enjoyed it as much was in London's Garrick Club. At Reading I'm selecting from a menu including 'Silver Mullet with Roasted Garlic' and 'Grilled Somerset Fillet Steak'. By Exeter I'm wondering if I can squeeze in the 'Chocolate and Salted Caramel Pudding' as well as the 'Artisan Cheese selection with Quince Jelly'. As we pass along the coast at Dawlish, one of the most sublime views from any railway carriage in the world, I'm seriously starting to wonder if this could be the Second Coming. Well, at least of the Golden Age of Travel.

As we pull into Plymouth at 3 p.m. Chef Neal, weary from a 5.45 a.m. start, explains the secrets of cooking the perfect soufflé ('Get the oven hot at the start') and a medium-rare steak ('Regard each piece of meat as an individual') on a train. But the future is uncertain. His kitchen dates from the British Railways days of the 1970s, and soon a new generation of Japanese-built trains called IEPs will come on stream. Let us pray that dinner in the diner, like Neal's today, might once again become routine on the trains of the future. But in the world of the modern railway, where newer often means worse, we shouldn't perhaps hold out much hope. I cannot help recalling the words of my British Pullman steward Alan as I stepped down from *Audrey* onto the red carpet at Victoria, bathed in nostalgia, after my time shift back into the golden age.

Here is the accumulated wisdom of nearly four decades as an old-school veteran of dining-car service: 'The problem with catering on modern trains is that they have to get people ever faster from A to B. Our passengers come on board simply for the pleasure of enjoying a good meal on a lovely old train.'

Chapter Twelve
The country railway terminated

Thousands of miles of secondary railways once passed
through the villages and hamlets of rural Britain. None
was more typical than the Withered Arm, Betjeman's
favourite, running into the loveliest and loneliest reaches
of Devon and Cornwall.

Might there be anything closer to paradise? It's a golden
midsummer evening and I'm dangling my legs over
the old station platform by the quay at Padstow. From here
I can watch the trawlers bobbing home over the bluest of
seas, while chomping on the flakiest and freshest battered
hake from the upmarket chippie run by celebrity chef Rick
Stein. Once it was the fish trains that defined this place,

now it is Rick, who has transformed a fading north-Cornwall resort into a mecca for supercool urban foodies.

Long gone are the insulated vans dripping with ice that raced along the North Cornwall Railway in double-quick time to deliver the cod and haddock to London's Billingsgate Market with the bloom still gleaming on their scales. These days posh Londoners flood down the A39 to tuck into Rick's fashionable fish – witness the families in their Range Rovers and BMWs stuffing down a salt and vinegary supper in the car park where the fish sidings once were.

As for the rest of us, getting to Padstow – surely one of Britain's prettiest towns without any trains – has been the journey from hell ever since the railway closed in the 1960s. In recent memory you could board a mighty express at Waterloo and arrive here without leaving your seat – apart from strolling down the corridor for a three-course meal served on the crisp white tablecloths of the restaurant car. Now it could not be more different. Stepping down from the London train at the nearest station, Bodmin Parkway (nineteen miles from Padstow), I stand forlornly at the roadside waiting for the delayed 555 service of bus operator Western Greyhound.

But no greyhound this – rattling along the lane is a delivery van with seats, which clatters for a stomach-churning hour over switchback roads to reach its destination. So packed is it that the driver is forced to leave a party of elderly people behind at a remote wayside stop to wait an hour for the next one. It is a reminder of how the legacy of Beeching, now half a century old, still hangs heavy over rural Britain.

Padstow was the furthest-flung outpost of what was famously known as the Withered Arm, perhaps the most perfect example of the country railway networks that threaded the land in their own undisturbed way until the

national cull of the 1960s and 1970s. Self-contained and
enclosed in their own worlds, they were the main form of
communication for the small communities of Britain for up
to a century. These railways were as much part of the rural
scene as cricket on the village green, Mothers' Union jam-
making, church fetes and labourers working in the fields at
harvest time.

In most rural areas most comings and goings were by
train for at least two generations. As David St John Thomas
writes in his classic book *The Country Railway*,

> The pair of rails disappearing over the horizon stood
> for progress, disaster, the major changes in life: the route
> to Covent Garden and Ypres, the way one's fiancé paid
> his first visit to one's parents, one's children returned
> from deathbed leave-taking, the way summer visitors,
> touring theatricals, cattle buyers, inspectors, came. Even
> when most people made the journey by road, the railway
> retained its importance for the long, vital if occasional
> trips to the rest of the world. But the country railway
> provided more than transport. It was always part of the
> district it served, with its own natural history, its own
> legends and folklore, a staff who were at the heart of
> village affairs, its stations and adjoining pubs places for
> exchange of gossip, news and advice.

None of this could be truer than along the arteries of
the Withered Arm – so named because its routes, mostly
single tracks, meandering west of Exeter across the remotest
and most beautiful parts of Devon and Cornwall to
Plymouth, Barnstaple, Ilfracombe, Bideford, Torrington,
Bude, Launceston, Wadebridge and Padstow, resembled on
a map the branches of a rather sickly tree. Born out of a
territorial war in the west between Brunel's all-powerful

Great Western Railway and the London & South Western Railway at Waterloo, its smug Great Western detractors revelled in the name because they liked to think that the LSWR had come off worse.

No wonder they were smug – Brunel's GWR operated the choice direct routes along the coast south of Dartmoor, feeding the prosperous seaside resorts of Torbay before heading on to the far west at Penzance. The folk at Waterloo, meanwhile, were left with a circuitous route north of Dartmoor and a clutch of rocky, windswept, underpopulated destinations in north Devon and Cornwall. But the connoisseurs knew different. The Withered Arm, right to the end of its life in the 1960s, was always, in the eyes of those who knew, the more romantic, poetic and charming way to the west.

Its magic is best defined in a famous celebration of the line by the historian T. W. E. Roche, who wrote of his fondness for

> that Other Railway, the Great Western's rival in the West, whose 'Withered Arm', as the cynics called it, stretched its long, tortuous limbs west and north east from Exeter to the Atlantic coasts of Devon and Cornwall. It shunned the great tourist resorts of the south and sought out the high places and the lonely places; no other main line could look up directly to the towering peak of Yes Tor, no other railway called its engines after it. It was the Dartmoor main line, but it was also the railway which penetrated into King Arthur's land.

There were, Roche observed,

> endless stops in all those endless miles. The Withered Arm was a railway of great distances, whose towns were far apart and populations sparse, yet however far apart

there were always green coaches proudly flaunting the legend WATERLOO to remind one of the links with the outside world. And to show those remote towns were not forgotten it paid them the compliment of naming the great 'West Country' Pacifics after them and actually bringing them to receive their names at the place itself and then to work on those lines afterwards.

And not just locomotives. The Withered Arm had its own dedicated express train from London too, in the shape of one of Britain's most celebrated named services. Many would claim that the Atlantic Coast Express was the greatest of all – even more distinguished than its world-famous Great Western rival the Cornish Riviera Express – busier and with more through carriages to the towns and villages it served than any other train in Britain. Its name derived from a competition run by the Southern Railway's staff magazine, for which a guard from Woking won a prize of three guineas. The man, a Mr F. Rowland, moved to Torrington, one of the most delightful towns served by the Withered Arm, but sadly was killed in a shunting accident not long after.

This unhappy incident, fortunately, did not jinx the Atlantic Coast Express, which ran from Waterloo every weekday, apart from wartime, until 1964, conveying through carriages to Plymouth, Bude, Padstow, Torrington and Ilfracombe in the far west, sometimes dropping off portions on the way at Exmouth, Seaton, Sidmouth and Lyme Regis. Hardly the Atlantic coast, but who was worrying when the journey was so glamorous, with a polished green Merchant Navy Class, pride of the Southern fleet, at the head. Such was the demand for tickets that on peak summer Saturdays the ACE would set off in five separate sections from Waterloo.

The most atmospheric of the places where the attaching

and detaching of the various coaches of the ACE took place was lonely Halwill Junction in north Devon, the Clapham Junction of the Withered Arm. All the best country railways had junctions in places miles from civilisation – mini-Claphams or -Crewes. These lonely points of arrival and departure in the middle of nowhere often had romantic names, such as Melton Constable, a tiny Norfolk village that became the nerve centre of the old Midland & Great Northern, or Three Cocks Junction in Brecknockshire, the knot tied in a small bundle of railways that meandered through mid-Wales.

The atmosphere at Halwill, even as recently as fifty years ago, was unlike anything we would recognise on the railways of today. Here, far from anywhere, were services connecting in four directions, and when they arrived all at once there would be a cacophony of hooting whistles, the squealing of carriages being shunted, the clamour of porters and the tinging of signal bells. You could hardly hear yourself speak above the engines impatiently blowing off steam. As the choreographer of the performance, the signalman had an extra-tall box with forty levers – which would have been just as handy for counting sheep in this isolated place. And then all would go silent, except for the songbirds and the slow tick of the station clock, which would measure out the hours until it all kicked off again several hours later.

The veins of the Withered Arm passed through other junctions too – at Exeter, Barnstaple, Wadebridge and Bere Alston – but its blood – if it can be so described – flowed most strongly through the long lonely artery of the line of the old North Cornwall Railway from Okehampton, around both Dartmoor and Bodmin Moor to Launceston, Wadebridge, eventually ending on the coast at Padstow, the Southern Railway's most westerly station, 260 long miles from London.

This remotest of lines offered perhaps the most enchanting

country railway journey in Britain. On the face of it, here was a rural landscape of scattered villages and hamlets with many stations far from the places they served. The names of Port Isaac Road and St Kew Highway were a clue to prospective passengers of the long trek they faced at their destinations. Woe betide anyone booking a ticket to Tower Hill, thinking they might explore a famous London landmark. This particular Tower Hill was named not after William the Conqueror's great fortress but a modest local farm. But oh, what drama otherwise on this romantic Cornish coast, with its legendary historical and literary landmarks – King Arthur's Tintagel and Daphne du Maurier's mysterious Bodmin Moor among them. It was through this landscape of harsh weather, swirling mists and intrigue that the North Cornwall trains slowly wended their way.

Few railway lines in history have inspired such powerful poetic impulses as this one. We have already encountered Edward Thomas's 'Adlestrop' on the Oxford to Worcester train, Philip Larkin's 'Whitsun Weddings' viewed from the Hull service to London, and W. H. Auden's 'Night Mail' famously 'crossing the border'. But no line has touched the imagination so strongly as this Cornish paradise, singled out by Poet Laureate Sir John Betjeman as the 'most exciting train journey I know'. Betjeman's early-twentieth-century boyhood summers began aboard the Atlantic Coast Express from Waterloo to Padstow. He wrote that the final stretch of line along the Camel estuary was the most beautiful he had ever experienced, and at its end a different world awaited: one of 'oil-lit farms' and 'golden unpeopled bays', of shipwrecks and haunted woods. As an adult he continued to make annual pilgrimages to the area, capturing its melancholy and majesty in numerous poems and essays.

A horse and cart would have met him at Wadebridge station and taken him to the Betjeman holiday home at

Trebetherick. In his autobiography *Summoned by Bells* Betjeman evokes his boyish joy and excitement when he would

> Attend the long express from Waterloo
> That takes us down to Cornwall. Tea-time shows
> The small fields waiting, every blackthorn hedge
> Straining inland before the south-west gale.
> The emptying train, wind in the ventilators,
> Puffs out of Egloskerry to Tresmeer
> Through minty meadows, under bearded trees
> And hills upon whose sides the clinging farms
> Hold Bible Christians. Can it really be
> That this same carriage came from Waterloo?
> On Wadebridge station what a breath of sea
> Scented the Camel valley! Cornish air,
> Soft Cornish rains, and silence after steam.

Rhapsodic experience though it was, the North Cornwall Railway came very late and was only a few years old when Betjeman first experienced its charms. The LSWR first obtained an act to build the line in 1882, but the difficult terrain and a shortage of funds meant that it didn't get to Wadebridge until 1885, finally arriving in Padstow in March 1899.

Although the route ran for many miles through unpopulated, often treeless territory above the 300-foot contour line, with the breakers of the Atlantic Ocean crashing on the rocks on one side and the granite mass and peaty bogs of Bodmin on the other, there were also some choice commercial jewels in the crown. Launceston and Wadebridge were prosperous market towns, exporters of cattle, sheep and pigs. Wadebridge, on the Camel, was a busy little port too. Then there was the vast slate quarry at Delabole along the way. And the remoteness of the fishing village of Padstow had its compensations; its role as an emigrant port had meant that it had until hitherto been in better communication with Canada than London. Now tourists poured down from the 'Smoke' and fresh fish headed in the other direction. How good for business was that?

It was a truly auspicious day on Thursday 23 March 1899 when the new railway finally reached Padstow. A light snow had fallen overnight as dignitaries from the town, contractors and London & South Western Railway bigwigs assembled on the quay. Joining them amid the crowds was the lord of the manor and six sea captains. The first train steamed in at 12.30, breaking a tape across the line, while the Padstow Artillery and Delabole brass bands played 'See the Conquering Hero Comes'. A royal salute of twenty-one guns was fired from the quay before the serving of a leisurely lunch, punctuated by toasts and speeches. Special trains were run up to Wadebridge, where 600 children were each treated to a Cornish pasty, and in the evening a splendid cold meat tea was served to the locals. Such was the confidence that the coming of the railway bestowed on the town that, while the crowds were celebrating on the quay, workmen were simultaneously putting the finishing touches to the vast new Metropole Hotel above the station, still the largest building in Padstow.

In those early days we might have travelled along the line behind one of the elegant T9 Class locomotives of the London & South Western Railway, which made their first appearance here when Victoria was on the throne and stayed with the line almost until its 1960s closure. Unlike today's rickety buses, these venerable engines truly earned their nickname of greyhounds. But let's move on in time to imagine ourselves on a post-war summer Saturday, in the line's heyday.

Heading west on holiday are mother and father, just

emerging into the never-had-it-so-good world of post-austerity Britain, along with their eager children clutching tin buckets and spades and scuffed copies of *Swallows and Amazons* and Enid Blyton's Famous Five stories to read on the journey. The boarding house and the golden sands beckon. We have been able to stay in the same carriage all the way from London, after an engine change at Exeter, where we swapped our Merchant Navy for one of the equally impressive West Country Class Pacifics, perhaps *Wadebridge*, *Camelford* or *Yes Tor*. Maybe even *Padstow* herself? How privileged we are that such a railway backwater should lend the names of its towns to such magnificent express locomotives.

Continuing west past Okehampton, our train edges its way across the fragile-looking lattice piers of the romantic Meldon Viaduct, with its six 86-foot spans on stone plinths, 150 feet above the plunging ravine of the West Okement river. Even in the early 1950s the railway here was pretty much as it was built. All along the line were commodious stone-built stations (so solid that many survive as private homes today). Most of them still had sidings to handle the goods trains that kept the shops of the West Country stocked with the finest products of British factories and food from the empire, while transporting the farm products of Devon and Cornwall to the breakfast tables of London.

Pausing briefly at Halwill Junction to disgorge passengers for Torrington and Bude, we might note the prosperity the railway has brought to this tiny place, with its post office, police station, bank, pub, cottage hospital, garage, shops and egg-packing station. Here we might pass one of the mixed trains of freight wagons and passenger coaches that survived on this line long after they had disappeared from other rural railways. Then off we head down the valley past Ashwater, Tower Hill and over the Tamar into Launceston — 'the gateway to Cornwall', also served by the rival Great Western, whose own station was adjacent. Many members of the large staff here, ranging from stationmaster to booking clerks, porters, shunters, cattle checkers and shop assistants in the platform branch of W.H. Smith, would still have been bustling away in their jobs – unlike today, when there is no railway at all.

The summit of the line is reached just after the delightfully named Otterham, nearly 800 feet above sea level and nearly two miles from the village it purports to serve. In contrast to the image of jolly sunlit holidays, here is a bleak, windswept location. So chilly and damp are the squalls that blow off the Atlantic that the walls of the station building have had to be faced with slate to protect passengers from the cold. But rolling down to Wadebridge, with its busy little port on the Camel, all is different once again: sidings busy with livestock and farm produce, even consignments of ice cream heading off to fill cornets on the beach at Newquay. Hard to imagine in 2015, when the old station buildings house a day centre for the elderly, that the stationmaster here once had a staff of 140 under his command.

A treat here too for young trainspotters leaning out of the windows past the engine sheds, who might cop one of the ancient Beattie Well Tanks – the oldest design of locomotive in service on the railway. These old ladies, built for service on London suburban trains between 1863 and 1875, survived because they were the only locos with a small enough wheelbase to work the sharp curves of the mineral trains to Wenford Bridge on the flank of Bodmin Moor. Astonishingly, two survive in running order in 2015.

And soon to come is one of the most beautiful views from a train carriage in Britain. The vistas along the Camel estuary as the service steams slowly west from Wadebridge to Padstow exceed, in the opinion of many, every other carriage window seaside view in the land – including the waves foaming on the Dawlish sea wall, the blue Atlantic and golden sands of the St Ives branch or the North Sea panorama from the London to Edinburgh train as it races along the Northumbrian coast. Here, along the fringes of the Camel, the blue water, golden sandbanks and green fields herald journey's end for weary travellers as our London train pulls in after its haul of more than five hours from the capital. How we must regret in modern times that it was never part of Beeching's remit to save railways such as this simply for their outstanding scenic qualities, or the Padstow line would be with us still.

But the pleasures to be had along the line were not just linked to the scenery. The passengers on these lonely country routes were part of an exclusive club, who could enjoy their own company in a non-corridor compartment labelled to seat ten or twelve. 'Windows open, shoes off and feet up on the seats opposite, itinerary and timetable, refreshments and reading matter organised nearby, case and coat on the seats to discourage other passengers,' write David St John Thomas and Patrick Whitehouse in their book *The Great Days of the Country Railway*. 'This was your private room, ambling along at seldom more than 30 miles an hour, filled with the sounds and smells of the locomotive, as well as those of the countryside through the window, too.' But there was still 'rich companionship' to be had – 'with staff, driver and fireman during those long pauses for water; with the guard, and sometimes even with other passengers. Here were strangers from all walks of life – all had an interesting tale to tell when you had their interest in such a gentle environment. Business, education, entertainment, romance were there for the taking . . .'

At some stops along the Withered Arm you were more likely to witness a rabbit boarding the train than a passenger. This is no exaggeration. At Bridestowe, south of Okehampton (if you were local, you knew to pronounce it Briddystoe),

T. W. E. Roche reported that 'a statistician had worked out that the station sent away annually more rabbits than passengers. Certainly, when warrening was a considerable industry on Dartmoor, the rabbits were very much in evidence, boxes and boxes of them, their tootsies tied together, standing up on the platform. There were never many passengers.' And yet, in its excellent timetable, which rendered the Withered Arm superior to almost all other country railways, there was a daily service from Waterloo, in the shape of the 3 p.m. down, which got you back at 7.43 p.m. – in time to see a golden sunset over the Atlantic on a summer's night.

Daily life along the Withered Arm would have been typical of all country trains in pre-Beeching days. David St John Thomas describes the contents of the guard's van on these trains:

As well as the passengers' belongings there would be bottled gas, empty flower, fish and poultry boxes being returned to their owners, pigs and day-old chicks, pigeons (always being consigned everywhere), bags and parcels from a national food or other manufacturer to be cast off in twos and threes at stations along the line, mailbags, the railway's own registered letters and parcels, the pouch in which the stationmaster sent his daily takings and received weary official communications, boxes of glass, trees and shrubs, bins of ice cream. Return trips would bring back the produce of the countryside, including growers' specialities . . . calves to be exchanged with farmers elsewhere as genetic standards rose (nor should we forget the benefit to rural human genetics brought by the railway; with less intermarrying the 'village idiot' has disappeared).

Betjeman, in his regular journeys along the line, was inspired by somewhat loftier matters. 'I know the stations by heart,' he told a radio audience on the BBC Third Programme in 1949.

> The slate-and granite-built waiting rooms, the oil lamps and veronica bushes, the great Delabole Quarry, the little high-edged fields; and where the smallholdings grow fewer and the fields larger and browner, I see the distant outline of Brown Willy and Rough Tor on Bodmin Moor. And then the train goes fast downhill through high cuttings and a wooded valley. We round a bend, and there is the flat marsh of the Camel, there the little rows of blacking-green cottages along the river at Egloshayle and we are at Wadebridge, next stop Padstow . . . The smell of fish and seaweed, the crying of the gulls, the warm moist West Country air.

A feast for the boy who was to become poet laureate, and, miraculously, it's still possible for energetic travellers on foot or with a bike to relive the old route. Setting off back home from Padstow, my 08.30 boneshaker to Bodmin Parkway is late again. 'We've got six buses down with engine failure this morning,' announces the driver. To hell with these old-fangled relics of the transport dark ages, why not set off east to walk along the old track, now converted into a footpath known as the Camel Trail? It's easy to follow — just head out of the station along the estuary. Not hard to imagine as you stride across the magnificent 133-foot iron spans of the Little Petherick Creek Bridge that you are the regulator of the London express, a scene depicted in a famous Southern Railway publicity poster by Eric Hesketh Hubbard to promote its route into Cornwall.

Still, it's a stiff walk and not for the faint-hearted. I'm fearing for my blisters when eventually there appears a mirage in the shape of an old Southern Railway station, complete with period green signs announcing BOSCARNE JUNCTION. Here is a stretch of line that is one of the oldest in Britain, opened to transport minerals in railway pre-history in 1834, long before the iron road came to Cornwall let alone most other parts of Britain. For years the haunt of the famous Well Tanks, it lived on to become the very last bit of the old Southern Railway in north Cornwall in revenue-earning service, staying open for freight until 1983. Today, simmering in the platform is my saviour – a former GWR 'pannier tank' steam locomotive at the head of four 1950s coaches and an old-school guard with red carnation in his buttonhole who tells me his train will connect me to the London service at Bodmin Parkway.

No mirage this, but a real service of the preserved Bodmin & Wenford Steam Railway, Cornwall's only steam heritage line. In pre-preservation days and after the demise of the Withered Arm this was the very last vestige of a passenger rail connection from London to Padstow, finally ceasing on 28 January 1967. Today at Bodmin my train discharges at least a couple of hundred passengers – times are clearly looking up. But to understand what went wrong, we must cast our minds back to when the bureaucrats at British Railways headquarters deemed these local lines to be hopelessly uneconomic. What chance was there for the gnarled fingers of the Withered Arm, as the Ford Prefects and Morris Minors, polished pride and joy of Britain's growing post-war army of affluent workers, filed nose to tail along the A30?

The omens began to come true when control of the Withered Arm was transferred to the Western Region of British Railways on 1 January 1963. The desire for revenge on the Great Western's upstart rival had never been forgotten, and now at last was the chance to exact retribution. First the Atlantic Coast Express was withdrawn, departing from Padstow for the last time on 5 September 1964 behind West Country Class No. 34023 *Blackmoor Vale*. Next to go were passenger trains on the Halwill to Torrington branch in 1965. Since the 1950s this line had had scarcely any human footfall at all; barely one passenger a week used the biggest station at Hatherleigh. Hardly anyone went, nor anyone came, on the neat platform with its tended flower beds and polished brass, even though it was served by two single-coach trains daily. David St John Thomas writes,

> Finding various excuses to visit this living but empty museum over the years, I once drove the evening train from Halwill and arrived at Petrockstowe so early that the crew played cards for half an hour in the station and still reached Torrington ahead of schedule. On the twice-daily trains, fireman, guard and signalman were 'amazed' if any passenger were ever spotted.
>
> Once a story did the rounds of a passenger on the line who asked the guard: 'Do I have the train to myself?' as the single coach was hauled in leisurely fashion behind a spanking new British Railways 2-6-2T tank locomotive. 'Yes,' said the man, whose face looked as though it had been chiselled out of red marble. 'But you can't count on it. On Wednesday we took Mrs and Miss Thomson to Halwill. They were going to Bude, you know. They'll be back some time next week.'

No wonder that soon the other gnarled fingers of the Withered Arm would be lopped off one by one. Goodbye, Bude, Callington, the main line to Tavistock and Plymouth, and Ilfracombe. Farewell, services to the ancient towns of Bideford, Launceston and Bodmin.

Amid the wreckage it is astonishing that the fifty straggling miles of the North Cornwall Railway survived until as late as 1966. Economically it was an example of staggering inefficiency, yet for enthusiasts and many of its passengers, it was a beacon of old-world charm. Stopping trains averaged just 27 mph, and there were manually operated signal boxes at each of its ten stations. Just one steam locomotive, operating on the line over a fifteen-hour period, needed servicing and turning several times, involving eight men. In the background were the traffic staff, the signalmen, station staff, permanent-way and telegraph men, let alone the night shed men in the locomotive depots.

As closure loomed, time had stood still too long for the clock ever to be put back. David Wroe, historian of the North Cornwall Railway, describes the passing of the last down train and the last up train of the day at Tresmeer in the early 1960s. It is a cameo that could equally have dated from 1900.

Imagine a drizzly wet winter's evening. Dim oil lamps light the platforms, local people from Launceston market preparing to walk a mile or so to Tresmeer village – some lucky to be fetched in a pony and trap or (later) a motor car. Parcels to be dropped off, Cornish voices in the dark, the single line tablets handed over to the drivers. Then, with a toot of the whistle, one 'T9' sets off with a resounding bark up and around to Otterham while the other drifts off to Egloskerry. Signal restored with a clank of levers, final bell codes as the lines clear and Tresmeer shuts down for the night.

The words could be a requiem for all country railways of the period entering their final days. The pattern was nearly always the same. First the steam services would be withdrawn, followed by a burst of optimism as new diesel trains were delivered. But this was very often the harbinger of closure. The omens for north Cornwall were especially inauspicious. The locomotive on the last steam service – the 1.19 p.m. Exeter St David's to Padstow on 3 January 1965 –

was in such poor condition that it had to stop twice on the journey to raise steam, even though No. 84025, which bore the headboard LAST REGULAR STEAM TRAIN PADSTOW TO EXETER, was itself only a few years old. The freight service had already gone the previous year.

Efficient though not necessarily clean the new diesels might have been; the timetable nevertheless deteriorated. Connections were missed and the Sunday service reverted to a Southern National bus. The line's chronicler T. W. E. Roche undertook a pilgrimage in the final days. Under 'lowering clouds' he reported a scene of utter melancholy: rusted tracks, deserted goods yards, empty station buildings converted to halts. Arriving in his own vehicle, he heard staff at Wadebridge talking to the guard: 'Car, 'ave 'ee? Us ought to charge 'n' car parkin'. 'Tis they cars be killin' us.'

Roche responds emotionally: 'I felt a wave of resentment against Dr Beeching and everyone else who was bringing about the demise of this most delightful station in this most charming West Country town.' Soon the train onwards to the little platform at Tower Hill arrives.

Along came the driver with a pot of tea, new-made in the signal box; the guard's whistle shrilled and we were off . . . Up through the lovely country we ran and so to Tower Hill, where, wonder of wonders, one of the other passengers alighted; the guard ran up to take my ticket and waved to me as the train ran by; I stood on the platform listening to its sound growing fainter, then echoing louder again, then dying up the valley of the hanging woods, while the wet Western evening wept for the North Cornwall line.

No one was surprised when the inevitable took place on 3 October 1966. The line's last day was filled with sadness. As one observer describes it, 'The younger enthusiasts gave what cheer they could to the final day's services. The older generation bought last tickets and thronged the trains.' As always on these occasions, the last extinguishing of lamps, the locking of gates and doors and the final replacement of single-line tokens in their machines underlined the awful melancholy of those railway closures of the Beeching years.

All that was left of the Withered Arm were three truncated stumps. In the near half-century since then one of those stumps – the Tarka Line from Exeter to Barnstaple – has prospered, doubling passenger numbers. The western end of the old main line along the Tamar Valley to Bere Alston and Gunnislake has also done well, reinventing itself as a commuter route into Plymouth. At the other end of the line, Okehampton has scraped by, albeit with a limited summer Sunday service. Meanwhile, Padstow, Wadebridge, Launceston and Bodmin have worse connections than at any time since modern public transport was invented.

For five decades since the last trains ran, the closed sections of the Withered Arm settled on a future of infinite decay, the worms eating away at the last bits of infrastructure, and the embankments and viaducts appearing to modern generations as mysterious as prehistoric tumuli. Then, out of the blue at 10 p.m. on 4 February 2014, the railway gods intervened in the form of the worst storm to batter the Devon coast in living memory. With an unprecedented 'black warning' in force, a furious sea washed away Isambard Kingdom Brunel's historic 1846 railway to the west along the sea wall at Dawlish. Cornwall was entirely cut off from the rest of the United Kingdom, with 109 miles of track isolated and twenty-five trains trapped. The cost of the closure, until the line was reopened two months later, was reckoned to be £20 million a day.

Back in the 1960s this would have been little more than an inconvenience. There was still a commodious service of expresses from Waterloo to Plymouth on the Withered Arm main line along the Dartmoor route via Okehampton, the fastest of which took only ten minutes longer than Brunel's route. And weren't the Waterloo trains much nicer, with their spacious Bulleid corridor carriages, through coaches from London to the tiniest of wayside stations, restaurant cars with generous menus, all pulled by Britain's most modern and sophisticated express steam locomotives in the form of the Merchant Navy and West Country Classes?

No wonder all the chatter now is about reopening a railway that the powers that be happily put in the bin half a century previously. Not so long ago anyone raising the question of resurrecting the Withered Arm would have been regarded as a deluded fantasist. Now metrics are being studied and cost-benefit analyses drawn up, part of a pattern since Beeching in which political will can suddenly become potent in raising 'trains now departed' from the dead. A Network Rail study in the summer of 2014 found that the entire Exeter to Plymouth line via Okehampton could be rebuilt for £875 million, a drop in the ocean compared with the tens of billions reserved by the Treasury for HS2.

The tracks already run to Bere Alston from the Plymouth end of the line – and to Meldon Junction just past Okehampton at the Exeter end. Preparations are already well under way to reopen the line from Plymouth as far as Tavistock. Optimists say that only eleven miles of the old main line would need to be totally rebuilt. Maybe it could be done, people say, for £500 million, peanuts compared with the cost of another great storm at Dawlish. Who knows where it might end? Perhaps one day London's well-heeled will leave their Chelsea tractors at home to head along the north Cornwall line aboard a revamped Atlantic Coast Express to dine chez Rick Stein. Or enjoy some delicious grilled Padstow sole in the restaurant car on the way home. Well, you can but dream.

Chapter Thirteen

Final whistle for the grand stations

Victims of a barbarous age, mighty cathedrals of steam
such as Birmingham's Snow Hill, London's Broad Street
and Euston, with its heroic Doric arch, fell cruelly to the
wrecker's ball. There were others, too, less famous but no
less glorious. A journey among the ruins . . .

How ironic. I'm on my way to visit what must be Britain's
meanest and most wretched apology for a once-grand
city railway station, aboard one of the last truly comfortable
trains in Britain. My newly refurbished Chiltern Railways
carriage, built in the days before coaches were designed for
emaciated stick insects, is commodious indeed, with generous
armchairs and wide windows to absorb the view. Never mind

that it is an old British Rail Mark III coach dating from the 1970s; it has been reinvented with a slick black and grey interior and Wi-Fi at every seat. Best of all, in the increasingly cramped world of modern rail travel, the seats line up with the windows. All the better to enjoy the vista of the Warwickshire countryside rolling by on this early spring day.

Once we thought we would lose it all – hard to believe that this grand former Great Western main line over the Chiltern Hills, through the tranquil fields of Buckinghamshire and Warwickshire to Birmingham, was once regarded as redundant. This had been the hallowed fiefdom of the famous Castle and King locomotives – all burnished brass and Brunswick green – along with mighty expresses with names such as the Inter-City and the Birmingham Pullman, dashing up and down the line to London in two hours. It survived by the skin of its teeth through the closure blitz of the 1960s, though relegated to a route primarily for commuters, and terminating no longer at Brunel's Paddington but at Marylebone, a station likened by Sir John Betjeman to a suburban public library.

In its heyday, the vast Birmingham Snow Hill station bustled day and night with trains to and from all corners of the land. Yet inside little over a decade, between the 1950s and 1960s, it had turned ignominiously into the 'biggest unstaffed halt in Britain'. These days the crack trains, like the Chiltern Mainline Silver service that I'm on today, don't even bother to travel the full distance to what was once one of the most important city-centre stations outside London. Short of total closure, no grand station fell more egregiously and precipitately than this.

Which is why I'm dodging the traffic of Birmingham's ring roads, wending my way from Moor Street – my 'final station stop', in the language of today's train conductors – to find what survives of the ashes of the old Snow Hill.

Past the brutalism of New Street and Colmore Circus, here's a pretty little Victorian arcade built by the railway as the station approach above the tunnel containing the railway. Now twee shops sell artisan bread, vintage fountain pens and brightly coloured sweets from the olden days. But don't get lost in a reverie; prepare for a very modern shock when you emerge.

Where the palatial Great Western Hotel once dominated is a characterless solar-glass office block above a fume-filled subterranean platform. Where the old station once stood, buzzing with the ferment of Brummie commercial life, is a depressing multi-storey car park with a large sign reading, WELCOME TO THE SNOW HILL CAR PARK — BIRMINGHAM CITY COUNCIL. Goodness, those councillors must be proud of themselves!

The fate of the old Snow Hill is a case history of what happens when railways fall out of fashion. The 1963 Beeching Report, which promoted blinkered short-term economic demand above community need, ripped, as one commentator put it, the steel backbone out of the nation. More than two thousand stations were lost as a result. Bad enough, but in their misguided quest for modernity architects and planners inflicted equal damage on many of the stations that survived. Magnificent buildings were felled by the wrecker's ball and deleted from our heritage with callous disregard for tradition or merit. Some were blitzed from the landscape entirely, with every trace obliterated. Even more were replaced by hideous concrete bunkers. Others were incorporated into shopping malls or car parks, dumbly commemorated by some meaningless name from the past or a redundant piece of stonework that the developer couldn't be bothered to put in a skip.

Although the loss of countless smaller stations was devastating enough (and not just for social reasons; many of them were minor architectural gems), there is something even more poignant, more tragic about the loss of the great city stations. These mighty termini and junctions were as emblematic in the cityscape as palaces or castles or cathedrals. But in the heart of British life they stood for something profounder still. As Jeffrey Richards and John MacKenzie point out in their book *The Railway Station: A Social History*, 'The railway station, in its latter-day incarnation as cathedral, castle and caravanserai, was yet one more gigantic stage on which drama could daily unfold, casts of thousands could cavort and modern technology could convey its marvels and miracles.' And it wasn't just that.

The great termini represented the last great age of travel before the joys and mysteries and individualism of travel were taken over by the bland, prepackaged age of tourism, when long-distance flights with their second-rate movies, plastic food and attendant jet lag replaced for ever the slow boat to China and the stopping train to Samarkand. It was the last age when the railway station was an essential ingredient of every traveller's itinerary: point of departure, point of arrival, point of contact en route with everyday life as it teemed and flowed outside the protective cocoon of the train.

No wonder the great stations inspired the finest poets and writers. Théophile Gautier said of them, 'These cathedrals of the new humanity are the meeting points of nations, the centre where all converges, the nucleus of the huge stars whose iron rays stretch out to the ends of the earth.' E. M. Forster was similarly moved. 'They are our gates to the glorious and the unknown,' the author of *A Room With a View* wrote. 'Through them we pass out into adventure and sunshine, to them alas! we return. In Paddington all Cornwall is latent and the remoter west; down the inclines of Liverpool

Street lie Fenland and the illimitable Broads; Scotland is through the pylons of Euston; Wessex behind the poised chaos of Waterloo.'

These great termini were intensely romantic places, says John Minnis, a senior architectural adviser with English Heritage who has made a study of lost stations.

There was a sense of otherness to them, as though they were somehow detached from the outside world. True, there were kiosks of W.H. Smith's or Wyman's or John Menzies, selling little but newspapers, books and magazines, the stalls of the Empire Fruit Co. and the sweet shops of Maynards. But these were merely a prelude to travel – one did not go to stations for a 'retail experience' . . . . No, they were a point of departure for far-off places, a process accompanied by arcane ritual – even into the 1960s, the stationmasters of the great London stations wore silk hats.

The sense of romance, as Minnis points out, was heightened by the names of the trains that served them – 'the Royal Scot, the Queen of Scots, the Cornish Riviera Limited, the Cathedrals Express, the Red Dragon, the Golden Arrow, as did the names as well of the locomotives themselves – *Wolf of Badenoch, Quicksilver, Lord of the Isles*. The architecture added to that sense of anticipation.'

The milestones of my own early life, as for many of us, were counted out in rail journeys from these great termini, which always seemed to offer an aching and infinite sense of possibility. The terrifying hiss of steam for a small child heading off on holiday from Waterloo; the thrill of standing as an eleven-year-old at the end of the platform at Euston or Paddington, jotting down the numbers of mighty machines whose glamour was celebrated far and wide. Here was my first long-distance journey away without my parents – tingling with anticipation and fear as the Scottish train from St Pancras prepared to depart.

When I left home for the final time, for a new life at university, I recalled the words of T. S. Eliot in *Four Quartets*. Here was a journey that would turn out to be much more than a physical departure:

When the train starts and the passengers are settled,
To fruit, periodicals and business letters
(And those who saw them off have left the platform)
Their faces relax from grief into relief,
To the sleeping rhythm of a hundred hours.
Fare forward, travellers! Not escaping from the past
Into different lives, or into any future;
You are not the same people who left that station
Or who will arrive at any terminus,
While the narrowing rails slide together behind you.

None of this helped to save Birmingham Snow Hill, of course. Prowling around the perimeter of the car park as afternoon twilight falls, I can find very little evidence of what was once a focus of Birmingham life, with its packed platforms a third of a mile long, elegant canopies and salt-glazed wall bricks. The booking hall was famously elegant – dressed up a treat with buff terracotta and white Carrara marble. The refreshment rooms were the finest in the country – walls lined in fumed Austrian oak and the countertops finished in red marble.

All smashed up, all vanished now. The best I can find today is a bricked-up gateway halfway along a side street, whose provenance is recognisable only by a Great Western Railway coat of arms. A commuter who sees me peering at it comes up to say, 'Shame what we did to our city! Now we're trying to get it back. But they'll never manage to do that here. Too much gone . . .'

The end for Snow Hill came fast and brutally. Rail staff and passengers were shocked when it was announced that main-line trains would come to an end in the spring of 1967. By 1968 only one service was left in this huge echoing train shed – a single railcar to Wolverhampton which made its way through weeds so high that it was christened the Dandelion Express. Posters peeled and pigeons flapped as the building crumbled. The hotel had already been demolished when the final services ran on 4 March 1972. The journal of the Standard Gauge Steam Trust reported the event in melancholy tone: 'Now the stage was set for the departure of the very last train of all. As one gazed around, one realised what a great place of activity Snow Hill had been. The imagination returned to the mid-fifties when a "King" or a "Castle" would sweep majestically into Number 7 platform on a London express, or even further back to the sound of troops singing as they went off to war . . .'

For some years afterwards, the decaying building remained a gaunt citadel of the past as Birmingham turned itself into an infamous concrete jungle. It was just waiting to die. As one local humorist observed, the next whistle to blow would be for the demolition men's tea break. In the meantime, it languished in various guises – as a car park, a spooky set for films (famously used as a setting in the BBC TV series *Gangsters*) and a paradise for scavengers, who had a field day stripping out every piece of metal they could lay their hands on.

Snow Hill was not alone in its fate. In many of Britain's other great cities majestic railway terminals went out of use and lay rotting for years – as one writer put it, 'like great beached whales in the noonday sun'. Even those that have been saved for other purposes, such as Manchester Central, now preserved as an exhibition hall, have in a real sense ceased to be. Minus the ebb and flow of passengers, the arrival and departure of trains, they are little more than mausolea. The fire and steam that forged them has been doused, leaving them as dead things, devoid of spirit.

In mitigation it may be argued that some were victims of a necessary rationalisation, redundant products of that nine-teenth-century railway mania during which rival companies insanely vied to block each other's moves on the railway chessboard. In Britain as a whole, because of the intense rivalry of the train companies, only four major cities – Newcastle, Aberdeen, Stoke-on-Trent and Carlisle – managed to amalgamate their railway traffic into a single station. Manchester and Glasgow had four central stations, Leeds, Liverpool, Leicester, Belfast, Plymouth and Nottingham three, and Birmingham, Sheffield, Edinburgh, Bradford and Bath two. Few of these were actually in the city centre, Birmingham New Street, Edinburgh Waverley and Glasgow Central being the main exceptions.

Inevitable though it may have been, the cull was still heartless and brutal. Poor Nottingham Victoria, axed in favour of the city's Midland station in 1967, was the most high-profile victim of Beeching's destruction of the entire Great Central Railway route to London. Built in 1900 in glowing red bricks and Darley Dale stone, this Victorian extravaganza, with its hundred-foot clock tower, complete with cupola and weathervane, dominated the city centre. Its northern renaissance style 'would have passed muster for a town hall in some Flemish port', wrote John Minnis in *Britain's Lost Railways*. 'It was a glorious affair, beautifully proportioned in a slight asymmetry, and its facade given tremendous vigour by the heavy blocking of the paired attached columns at first-floor level and the rhythm set up by the repetition of elegant pedimented gables.' Praise that might have been accorded to a cathedral, yet the site is now the faceless Victoria Shopping Centre. The tower survives, but these days presides over the emptying of wallets rather than the departure of trains.

Its namesake, Sheffield Victoria, further down the same line, suffered a similarly tragic demise, with the last trains running in December 1970. Never mind that its great glass roof had once been likened to that of the Crystal Palace, that it had been the destination for such famous expresses as the Master Cutler and the Sheffield Pullman or that it was the terminus of one of the most modern and superbly engineered lines in Britain – the Woodhead route across the Pennines to Manchester, electrified only fifteen years before. The politburo at British Railways HQ in London decreed its demolition and there was no reprieve. Now a hotel car park is on the site.

Neither city, though, fared as badly as Liverpool, which lost two grand city-centre stations in the Beeching years. The last trains ran from the palatial Liverpool Exchange in 1977 (World War I poet Siegfried Sassoon stayed for long periods in the hotel there). It too ended up as a car park, although the frontage still survives. Liverpool Central, with its overall glass roof looking like a lesser St Pancras, had a superb position in the heart of the city's shopping district – no wonder the developers wanted to get their hands on it. I recall its final days at the end of the 1960s, when I used its rare trains to get home to my university hall of residence in the south of the city. By then it was a ghostly, deserted skeleton of a place, where emaciated rats and pigeons had usurped passengers as the main occupants. Feeling sorry for poor Liverpool Central, I rather fancied that by using its largely empty trains rather than the more convenient buses I might help to save the place. What a hope! The final services were withdrawn in April 1972.

Just across the Mersey there was another tragedy when Birkenhead Woodside, terminus of the Great Western Railway's services to Birmingham and London Paddington, was axed. Never mind that it was praised by Marcus Binney of Save Britain's Heritage as 'a station of truly baronial proportions and being worthy of any London terminus'. No matter that the father of the poet Wilfred Owen had once been stationmaster here. The station closed to passengers on 5 November 1967, and its two great curved train sheds were ripped down shortly afterwards.

When Manchester Exchange closed in 1969, the record books had to be rewritten since its link with one of the platforms at the neighbouring Victoria station formed the longest single platform in Europe – 2,238 feet. The platform has gone now and Victoria is diminished, although the mighty wrought-iron single-span roof at Manchester Central, terminus of the old Midland route to London, survives. The station beneath, however, has never seemed happy in its modern role as a conference centre, although it has fared better than that other great terminus of main-line trains from St Pancras, Glasgow St Enoch, all traces of which have been eradicated.

With its gorgeous glass roof, similar to its London and Manchester counterparts, St Enoch's 1966 closure and subsequent demolition was the grossest act of post-Beeching vandalism north of the border. St Enoch had many fine features, including a special room for travelling salesmen to show off their samples – the only one in Britain. The scandal of its demolition is exacerbated by the fact that the shopping centre which replaced it has been widely reviled – even by many of the architects who design such things.

London was more fortunate, although there were several narrow squeaks. A terrible tragedy at St Pancras was averted in the 1960s when Sir John Betjeman fought British Railways' plan for demolition – and won. Lavishly refurbished as the London Eurostar terminal, the restored ensemble of George Gilbert Scott's fairy-tale Gothic hotel and William Barlow's soaring single-span roof makes it, for many, the finest railway station in the entire world.

There were few tears when Holborn Viaduct closed in 1990 and was replaced by the prosaically named City Thameslink. Its charismatic hotel had already gone in 1963, damaged beyond viable repair in the war and subsumed into a faceless office block. Here was a rare example of a benign demolition, with the introduction for the first time ever of a proper through service for commuters from north to south through central London at the replacement station buried below ground. A sadder loss was the Nine Elms terminus of the old London & Southampton Railway, opened in 1838 but damaged beyond repair by Nazi bombers and demolished in the 1960s.

Far more cruel was the way Broad Street station, in the heart of the City, was killed off in the 1970s – the only major London terminus to be expunged entirely from the landscape. It is hard to believe from the ravaged state in which it ended its life that this splendid Italianate cathedral of the North London Railway once had more passengers than any other London station bar Liverpool Street and Victoria. Armies of clerks commuted through here, while expresses would carry City businessmen to the Midlands, supported by railway typists churning out their memos on the way.

Broad Street's demise was a case history in how to kill a station. Beeching condemned it in 1963 and the campaign to save it was undermined by a slow war of attrition – services slashed, facilities withdrawn, creeping dereliction. This was a technique used across Britain, deliberate and wanton neglect creating the justification for closure. The

Victorian ticket office was shut and an ugly 1950s brick booth slapped up in the concourse. The great wrought-iron and glass roof was hacked down, forcing passengers to brave the elements to get to their trains. At the end, when the last trains ran in June 1986, it was an eerie place with a forest of small trees growing between the neglected platforms

As the inevitable end approached, Betjeman caught the mood, writing in 1972,

There is one station which hardly anyone uses at all – Broad Street, which is given over to ghosts of frock-coated citizens who once crowded the old North London trains from the steam suburbs of Highbury, Canonbury and Camden Town. Often do those sumptuous LMS electric trains swing across from the North London suburbs on that smooth, useless, beautiful journey to Richmond. At no time of day have I known it impossible to find a seat in their spacious carriages. And the frock-coated ones are dead and gone like the rolling stock which carried them, their houses have been turned into flats, their gardens built over by factories. The North London was the last line to use wooden-seated third class carriages as it did on its Poplar branch, now closed, the last line in London to use no trains during church time on a Sunday morning, and within living memory the General Manager of the line refused to allow Smith's bookstall on Broad Street to sell any vulgar-looking papers. Still the train ran through haunted gas-lit stations, on the most revealing journey London can provide.

But Broad Street was never quite humbled – retaining its dignity to the end even as the facade crumbled – unlike some other historic London stations such as Paddington and Liverpool Street, which did Faustian deals to convert themselves into the railway equivalent of airport retail malls in exchange for their restoration. Once upon a time the Lawn at Paddington was a spacious area at the end of the platforms where you might meet your great-aunt up from the country; now it has been replaced by an ugly development of shops and bars, dominated by the usual corporate names. Some of these changes were clearly defined in 1995 by a character in Martin Amis's novel *The Information*: 'The railway station had changed since he had last had call to use it. In the meantime, its soot-coated, rentboy-haunted vault of tarry girders and toilet glass had become a flowing atrium of boutiques and croissant stalls and unlimited cappuccino.' In this sense, Broad Street was the last of the unadulterated grimy old stations, macerated in the world of the traditional railway.

A Broad Street passenger during its last years might have appreciated the words of a writer in the *English Illustrated Magazine* in 1893, who saw in the great London termini something of the temples of ancient Egypt: 'Go at night,' he wrote,

> at an hour when no trains are leaving. Walk along [the] platform as far as the first seat and then look back. If you are fortunate enough to catch . . . a hidden engine belching out clouds of steam that mingle with the fog overhead, it does not need a very powerful imagination to fancy you are in some great temple. The white clouds come in from the altar fire; above it, half lost in vapour is the great clock, its huge round dial like the face of a monstrous idol before which burn in solemn stillness the hanging lamps, silver, white and rose.

O tempora! O mores! But the biggest travesty, the grossest act of barbarism, even bigger than that at Broad Street or

Snow Hill, or indeed anywhere else in Britain, was at Euston, whose mighty Doric Arch was demolished in 1962 as the world watched horrified. This, remember, was before Beeching, and had nothing to do with cuts to the railway network. It was a time when architectural philistines stalked the land, seeking out anything Victorian that they could cull in the name of modernity. Never mind the treasures the Victorians gave us – intricately wrought ironwork, sculpted columns, mullioned windows, stained glass, mosaic floors, tiled malls, delicate portes cochères, exquisite stone tracery, clock towers, crenellations, campaniles. Out too with wood-panelled booking halls, friezes, glass canopies, triumphal arches, balustrades, gables, chimneys, turrets, spires, drinking fountains, ornate platform seats, coats of arms, baronial fireplaces, even majestic gentlemen's conveniences in monumental marble. To the devil with everyone who did not worship at the shrine of functionalism, whose gods were concrete, neon and plastic. Soul and romance were words used only by heretics.

Stations such as Birmingham New Street, Stafford, Plymouth, Swindon, Coventry and many others were rebuilt in the bland, soulless fashion of the day. But it was the new Euston – memorably described as an 'all-purpose combination of airport lounge and open plan public lavatory' – that was the supreme symbol of the new brutalism. But why object? In 1947 the Great Western Railway regarded even the possible demolition of Brunel's masterpiece at Paddington with equanimity. Its prospectus for post-war modernisation cheerfully pointed out that 'many will miss the Paddington of Brunel and Wyatt and Paxton with its aisles and transepts and its slim wrought iron arabesques . . . London will be the poorer for its passing; yet London requires that it must go.'

It says much about the relative values of the nineteenth

and twentieth centuries – as Richards and MacKenzie observe in their social history of the railway station – that 'where the Victorians modelled their stations on cathedrals, temples and palaces, Modern Man models his on shopping centres and office blocks'. The demolition of Euston station – the world's first railway terminal in a capital city – 'signalled conclusively the end of the age of giants and the arrival of the age of pygmies'.

That was precisely how it turned out. Half a century on from the pulling down of the arch and station, I'm sitting writing this in what passes for a public square outside Euston, where scrawny pigeons peck at half-eaten burgers from Ed's Easy Diner and defecate on the shoulders of the statue of Robert Stephenson. Equally emaciated commuters gasp on their last fag and slurp down a Pret A Manger Americano before heading into the dungeon of the platforms to catch the train to Milton Keynes. I am reminded of the newspaper commentator who wrote that the station design gives the impression 'of having been scribbled on the back of a soiled paper bag by a thuggish android with a grudge against humanity and a vampiric loathing of sunlight'. What a squalid and unprepossessing gateway to the most historic, and one of the busiest, of main lines in the world.

Hard to believe how magnificent it once was. The opening of the terminus of the London & Birmingham Railway on 20 July 1837, according to Betjeman, who would fight in vain more than a century later to save it, was simply the greatest railway event in the world. Euston's magnificent design reflected the view that the buildings of ancient Greece and Rome radiated a higher nobility – which is exactly how the railway promoters liked to see themselves. Brass-headed moneymen though they were, they were also romantics in the spirit of their time. They quite rightly regarded the railways as achievements without previous parallel, eclipsing

everything that had gone before and completely revolution-
ising society. It was therefore entirely fitting that stations
should become the symbols of the new age.

Nothing expressed this better than Euston's great Doric
arch. The railway's directors saw it as the beginning of a
'Grand Avenue for travelling between the midland and
northern parts of the kingdom – well adapted to the national
character of the undertaking', as they put it to their shareholders. And why not? Napoleon had been trounced and
Britain's rapidly spreading influence confirmed her status as
leader of the world.

Philip Hardwick, the Duke of Wellington's architect, was
given the brief to design this gateway 'from England's capital
and heart, London, to her stomach and toyshop, Birmingham',
as Betjeman put it. The finest hard sandstone in the land
was used – lugged in great blocks almost as if for the
construction of the Pyramids or Stonehenge. The four great
columns of the portico were heroic in themselves – 8 feet
6 inches in diameter at the base, with one cleverly containing
a spiral staircase so staff could reach the offices and store-
rooms hidden inside the pediment. It says much about the
lavishness of its construction that the contractors, William,
Thomas and Lewis Cubitt, were then invited to build King's
Cross station, although they remarked that 'a good station
at King's Cross could be built for less than the cost of the
ornamental archway at Euston Square'.

The grandeur did not finish with the arch; either side of
the portico were pairs of square stone lodges, adorned with
flat pilasters. Each lodge had a Doric grand central door,
and the whole composition was joined together by a lofty
ornamental cast-iron screen of gates by J. J. Bramah, one
of the most famous locksmiths of the day. 'The railway
builders were moved by the spirit of the conqueror, and
nowhere is this spirit more clearly visible than the portico

of Euston,' wrote the architectural historian Christian Barman. 'Moving southwards for the attack on London we can see they understood the greatness of their mission. And so when finally they had invaded the greatest city in the world, they built the portico to proclaim as a memorial their victory to posterity. For this portico, though designed in the manner for porches attached to buildings, is by virtue of its starkly isolated position a genuine military *arc de triomphe*.'

People from across the land flocked to see it. 'It is seen not as a railway station, but a spectacle,' wrote one commentator in 1896. Aubrey Beardsley was even more ecstatic when he wrote in 1920, 'I can never understand why people should seek Egypt in search of the Sphinx and the Pyramids when they can visit Euston station and survey the wonders of the stone arch.'

But that was not all. The railway's slogan, 'The Premier Line', was no hyperbole, since by mid-century the London & Birmingham had become, through its various amalgamations, the London & North Western Railway and the largest joint-stock company in the world. In 1846, by way of celebration, Philip Hardwick, with the aid of his son Philip C. Hardwick, was commissioned to design the Great Hall of Euston station. This magnificent chamber was built in the Italian Renaissance style, and influenced by the Berlin Opera House and the Palazzo Massimi in Rome. No wonder it was called the grandest waiting room in Britain.

Here passengers could repose in palatial splendour until officials rang a bell and announced the departure of their train. They could either wait on the ground floor or ascend by a double staircase and watch the crowds below from a gallery which surrounded the whole enormous hall. The columns were in the Ionic style, and the chamber was lit by attic windows, which illuminated the elaborately corbelled and coffered ceiling. At 125 feet 6 inches long and 62 feet high, this was believed to be the largest unsupported ceiling in the world. Copied from the church of St Paul Outside the Walls in Rome, it was rivalled in the secular world only by that in the ballroom at Buckingham Palace. The cost of this sumptuous waiting room was a mere £150,000. (Although the keen price may have encouraged a degree of jerry-building, with a column collapsing during construction, killing three workmen.)

There were further marvels. The circular counter in the station's refreshment room marked the first appearance in Britain of a bar where it was possible to stand and drink or eat. Thereafter the habit became common at stations long before it arrived in pubs. (Even at the most primitive village inn customers' wants were met by serving maids, and it was the railway station refreshment room that inaugurated this new way of buying drinks.) During this period too a royal waiting room was built in the Greek style with white and buff walls, featuring a private entrance from the street and French windows opening out straight onto the platform so Her Majesty could step directly aboard the train.

Euston had other distinctions. The station was renowned, for instance, for the variety and comprehensiveness of the items contained in its lost property office. One reporter in 1849 gave a minute inventory of its contents: 'It would be infinitely easier to say what there is not, than what there is, in the forty compartments like great wine bins in which all this lost property is arranged. One is choke-full of men's hats, another of parasols, umbrellas and sticks of every possible description. One would think that all the ladies' reticules on earth were deposited in a third.' But there were items of great value too. 'Some little time ago, the superintendent, upon breaking open, previous to a general sale, a locked leather hat box which had lain in this dungeon two years, found in it under the hat 65 pounds in Bank of England notes, with one or two private letters, which enabled him to restore the money to the owner, who, it turned out, had been so positive he had left his hat box in a hotel in Birmingham that he had made no inquiry for it at the railway office.'

But none of this counted as the age of pygmies dawned a century later. In 1960 Euston's death knell sounded as British Railways proposed total demolition. The line to the north was to be electrified, and the fuddy-duddy old structure hardly fitted in. Demolition was approved by Transport Minister Ernest Marples, whose family firm's main activity was the construction of roads, notably the Euston line's rival and Britain's first motorway, the M1. He didn't stick around to see the results of his decision, fleeing to his chateau in France to avoid being arraigned for tax fraud in 1975.

Despite the outcry from preservationists (Betjeman called the arch 'the noblest thing in London'), the London County Council and even the Royal Fine Art Commission, nothing could prevent the architects of British Rail from destroying the majestic old Euston. In a final bid to save it, the editor of the *Architectural Review*, J. M. Richards, went to lobby Prime Minister Harold Macmillan. As he recalled, 'Macmillan listened – or I suppose he listened . . . He sat without moving with his eyes apparently closed. He asked no questions; in fact he said nothing except he would consider the matter.'

Even the demolition contractor, Frank Valori, was distraught at having to destroy the portico so loved by Londoners, and he offered to number the stones and re-erect them at his own expense on a site chosen by British Railways. The government ungraciously refused this offer on the flimsy pretext that no site could be found. The sad Mr Valori presented to the newly formed Victorian Society a silver model of the propylaeum, which the late Lord Esher, the society's chairman, received with the observation that it 'made him feel as if some man had murdered his wife and then presented him with her bust'. Valori later used some of the stones from the arch in his own house at Bromley in Kent.

Betjeman later wrote sourly,

What masterpiece arose on the site of the old station? No masterpiece. Instead there is a place where nobody can sit; an underground taxi entrance so full of fumes that drivers, passengers and porters alike all hate it. A great wall of glass looks like a mini-version of London airport, which it seems to be trying to imitate. On its expanse of floor and against its walls passengers lie and await trains . . . Hygienic and slippery buffets may be glimpsed on upper floors and less hygienic and more slippery bars are entered from the hall itself. The smell of sweat and used clothes, even in winter, is strong in this hall, for there is something funny about the air-conditioning. In hot weather, it is cooler to go to the empty space in front of the station where the portico could easily have been rebuilt. In cold weather, it is advisable to retreat into one of the shops. The only place where the air approaches freshness and reasonable temperature is down to the Underground station, with its manifold passages.

Not much of the old station survives today. The bronze statue of Robert Stephenson by Carlo Marochetti presented to the LNWR by the Institution of Civil Engineers in 1870 still stands disdainfully outside All Bar One — abused by commuters, who wedge coffee cartons and discarded copies of the *Metro* free newspaper between his feet. The twin

Euston Road lodges, designed in 1869 in Portland Stone by the company's architect J. B. Stansby, are now real-ale and cider bars where City boys neck impossible quantities of alcohol, anaesthetising themselves for the commute home. You don't need a pint to be dazzled by the impressive list of destinations once reached by the LNWR, carved into the lodges' quoins. Now long out of date, they include such unlikely places as Swansea, Cork, Cambridge and Newark – a reminder of the fierce competition between the old railway companies. Of the seventy-two stations listed, only thirty-seven were ever on reasonably direct routes.

With the destruction of the arch, the spirit of the old Euston disappeared. Right at the beginning the carriages had been hauled by a cable up the steep slope to Camden Town, but in its heyday, the years before and after World War II, it was home to the mightiest locomotives – the Duchesses, Princesses, Royal Scots and Patriots, and their crews – aristocrats of labour at the controls of the fastest expresses. Here is the Reverend Roger Lloyd, known as the railway canon, writing in 1951 in his book *The Fascination of Railways*.

Come and stand at the far end of the No. 12 platform at Euston. It is the only spot from which every train passing in and out of the station can be seen; and there is a blackened signal post on which somebody (probably one of the small boys who are invariably to be found there) writes in pencil the names of some of the famous Camden drivers who bring their engines down to the platform to join their trains – Bishop, Copperwheat, Laurie Earl and others.

There it was I met a little tiny man with a very humorous expression waiting to take the 10.08 Perth train with a streamlined engine. It was a lovely June day, but he perversely disapproved of that, since he wanted a March gale, the only 'right weather' for the Carlisle run. 'It's not my sort of day. What I like is to drive through the lonely hills around Shap when it's wild and stormy. You get the wind in your lungs and it's grand.' The whistle blew, and off he went up the Camden bank, and a porter came up to me and said: 'Do you know who you were talking to? That was Laurie Earl.' There was reverence in his voice.

But there is hope yet. In our present, less philistine age we have come to understand the virtues of what we have lost. The millions spent on the recent restoration of St Pancras and King's Cross along the road have undoubtedly made them nicer places. How much more pleasant to scoff a gourmet meal in the restaurant that occupies the old booking office at St Pancras than to join the queue, as one did in the old days, for a grumpy British Railways ticket clerk. However, even where the great stations have been preserved and survive, much of the paraphernalia that added to the atmosphere has gone. The clatter and chatter of the mechanical arrival and departure indicators, the racks of roof boards bearing the names of grand expresses, the pigeon baskets and milk churns, the machines that stamped the names of excited children on a little strip of aluminium, water tanks with hoses for replenishing restaurant cars, chocolate dispensers with clunking drawers, glass cases with models of the *Rocket* with wheels that would rotate for a penny in the slot to help widows and orphans in the various railway homes. And that late-evening burst of excitement as the newspaper vans raced up from Fleet Street fresh with the smell of ink, and the thumps and thuds as the bundles were tossed onto the trains that would speed them to distant destinations.

Gone too are other assaults on the senses. 'All large railway stations had smells,' says Gordon Biddle in his book *Great Railway Stations of Britain*, 'usually a compound of steam, smoke, hot oil, gas, and near the luggage lift, dirty water that oozed out of a hydraulic cylinder with a distinctive sighing sound'. The railway historian Michael Bonavia writes of 'spilt milk, stale fish and horse manure blended in as well'.

But we must be thankful for what is left. Heading back from Birmingham after my homage to Snow Hill, I can just spy from the train out of New Street a classical arch looking curiously like Philip Hardwick's mighty structure at Euston sitting forlornly in the midst of a wasteland of brick rubble. This is Curzon Street station, the Euston arch's twin sister and just as handsome, with columns forty-five feet high and a superb carved London & Birmingham coat of arms still surviving haughtily over the original front door – though purists would point out its columns are Ionic not Doric. This was, for a time, the northern terminus of the London & Birmingham Railway.

Too provincial for anyone to take much notice over the years, Curzon Street quietly slumbered on unscathed as a goods station, but it is now destined for glory as the city terminus for HS2, the new high-speed line to the north. Its resurrection would be a fine revenge for what the wreckers did to Snow Hill. If it happens we should not be surprised if that forlorn statue of Robert Stephenson steps down from its plinth outside Euston and dances with delight.

Chapter Fourteen

A day return on the Heath Robinson special

The wacky world of the Shropshire & Montgomeryshire
Light Railway, Britain's most eccentric line, run by railway
history's dottiest proprietor. Even Heath Robinson might
have struggled to invent it . . .

Out of Shrewsbury station and over a rusty bridge,
ducking and diving through some back alleys down
onto the bank of the Severn, where I'm sidestepping the
puddles and already out of breath. 'Could you imagine
carrying your luggage all this way just to change trains?' My
guide, Mansel Williams, a town councillor with a curious

resemblance to the former Labour leader Neil Kinnock, is leading the way from Shrewsbury's main station to the site of the almost mythical and long-closed Abbey Foregate Street, terminus of the Shropshire & Montgomeryshire Railway, perhaps the most hopeless line ever built in Britain. If there was a prize for the lost causes of British railway history, then this obscure branch line would surely deserve to be the winner.

'It never had much of a chance from the start, since the Great Western and London & North Western Railways ganged up to block its trains, forcing the little railway to open its station in the badlands of town,' Mansel explains as Shrewsbury proper starts to peter out amid derelict shops. 'Nearly there,' he says as a huge Asda looms up in the distance. At least there's some relief in the form of the glowing red sandstone of the ancient Benedictine abbey, which gave the Shropshire & Montgomeryshire's mighty HQ its name.

Mighty? Well, that's how it liked to think of itself. In reality, it was a platform and a modest single-storey building, with the stone pulpit where monks once preached against sin in the Benedictine refectory sternly overseeing the arrival of passengers at the end of the platform. And woe betide any passenger with bladder issues, since the construction budget did not run to the provision of toilets.

Astonishingly, it is nearly all still there, complete with pulpit though minus track, more than half a century since the last passenger trains ran. Spiders scuttle away as Mansel turns his key in the booking-office door, and here is the old ticket-issuing window, surrounded by peeling chocolate and cream paint, where once you could buy a day return to Wern Las or Chapel Lane. One day Mansel and his group of enthusiasts are hoping to have it restored to its former (non) glory. 'Can you imagine buying a ticket here?' A faraway look appears in his eyes. 'And one day we may even lay some track . . .'

Yet the omens for Mansel's dream and a Shropshire & Montgomeryshire revival may be no better than they ever were. By a bizarre quirk, the clock on the abbey tower uses the letter F instead of the Roman numeral X, so a quick time check (it is now around 11 a.m.) reveals the word IF.

'If only . . .' might be the motto of the line. The S&M fulfilled every stereotype of the uneconomic bucolic branch line at its most hopeless, with slow, unreliable services, creaking tracks, rickety bridges, remote stations in the middle of nowhere and the most bizarre assembly of clapped-out rolling stock ever assembled on a British railway. Think of Rowland Emmet's cartoon engine *Nellie*, crossed with the Reverend W. Awdry's *Thomas*. Add a dash of Heath Robinson, the Titfield Thunderbolt and Oliver Postgate's *Ivor the Engine* and you are almost there (or not, if you happened to be unlucky enough to be a passenger on one of Shropshire & Montgomeryshire's interminable journeys).

For the whole of its struggling life the Shropshire & Montgomeryshire was like a railway purgatory, where ancient locomotives and carriages lived on in a kind of rusty limbo of dark sheds and overgrown tracks, conveying passengers like lost souls on their way to Hades. (Fortunately, Freud's couch was way in the future when the line opened, and psychoanalysts specialising in S&M had not yet been invented, although the initials may be applied perfectly to the little railway's penchant for self-flagellation.) Yet its survival for a century through bankruptcies, closures and yet more closures until its final demise in the 1960s has given it legendary status in the pantheon of lost railways.

The whole doomed empire was presided over by perhaps the most eccentric entrepreneur in the history of the railways, in the form of Colonel Holman Fred Stephens, a civil engineer and the son of Frederic George Stephens, the eminent Pre-Raphaelite painter and critic, some of whose works are in Tate Britain. Stephens planned, built and collected a whole portfolio of failing small branch lines around the country and ran them with evangelistic fervour from a terraced house in Tonbridge, Kent. There was nothing too hopeless, too woebegone, too run-down that this patron saint of lost railway causes couldn't espouse.

But we cannot blame the colonel for bringing this unfortunate railway on the English–Welsh borders into the world. Even by the overexcitable standards of the mid-nineteenth century's railway speculators, it is fair to say that any individual who had the idea of making money from a railway connecting Shrewsbury to the tiny border village of Llanymynech (population 887) was either clinically deluded or the most outrageous optimist and probably both. The route originated as the only constructed portion of a grandiose scheme to connect the Staffordshire Potteries with the mid-Wales port of Portmadoc. Originally promoted as the West Midlands, Shrewsbury & Welsh Coast in 1860, revived five years later as the West Shropshire Mineral Railway and later renamed the Potteries, Shrewsbury & North Wales, none of these titles exactly rolled off the tongue. The idea was to concentrate on goods and minerals, and if the occasional passenger came along, well, this would be a bonus. Oh, what dreams were encapsulated in the geographical reach of those titles. It was under the latter name that the line set out bravely from Shrewsbury, only to have its ambitions resoundingly crushed not long afterwards.

The Potts, as it was known, never managed to get further east (so no lucrative traffic from Stoke-on-Trent), and westwards it only struggled as far as the Welsh border. Even so, minus any connection with the capital of the world's ceramics industry, the line's nickname stuck for a century. Optimism lived on too. Years later, in dusty booking offices along the line the railway still carried printed tickets for the use of

'Shipwrecked Mariners', even though a terminus at the Welsh coast would never materialise, and there weren't many shipwrecks in Shrewsbury!

For its whole life the line would teeter on the edge of financial ruin, occasionally plunging over the fiscal cliff before being recklessly hauled back up again. There were never going to be many passengers in this lush but thinly populated part of Shropshire in the flood plain of the River Severn, where the small farming villages and hamlets had scarcely changed since medieval times. But even worse — before the tracks were laid, there was a terrible augury. The company was refused permission by the combined might of the Great Western and London & North Western railway companies to operate into the main station at Shrewsbury General, and was banished to the edge of town to a little station with no connections to anywhere.

The trains eventually got under way on 13 August 1866, and according to the *Shrewsbury Chronicle* crowds of passengers turned up at Abbey Foregate to try out the new service. Many were walkers heading for the scenic Llanymynech Hill; others were loaded with fishing tackle for a bit of sport on the River Vrynwy. But a different kind of liquid flowed through Llanymynech too, since the English–Welsh border ran down the middle of the high street. Its legendary pubs, where drinkers from dry Wales could get legless on Sundays merely by crossing the road, attracted tipplers for miles around.

The attraction, if not the hangovers, wore off quickly, and the line was in financial trouble within months. Debt collectors turned up at Abbey Foregate station and seized a train. After some haggling, it was allowed to leave but only with a bailiff on board. With suitable deference the man was shown into the train's sole first-class carriage. After a while, mystified that his coach hadn't moved, he poked his head out of the window and saw the engine and the remaining carriages vanishing off into the distance. As it was the last train of the day, he had a weary journey home on foot. For the record, he was told that a coupling had broken, but the canny staff of the Potts whispered a different and more subversive tale as they cackled into their pints in the local pubs that night.

The downhill struggle continued, and on 11 December 1866 the company went formally bust and was forced into a fire sale of some of its assets, although three of its five locomotives were allegedly so worthless that they failed to find buyers. Two years later the line ground back into action, although the track had to be reduced to a single line to cut running costs. But, almost unbelievably, the directors scraped together enough cash to open passenger services on two short new branches in the early 1870s. One was to the mining community of Criggion, where the plan was also to pick up some business transporting aggregates from a vast quarry at the foot of the Breiddon Hills famous for its green gravel. The other went west to Nantmawr, where it was hoped to milk some revenues from another quarry producing lime-stone for the fluxing process in iron furnaces.

Some hopes! In 1880 oblivion loomed again and the line closed abruptly. In the words of the engineer and writer L. T. C. Rolt, who visited the line several times over his life, it was 'like the crew of the *Marie Celeste*, the staff had been mysteriously spirited away and all was left to rot exactly as it stood. As the years went by the effect was eerie in the extreme'. The wooden bridge over the Severn at Melverley sagged crazily. Kinnerley Junction, the Crewe of the system, was like some ghost town in the American Midwest.

Locals crowded in for bargains when the rolling stock was again auctioned off in 1888. Trucks were a snip, going for as little as a pound each, but the bargain of the day was a handsome 2-4-0 tank called *Hope*, which went under the hammer for a mere £200. (*Hope* lived up to its name, lasting for another three quarters of a century, finally going to the scrapyard in 1955 after serving as a shunter for the National Coal Board.) Some repairs were done to the track in 1890, but no trains ran, and the line slumbered on, buried ever deeper beneath the weeds, for seventeen years.

Fast-forward to 1906, when the unlikely figure of Colonel Stephens strode onto the scene, hacking through the undergrowth, in Rolt's words, to 'awake Sleeping Beauty'. Grass and thistles were scythed from rusty rails; pigeons were evicted from buildings and a number of new line-side halts opened. A primitive signalling system was installed, and trains were permitted to run again under a provision known as a light railway order. The less demanding standards for track and infrastructure this required meant trains could run even more cheaply, though it was hard to know where costs could be cut any further.

This was a world away from slick modern light rail operations such as London's Docklands Light Railway. In the agricultural depression of late-Victorian times farmers in remote rural areas needed to get their produce to market. In those horse-and-cart days roads were terrible; there were no vans or lorries and the great days of railway building were long past. So, ever innovative, the Victorians came up with a new concept, made legal by the Light Railways Act of 1896. The idea was to rip up the rule book, cut the frills, avoid the hills, lighten the rails and pack in as many curves and gradients as might be needed. It was a principle that had been applied throughout the empire, so why not at home?

It was with this Act under his arm that Stephens entered the scene, acquiring old railways as an art collector would seek out Old Masters or a wine buff fine vintages. The difference was that instead of increasing in value, the worth of his portfolio was eternally diminishing. But whatever it lost in monetary worth, this empire of tiny railways with quaint names – its possessions extending from the Snailbeach District Railways via the Rye & Camber Tramway to the Weston, Clevedon & Portishead Light Railway – accumulated ever more charm and character as the years rolled by.

What a shame the life of the colonel has not been more celebrated, since here was an extraordinary Englishman. What Colonel Sanders would be for the fast-food industry and Colonel Parker to rock and roll, Colonel Stephens represented in spades for beleaguered railways. He was born in 1868 and remained a single man with few women friends – not surprising in view of the passion for obscure railways that dominated his life – and lived mainly in hotels and gentlemen's clubs. It was in one such establishment, the Lord Warden Hotel in Dover, which he cherished for its clubbability, that he died in 1931.

Tall, with a clipped moustache, bowler hat and cane, he played to the gallery with his military bearing. Some muttered though that he wasn't quite the real thing, since his rank had reputedly been acquired through service in the Territorial Army, though no one knew for sure. But his devotion to the survival of his railways was such that if traffic receipts at the end of the week weren't enough to pay the wages, he would stump up the cash himself. He had other curious habits. He would set off from his modest three-storey terraced HQ at 23 Salford Terrace in Tonbridge, pouncing at random on any one of his railways around the country that took his fancy, and order an immediate inspection.

If all was well he would beam, hand out cigars and tip staff with cash out of his own pocket. He even paid for one employee's false teeth. But the atmosphere would turn thunderous if not, and blistering memos would ensue. Typical is a note written to a manager on one line – the Ffestiniog in Wales – on 10 August 1925: 'Why are the windows of the 1st class compartment allowed to be open during heavy rain? Letting the windows down for air does not mean letting them down for rain to beat in. You seem to have some perfectly stupid people to deal with . . .'

But the colonel was in a rather more generous frame of mind on a delightful spring morning on Thursday 13 April 1911, when the Shropshire & Montgomeryshire sprang to life once again with a special inaugural train from Abbey Foregate drawn by an antediluvian 0-6-0 locomotive called *Hesperus*. Holding the town's loving cup aloft at the opening ceremony, Major Wingfield, the deputy mayor of Shrewsbury, delivered an oration to the crowd from the roof of a carriage which was reported thus in the *Shropshire Chronicle*: 'We are assembled here to open the Shropshire & Montgomeryshire Light Railway, which I trust and think will be of great benefit to this borough and the country districts which it serves [Cheers] . . . I hear the engine blowing off steam, so for fear it should burst, I curtail my remarks and drink out of the loving cup: "Success to the Shropshire & Montgomeryshire Light Railway." [Cheers]'

Amid a fusillade of detonators, the train – including a borrowed Cambrian Railways saloon that was famous (at least locally) for once having carried no less a celebrity than King Edward VII on a trip over the Birmingham Waterworks Railway – set off past a sea of waving flags. Arrival at Llanymynech was celebrated with a feast of sandwiches prepared by the parish council, the train arriving back in Shrewsbury in mid-afternoon. The train ran, according to the *Chronicle*, 'with a smoothness which would not compare unfavourably with some of the greater railways in the country'.

Unfortunately the script had to be rewritten two days later, when *Hesperus*, on its way to Shrewsbury, derailed with three coaches, damaging a long section of track. Although no one was injured, the new railway's pride was damaged far more than its assets, as a huge crowd turned out to watch the re-railing operation. But no sooner had the line reopened than it happened again just four days later, when the 1.25 p.m. to Shrewsbury tumbled off the rails. The *Chronicle* reported tartly that the interval between inspection and accident had been 'amazingly short'. The colonel's policy of 'never spend more when you can spend less' was laid bare for all to see.

A postcard depicting the railway at the time, sent by a local enthusiast on 17 May 1911, says it all. Captioned 'Our Local Express', it shows a train being pulled by a donkey, helped by passengers tugging it along. Someone on the track holds up a sign saying NOT SO FAST, while the signalman appears to be asleep in his signal box and the driver puffs a bellows into the firebox. Still, the colonel did his utmost to bring prosperity to the line. He invented 'Support your local line' long before it became a national slogan in the Beeching era. He was also decades ahead of his time in introducing the internal combustion engine in the form of two sets of Ford railcars. They each consisted of two wheezing Model T Ford buses coupled back to back, equipped with a steering wheel at each end with no function (it was there only because the engine controls were mounted on the steering column). At each terminus the driver had to switch off the engine at one end before moving seats and starting the motor at the other. Their hollow steel wheels made such a racket that they scared the animals for miles around in the quiet Shropshire countryside. Smelly, noisy and uncomfortable, they were reckoned some of the worst rail vehicles ever built – and were a terrible advertisement. Staff were frequently forced to apologise in the face of unprintable comments from passengers. As one driver retorted, 'Well it ain't a bloody railway any more; just a broken-down bus on rails.'

The infrequent steam services were marginally more comfortable but slower because they also trundled a variety of freight wagons along with the coaches, performing laborious shunting operations on the way. So slow were the trains in fact that it was said that you could keep to the timetable by pushing along a platelayers' trolley without too much physical exertion. But the colonel was undeterred, pouring energy into his vision by producing a threepenny guidebook for tourists, introducing passengers to the pleasures of the Severn and Vrynwy, and the hills around Llanymynech. The enterprising railway company even set itself up as part of the nascent tourist industry, building camping huts for hikers in the scenic Breiddon Hills and offering rowing boats for hire on the Severn. The huts were a snip at a mere seven shillings a week, and there was the lure of a weekly ticket over the line at a bargain rate.

The guidebook waxed:

This line runs through a delightful country and affords the travelling public every possible facility for pleasure and trading . . . A journey by rail direct from Shrewsbury to Llanymynech is reminiscent of a past generation. For 30 years the line which links up these two stations had lain derelict, grown over with briar and bramble, and in parts buried in brushwood and copse. But in 1911, the old railway, little the worse for its long sleep, once again rattled to the running of the train, and is now the scene of greater bustle and activity than ever marked its life in the early struggling years of its existence.

The colonel also erected a large sign on the S&M platform at Llanymynech, adjoining the rival Cambrian Railway, which boasted, SHROPSHIRE AND MONTGOMERYSHIRE RLY. SHORTEST

ROUTE TO SHREWSBURY. FREQUENT TRAINS. CHEAP FARES. Lucky for him there was no Advertising Standards Authority in those laissez-faire Edwardian times. Although 'shortest' might have just qualified in terms of distance, any passenger who spent what might have seemed a lifetime aboard one of the notoriously slow services on the basis of this claim would have been clamouring for their money back. As for 'frequent trains', they might be seen as such only in comparison with a service where there were no trains at all.

The colonel's philosophy was never to buy anything if something cheaper would do – his railways were the eBay, Lidl and Poundland of their day. This was especially true of his locomotive stock. The typical Colonel Stephens operation comprised a wheezing and rackety animated museum of railway history, with ancient second- and third-hand engines representing nearly every locomotive builder in the country and most of the old pre-grouping railway companies too. Neither age nor condition mattered very much – the only requirement was that they had a light axle loading so they did not cause expensive repairs to the fragile track or, worse, fall off. Though to be fair the colonel had an eye for a bargain locomotive in good condition. Typical of the S&M's ramshackle fleet was the *Severn*, which originated on the St Helens Railway back in 1853. It spent most of its time rotting and unserviceable, reposing in the nether reaches of the engine shed at Kinnerley.

Not unusual, since most Stephens locomotives were out of service at any one time in various degrees of decrepitude or disintegration, usually amid jumbled heaps of rusting locomotive parts quietly disintegrating in the coal dust. The inability of the maintenance staff to find anything to which these parts could be attached was why so many locomotives were acquired – on the off chance that one or two might be repaired and pressed into service.

Nothing, however, symbolised the bizarre world of Colonel Stephens better than *Gazelle*, a tiny 2-2-2 five-ton tank engine with wooden wheels – the smallest standard-gauge steam locomotive in the world, which looked for all the world like a pull-along puffer that might have belonged to Christopher Robin in an E. H. Shepard drawing. Not that *Gazelle* was exactly famous when Stephens bought her after she had been disposed of by the deputy mayor of King's Lynn, who had used her for private transport in his seed-corn business. She was said to have reached Chesterfield under her own steam once, though judging by appearances the hapless locomotive scarcely appears capable of reaching the buffer stops in a toy train set.

This toy for grown-ups was the quintessential Stephens engine – small, economical, and, more important still, it contained a bench seat for four passengers in the cab. This meant that no coach was required on quieter journeys – a money-saving wheeze brought to an end by a complaint from the Reverend Brock, the vicar of Criggion. Who knows whether this self-important cleric may have received a smut in his eye, but he complained indignantly to the Board of Trade that the arrangement broke safety rules. The railway eventually picked up an old London tramcar on the cheap and cut the top off to create a companion for *Gazelle*. Everyone observed that it looked a bit like a garden shed on wheels. Nothing went to waste, since the seats from the scrapped top deck were reused on the station platforms.

Who knows whether it was the influence of his artistic family, but the proprietor had a particular weakness for giving his locomotives classical names. The writer L. T. C. Rolt describes a visit to Kinnerley shed in 1929, where rusting bits of old engine were scattered around the trackside: 'Motive power then consisted of three Terriers: *Hecate*, *Dido* and *Daphne*; three Ilfracombes [ancient 0-6-0 tender engines

acquired from the London & South Western Railway],
Hesperus, Pyramus and Thisbe; the aptly named *Gazelle* and the
ancient *Severn.*

The Terriers were tiny tank locomotives pensioned off
from hauling suburban trains around south London (several
survive today, including *Stepney*, long the mascot of the
preserved Bluebell Railway in Sussex), and in their middle
age were scarcely up to even the undemanding standards of
the Potts. Unlike modern engines, they lacked an injector
– a device that fills the boiler of a steam locomotive with
water under pressure. Rather, the Terriers depended on a
primitive axle-driven pump to feed their boilers. Chugging
slowly up the gradients, water consumption sometimes
exceeded supply, and if the water level disappeared from
view in the gauge glass, the crew 'whistled up'. This was the
signal for the guard to jump down from his van and pin
down the wagon brakes. The engine then uncoupled and
careered briskly up and down the track, pumping water like
crazy until the level was restored and the journey could
resume.

'The stock of eight locomotives sounds impressive,' Rolt
observed, 'but in fact it was seldom that that more than two
were capable of service at any one time.' It was famously
said that no locomotive on the Potts was ever scrapped; they
simply faded away. This was certainly true of *Hesperus*, the
locomotive so celebrated on opening day, which, minus her
boiler, became a rusting landmark in Kinnerley yard, a wreck
like her notorious schooner namesake. It was characteristic
of the serendipity that defined life in Colonel Stephens'
world that in later years she was plucked from her resting
place in the weeds, and with a few repairs was put back into
service once more.

The carriages derived from equally eccentric sources,
boasting examples from the Midland, North Staffordshire,

Great Eastern and London & South Western Railways, so that the traveller trundling across the plain of Shropshire might find his or her compartment embellished by faded scenes depicting the Peak District, the Norfolk Broads or the waterfront of Lyme Regis. The plum of the collection was a royal saloon built by Joseph Beattie of the London & South Western and identified from contemporary illustrations as existing in 1844, if not earlier. But the canny colonel's rolling-stock acquisitions were not so random as might appear. As R. W. Kidner observes in *The Colonel Stephens Railways*, 'An ordinary railway, faced with the chronically infirm Melverley Viaduct [it had already collapsed once], would have spent time and money attending to the foundations. Not so the Shropshire & Montgomeryshire. Miraculously there were produced a three-ton locomotive and a horse tramcar, which could be relied on not to strain the timbers, and which, slightly modified, outlived the ordinary passenger trains on the line.' The acid test for a new engine, some reckoned, was not how efficient or powerful it was, but whether it might cause Melverley Viaduct to collapse.

But then nobody was in much of a hurry, and certainly not the trains. The journey from Shrewsbury to Llanymynech took an hour to cover eighteen miles, and in later years fifteen minutes longer as the trains crept ever more slowly over the deteriorating track. Passengers had to make do with three trains – timed to meet Cambrian's services at Llanymynech – each way on weekdays, with two extras on Thursdays and Saturdays and two each way on Sundays. The quarries provided stone for some freight trains, although general goods were carried by the passenger services, which usually had a wagon or two in the mix, which would be shunted off periodically as the trains dawdled along the line.

Nor did anyone exert themselves very much if they could avoid it. With its two through platforms and branch bay, Kinnerley Junction, where trains diverged for the Criggion branch, was by far the most imposing station on the system, boasting quite an impressive array of signals controlled from a frame of thirteen levers protected from the weather by a corrugated-iron shelter. Here presided as stationmaster the appropriately named Mr Funnel, plump, genial and rubicund, a character straight out of the world of Will Hay's *Oh, Mr Porter!*.

Rolt was a friend of his and recalls, 'He was also captain of the village cricket team, employing a runner when he went to the wicket because of his high blood pressure. Fortunately the proceedings at Kinnerley Station were not calculated to endanger his health by any call for violent exertion.' Only the up platform was used for passenger trains, the down platform and bay being usually filled with either goods wagons or coaching stock in various stages of decay. 'When Mr Funnel heard a down train from Shrewsbury approaching (the Ford railcars announced their coming as soon as they left the next station at Edgerley) he would indicate in a desultory motion of a flag that it was expected on the up side. This obviated an unnecessary effort in pulling off signals and crossing from one platform to another.'

There was a similarly relaxed mood in the locomotive shed. Bill Willans, who joined the line as an apprentice in 1928, describes his first day at work: 'I made my way to Kinnerley shed! Not a soul in sight! There were no lights of any sort and a general air of abandonment.' One of his jobs was to ride to the rescue after the frequent accidents along the line. 'I particularly enjoyed this work when the "Rattlers" [the Ford railcars] broke down away from Kinnerley. A platelayer's trolley was acquired and Sid and myself pumped our way to the scene of the disaster. This seemed often to take place when they were doing a run to Criggion, and failure usually took place in the vicinity of the Tontine Hotel! Among other things he taught me was that classic "It Was Christmas Day in the Workhouse".

With his ragbag collection of prehistoric locomotives and carriages, Colonel Stephens fought hard but eventually lost his battle against the motor bus. His appeal to prospective passengers to 'travel across country away from the dusty and crowded roads on home-made steel instead of imported rubber' fell on deaf ears. By the end of the 1920s the weeds were taking over the stations, the footboards on the bridges were rotting and the camping huts falling into disrepair. When this lovable oddball of the railways died, there was no will to keep services going, and in 1933 regular passenger services were suspended. The daily goods and excursion train ran till the outbreak of war, by which time the tracks had more or less retreated beneath the undergrowth.

But it wasn't in the DNA of the Potts to abandon hope, and soon another opportunity was on the horizon. World War II may not have been a blessing for many, but it was a godsend for the fortunes of the S&M. Britain became a huge military base, and rural Shropshire was chosen as the location for vast ammunition depots, among them a huge secret storage site at Kinnerley. Some twenty-three square miles of land was requisitioned around the railway, and more than 200 gargantuan storage sheds, camouflaged with turfed roofs, were built around the station, each served by a siding.

You might think that a dose of army discipline would have sharpened the line's operation, but that is to under-estimate the Potts' enduring eccentricity. The driver of the first train to enter Abbey Foregate under the new regime misjudged the gradient into the station. Smashing through the buffer stops, the engine burst through a large advertisement hoarding, ending up on the main road. The line may have lost its owner but none of its eccentric character. However, in other ways the little old railway was transformed by the military beyond the wildest expectations of the colonel. Before long as many as twelve locomotives including little *Gazelle* were in steam at any one time. At the end of the war modern 1940s-built Austerity engines were brought in to do what the old ones couldn't. The stations, bereft of passengers for years, crawled with servicemen who spared no effort in renewing and maintaining the line, including relaying the rotting wooden track with concrete sleepers. The new motto of the railway was, in the words of the 1930s American children's book *The Little Engine that Could*, 'I think I can.' As if to prove it, an astonishing million tons of military traffic was carried between 1941 and 1945.

After the war the line became part of the nationalised network, although remaining under military control. Figures made public at this time showed that after absorbing nearly £2 million of capital expenditure in the eighty-two years of its life, the Potts had a cash value of less than £30,000. Charm was always its most bankable asset though, and staff were very welcoming to nostalgic souls who turned up to ride on the one train a day that was run for civilians. Towards the end a group that asked for permission to walk along the line was delighted to find a railcar had been laid on to give them an impromptu tour of the track.

In 1959 the War Department closed the last depot and stone traffic from the quarry at Criggion ceased. The following year the line was returned to civilian status, to be operated by British Railways. But if the Potts was at death's door in 1933, what hope did it have decades later, with Dr Beeching around the corner? The last scheduled train from Shrewsbury to Llanymynech ran on 26 February 1960, and three days later the line officially closed.

Not much survives of the Potts today. But shades of the

colonel – ramrod straight as always – still stalk this country railway which was so eccentrically his own. By a supreme irony, the once wobbly Melverley Viaduct lives on, now rebuilt and providing a vital road link. Part of the Shrewsbury ring road is named Old Potts Way, commemorating where the track once ran and now reverberating to the thunder of the juggernauts that eventually took over the stone traffic.

A much more important souvenir also lives on, not in the Welsh borders but far away near Stephens HQ in the Garden of England, where *Gazelle* reposes in a charming little museum at Rolvenden on the preserved Kent & East Sussex Railway, another outpost of the colonel's empire. The army took such a fancy to her that they preserved her as a novelty, and she now forms part of Britain's national railway collection. Safe from the liquidator and scrap man now, although her custodians tell me she will never run again.

But just imagine how lovely she would look at the head of her little train with the evening sun setting off her shiny green paintwork against the mellow red sandstone of Shrewsbury Abbey. The clock chimes, the signal drops with a clatter, and we set off on our train of dreams. Well, stranger things have happened in the curious history of the line that refused to die.

Chapter Fifteen

We do like to be beside the seaside

Pack your bags and load up those crates of ale for a
railway excursion to the seaside. Today we're heading for
Blackpool's Golden Mile. Tomorrow we could be making
merry on a day trip to Scarborough, Morecambe,
Bridlington or Bournemouth. Hurry, though. The tickets
will soon be gone.

Slip off the seafront at the side of the tower. Nip along
the alley past Poundstretcher, Poundworld and the 99p
Store. (Don't forget we're in twenty-first-century Blackpool
now.) Dodge the wide boys handing out flyers for stag and
hen dos in dodgy nightclubs. Don't get seduced by the
dazzling banks of digital lights on the gaming machines in

Coral Island. Hold your nose past the stench of frying onions on the hot-dog stalls. Surely there must be some trace of what I'm looking for? Not so long ago everyone knew their way to Blackpool Central, the largest and busiest seaside station in the land, if not the planet.

But I'm struggling to find it today. Instead, where rails once reigned supreme is one of the biggest car parks in northern England. These days clues to the recent past are rare indeed. If you are especially sharp-eyed you might spot, all along the side streets, the rows of boarding houses, now mostly down at heel, where swarms of landladies once emerged to lure the tourists off their trains into rooms where the odour of boiled cabbage was ever-present and there was hot water only if you were lucky. (Let's hope life has moved on at the Central Hotel – still advertising its wares opposite the spot where the main station entrance once stood.) These Blackpool harridans, the world's first tourist touts, were so pushy that their activities led to a ban in 1869.

Industrial archaeologists might also pick out the gents' toilets – a vast bank of them – once urgently needed on arrival to relieve the pressure from all those crates of Tetley and Thwaites bitter consumed aboard trains without corridors. Now they are the coin-in-the-slot kind where stingy local councils force you to jiggle for change to open the door. Come off it – 20p for a pee? No self-respecting bladder would have put up with it in the old days.

But that's it. The rest – all fourteen platforms and a glorious chapter of social history – is buried beneath our feet. Here lie the fragments of a grand terminus that once funnelled tens of millions of holidaymakers directly onto the most celebrated stretch of promenade in Britain, just a 99 Flake's throw from the sea. For 101 years the twenty-three acres of Blackpool Central station annually transformed a backward coastal hamlet into Europe's top tourism resort.

The newly leisured masses of northern England poured through the ticket barriers straight onto the Golden Mile to a myriad of sensuous delights – the tang of sea spray on the air, the sugary whiff of candyfloss and the throat-catching aroma of salt and vinegar from a hundred fish 'n' chip shops. Crowning the concourse was that Lancastrian evocation of Paris, the Blackpool Tower. For a week or two the grim workaday reality of Lancashire and Yorkshire mill-town life would be swapped for the hedonistic delights of the seaside.

This was the kiss-me-quickest, fish-'n'-chippiest, sauciest, how's-your-fatherest station in Britain, if not the world. It was the Euston, King's Cross, Liverpool Lime Street and Manchester Piccadilly of hedonism rolled into one, as well as the apotheosis of the railway holiday by the sea. But then a tsunami rolled over the railways in the closure years of the 1960s, drowning not just Blackpool but the rest of the Fylde coast as well and delivering a fatal blow everywhere to the essence of the British seaside holiday as we once knew it.

As the lights were dimmed on a dank, foggy evening on 1 November 1964 at the finish of another season of the famous illuminations, the very last train pulled out of Blackpool Central station, tearing the heart out of the town. Station staff and local people alike wept as the 9.55 p.m. for London Euston slid out of Platform 3. Even on that last day there had been fifty-five departures, so the station was hardly moribund. After the final arrival – a local from Manchester Victoria – whose driver sounded his hooter mournfully before being given a kiss by his wife and a bottle of beer by his son, the stationmaster turned the keys in the tall iron gates for the very last time. The following day, the *Blackpool Gazette* reported, the once thronged station resembled a 'ghost town'. How could it have happened? The railways were Blackpool. And Blackpool was the railways. And both were an essential element of the alchemy that made the

British seaside holiday a unique experience in the world.

Originally the railway companies weren't too bothered with this dot on the Fylde coast, whose sands were regarded as a place more suitable for fishermen digging for lugworms than holidaymakers having the time of their lives. The target was Fleetwood, further north, where before the days of a fully fledged railway to Scotland the dream was for passengers to transfer to steamships for onward travel to Glasgow. But once the new Preston & Wyre Railway had laid its tracks to Fleetwood in 1840, it opened a branch to Blackpool in 1846 over land purchased from the Clifton/Talbot family, building a terminus called Talbot Road, now named Blackpool North. Meanwhile, the tracks of the new Blackpool & Lytham Railway were racing up the coast from the south, arriving at Hounds Hill, as Central was first called, on 6 April 1863. From then on, the hospitality industry that still defines Blackpool as a destination scarcely paused to take breath until the traumatic events of almost a century later unfolded.

The closure of the town's main station was a shock from which many say the resort has never recovered. True, Blackpool still has a railway, although much reduced – at Blackpool North on the fringe of town, as well as the stump of the old Central route at Blackpool South station, the line hacked back from the town centre to a single platform at the end of a siding with a meagre hourly service to the rest of Lancashire. But where I am standing now, where the weary hordes of the Lancashire and Yorkshire mill towns emerged to get their first glimpse of the sea, there is not a jot to show of what was once here. Today there are only sporadic long-distance services and no late departures.

What bathos! How terrible a comedown from its 1930s heyday, when six million people a year travelled to Blackpool and its adjacent resorts by rail – not to mention the myriad rail journeys made by local people around this huge coastal conurbation. In the week running up to August Bank Holiday in 1935 more than half a million passengers passed through the barriers. During the illuminations period at the end of the season there were some three quarters of a million visitors.

For those in charge of Central station this represented a superhuman feat of logistics. The main signal box at Kirkham North Junction on the approaches dealt with 600 trains in a 24-hour period, averaging one every 180 seconds. In the tangle of lines around the station there were 22 miles of track where 40 trains could be stabled and prepared for the return journey. In Blackpool's not-so-distant heyday you could party through the night in the Tower Ballroom and still get a train home. In 1952 the final departure was at 1.55 a.m., while passengers were already milling about at 4 a.m. to catch the early-morning trains. The late trains would often arrive at their destinations with scores of light bulbs missing – removed by courting couples before engaging in what the staff termed 'a bit of hanky-panky'. Even up to the end the scenes of passengers arriving and departing were like something from a Frith painting. There is a famous 1963 photograph of trippers off a train from Oldham – men with Brylcreemed quiffs, women in dresses from the set of *A Kind of Loving* – joyously surging along the platform to the sea. So huge is this smiling crowd that they are almost spilling over the platform edges.

But when the final whistle blew from that last train just a year later it signalled not just the effective end of the railways in Blackpool but an entire chapter of British social history. A family holiday at the seaside was one of the greatest inventions of the Industrial Revolution. In the years before motorways and easyJet, trains were the obvious way to get to the seaside. They were mostly comfortable, and the journey was relatively stress-free – certainly compared with security-dominated airports today. In many people's minds, right up to the beginning of the 1960s, the annual journey to the seaside aboard a train was associated with pleasure, relaxation, the joy of sharing simple delights with your children in an era before iPads, smartphones, Snapchat and Twitter. The mood was encapsulated by the historian C. Hamilton Ellis, who writes in his 1947 book *The Trains We Loved*, 'Surely it was always summer when we made our first railway journeys . . . Sun shone on the first blue engine to be seen, a Somerset & Dorset near Poole; there was sunshine, most dazzling, on a Great Western brass dome; the sun shone on an extraordinary mustard-coloured engine of the London, Brighton and South Coast, seen by three-year-old eyes.'

Until they were transformed by the railways, seaside resorts had tended to be haunts of the sick seeking healthier climes, a fashion going back to Roman times, when the waters of Bath and Buxton were associated with a host of cures, both physical and spiritual. Later, in the eighteenth century, they acquired a social function, with the Prince Regent savouring the waters at Brighton and the Yorkshire gentry dipping their toes in the sea at Scarborough. Blackpool was no exception, marketing itself at the end of the century as a place to take the waters, and in 1781 a direct stagecoach service was established from Manchester and Halifax.

Within a few years the resorts had started to multiply rapidly. Jane Austen catches the spirit in her last, unfinished novel *Sanditon*. '"Every five years," says Mr Heywood, "one hears of some new place or other starting up by the sea, and growing the fashion. How can half of them be filled?"' The answer was supplied by the burgeoning railway companies. As Jeffrey Richards and John Mackenzie put it in *The Railway Station: A Social History*, 'To bring the new holiday-makers to the sea a transport revolution was required. Steam was the great liberator.'

By the end of the eighteenth century the coastal resorts were undergoing the first stages of the process that was to transform the seaside holiday from an exclusive upper-class recreation into a national institution. The Industrial Revolution gave birth to a large and well-to-do middle class, which wasn't slow to emulate the aristocracy in travelling to the seaside to enjoy the air and waters. The final three decades of the nineteenth century were to see a similar move by the working class, keen to experience the benefits of fresh air and seawater, the chance of amusement and relaxation away from their work, or just a change of scene from the grim tenements and back-to-back houses in which they lived and the satanic mills and factories in which they toiled.

Enter another British invention that became a key ingredient in the mix — the seaside excursion train. The first railway in Britain to carry fare-paying passengers on a seaside excursion used horses and ran along the coast of South Wales near Swansea, between Oystermouth and Mumbles, in 1807. The line operated until 1960 and was unique in that it used five forms of power in its 143-year history: horse, steam, electricity, diesel oil — and even an experiment with wind propulsion using sails.

But organised group travel by train on a grander scale began with the celebrated Thomas Cook (1808-92), who started life as a carpenter's apprentice, then became a printer in Market Harborough and leader of the temperance movement. In the 1830s Cook covered some 2,000 miles a year, mostly on foot, addressing anyone who cared to listen to his teetotal message in towns and villages around Britain. After many tiring and tedious journeys, it was only a small step from preaching the evils of the devil's brew to setting up his own commercial enterprise specialising in railway travel. He organised his first trip on 5 July 1841 for 570 temperance believers and their families, a day excursion from

Leicester to Loughborough with tea, cricket and sandwiches – all for a shilling a person.

Another pioneer of the day trip by train was the eminent Victorian Rowland Hill, founder of the Penny Post and a director of the London, Brighton & South Coast Railway. Hill introduced the first excursion train from London to Brighton in 1844. Four locomotives were needed to haul the forty-five carriages, which departed from Norwood Junction in south London. By the time the train got to Croydon, twelve more had been added, together with two more locomotives. The 800 passengers reached Brighton at 1.30, four and a half hours after setting out, and despite the length of the journey, a good time was reckoned to have been had by all.

In the industrial north of England whole trains were booked by companies to enable their workers to have a day beside the sea. In 1844 a factory manager in Lancashire arranged a day trip by train to Fleetwood for 650 of his employees, most of whom had never been on a train before, nor visited the seaside. Initial fears of the iron monster were soon overcome, and the delights of a day by the sea were shared with friends and neighbours, who came along on the next excursions. During the August Bank Holiday week in 1850 a total of 202,543 passengers left Manchester and nearby towns by rail for holidays in Blackpool.

In the decade from 1863 the number of visitors to Blackpool at least quadrupled. In 1873 about 850,000 passengers arrived at the town's two termini during the season. According to the 1881 census, however, the town still had fewer than 13,000 residents, making it only the twentieth-biggest holiday resort, but the growth in visitor numbers was phenomenal. By 1883 the number of arrivals had increased by half a million, and in the early 1890s was approaching two million. By the start of the new century, numbers were hitting almost three million, zooming up to four million on the eve of World War I.

The new breed of holidaymakers brought with them their families, including young children, turning the seaside holiday into something which it had not been in its aristocratic heyday – a family affair. Horizons were expanding too. Before the advent of the railways most resorts, whether spas or sea bathing places, had drawn their visitors primarily from their own regions, with a few exceptions such as Bath, Cheltenham and Brighton. But the railways offered a new freedom of choice, helping to shape the holiday habits of the nation. The northern resorts tended to remain regional, whereas resorts such as Bournemouth had a more national appeal. As Jack Simmons puts it in his book *The Railways in Town and Country, 1830–1914*, 'It was perhaps one of the differences between north and south, with the northerner more tenacious of tradition, of the manners they were accustomed to, the food and drink.'

Each of the manufacturing districts had one or two favourite resorts. The West Riding visited mainly Bridlington and Scarborough; Sheffield patronised Cleethorpes; Nottingham and Leicester went to Skegness and Great Yarmouth; Lancashire favoured Blackpool, Morecambe and Southport; while Birmingham decamped to Weston-super-Mare and Welsh resorts such as Barmouth and Pwllheli. The first requisite for all these places was a good train service, not just in the summer but also all year round. By 1914 the residents of every large manufacturing city except Coventry could reach the seaside in less than three hours, even in winter.

But it wasn't all a smooth ride. There were frequent conflicts of interest. The genteel burghers of Weston-super-Mare saw the railway as an invader and forced the Bristol & Exeter to bypass their town. Excursionists were unpopular at smaller resorts. The residents of Sidmouth in Devon protested about their rowdiness in 1874, and it was fear of the riff-raff that kept the railway out of Cromer until the same year. Yet in

Ilfracombe on the north Devon coast the citizens had to beg for a new railway. When in 1863 a line was opposed by the powerful landlord William Williams and rejected in the House of Lords, the locals became so agitated that the Riot Act had to be read. Other resorts were almost entirely manufactured by the railway companies, such as the genteel resort of Hunstanton in Norfolk, created jointly by the L'Estrange family, the local landowners, and the Great Eastern Railway.

Eventually the main seaside resorts of Victorian England settled down into four groups, according to Simmons. First, the leading resorts that tried to remain 'select', attracting their clientele mainly from the middle classes. These were, pre-eminently, Bournemouth, Eastbourne, Folkestone, Torquay and Worthing. Then there were the ten big ones, catering mainly for the masses: Blackpool, Brighton, Cleethorpes, Hastings, Margate, Ramsgate, Scarborough, Southend, Southport and Weston-super-Mare. In a special category of their own were the fishing ports that became holiday resorts, such as Weymouth, Great Yarmouth and Lowestoft. Then there were smaller places that owed their existence to their particular attraction to one social group, whether to the working class, as at Clacton or Skegness, or posher folk, as at Cromer or Sidmouth.

Spurred on by the railways, development was phenomenal. In 1871 there were forty-eight seaside resorts listed in the official census of Britain, but by 1900 there were over 200. By the end of the nineteenth century the idea of a railway holiday at the seaside was embedded not just in the popular imagination but in the literary one too. 'He's always splendid,' one of Henry James's characters observes in *Complete Tales* in 1892, 'as your morning bath is splendid, or a sirloin of beef, or the railway service to Brighton.' The popular novelist R. S. Surtees proclaimed on the first page of his humorous work *Plain or Ringlets*, which featured a seaside resort as part of the setting, 'Thanks to George Stephenson, George Hudson and many other Georges who invested their talents and valuable money in the undertakings, railways have brought wealth and salubrity to everyone's door. It is no longer the class distribution that used to exist, this place for that set, that for another; but a sort of grand quadrille of gaiety in which people change places continually, and whirl about until they finally settle down, finding out beauties that none can see but themselves.'

It couldn't have been more perfect. The railways enjoyed the business the seaside resorts brought in – from first-class passengers and excursionists alike – and the resorts, with tills ringing, acknowledged their dependence on the railways. Among the biggest money-spinners were the trains laid on for the unique Wakes Week holidays in northern England. Originating as church festivals, these were adapted for a secular purpose after the Industrial Revolution, when most of the factories in a town would close at the same time. The workers would take their annual holiday, and essential maintenance would be carried out.

Industrial Lancashire once had the densest network of railways and the biggest concentration of factory workers outside London, which offered a potent economic combination. In the days before cheap package holidays from Manchester Airport, a week in Blackpool was the aspiration of workers in almost every northern industrial town, and they saved for it all year from often meagre wages in 'going off' clubs where they worked. 'The Wakes Week excursions provided a social safety valve for the toiling masses,' says Barry McLoughlin in his book *Railway Heritage: Blackpool & the Fylde*. 'Marx and Engels could never have predicted that the enlightened self-interest of the employers would find such an ingenious method of maintaining the health – and morale – of their workforce.' The leading Blackpool architect Thomas Mawson quotes from a chat with a visitor on the promenade: 'If it wasn't for Blackpool, there'd be revolution in Lancashire.

Men stick it as long as they can in the mill towns and once a year they must either burst or go to Blackpool.'

The frenetic mood of Wakes Week in Blackpool is caught by the crime writer Andrew Martin in his novel *The Blackpool HighFlyer*, about an attempt to derail an excursion train from Hind's Mill in Halifax in 1905.

> In Central you could hardly breathe from the green-house heat burning through the canopies and the press of people and the nosebag smell, for the cab horses were at their dinner as we came in at just after eleven. A porter was standing on a stepladder, trying to put the excursionists into the right channels by a lot of shouting and waving of arms. This was the busiest station in Europe . . . And you had never seen a day so full: tribes of excursionists going both ways on the Prom (they should have had an 'up' and a 'down' as on the railways) . . . The crowds went on for ever, like the sea. These people had all aimed for the bull's eye, and they had all *hit* the bull's eye. There was no point in thinking about the future or the past.

In the early years of the twentieth century the railway companies found ever more inventive ways of promoting their seaside trains. The LNER introduced a summertime day excursion train from Liverpool Street, which ran from the end of May to the end of September, with Pullman coaches for which a supplement had to be paid – 10s. 6d. for first class and 6s. 6d. for third class. Known as the Eastern Belle, it was unique in that it ran to a different seaside resort each day of the week, selected from a list that included Felixstowe, Lowestoft, Great Yarmouth, Cromer, Sheringham, Frinton, Walton-on-the-Naze, Hunstanton, Heacham, Aldeburgh, Thorpeness and Harwich. What fun it must have been to arrive in such style. The most popular destination was Clacton, since this was closer to London and made for a longer day out. The Great Western had its own Hikers' Mystery Express from Paddington, where walkers were invited to join 'the great adventure'. The trains were hugely popular and had a match-making reputation: the potent combination of a cheap ticket and a day out hiking over the cliffs could end up with wedding bells.

Potent too in promoting the happy holiday to the coast was the railway seaside poster. From the 1920s onwards, railway companies commissioned hundreds of designs from the best artists of the day, advertising travel to their resorts and the joys of a sojourn on the coast. With colourful images of sandy beaches, endless golden sunshine and families paddling in the surf, they combined fantasy with reality and enthusiasm with nostalgia. Who could fail to be charmed by the Southern Railway's heart-tugging 'South for Sunshine' campaign, or the LNER's 'Filey for the Family' or 'Skegness is so Bracing' – perhaps the most famous English holiday poster of all, originally drawn by John Hassall for the Great Northern Railway in 1908.

Sometimes publicity departments got carried away – the Great Western Railway issued a poster advocating 'Bathing in February in the Cornish Riviera' featuring what was popularly known at the time as a bathing belle frolicking in the sea off St Agnes. (Whether the goose pimples achieved their purpose of filling seats in the off season seems open to doubt.)

Travel by railway to the seaside reached its peak in the 1950s, when stations during the summer school holidays were thronged with crowds surging towards departure platforms, children with buckets and spades, strawberry jam and Marmite sandwiches, beach balls and cricket bats, and parents staggering along with brown leatherette suitcases. This was an innocent era, with father possibly in his best Sunday togs, boys in short trousers and girls in ankle socks. When the platform announcement came and the tickets were clipped, there would be a rush along the platform to find the seats on the seaward side for the best views on arrival at the coast.

The 1950s and 1960s offered a variety of crack trains dedicated to the institution of the seaside holiday. Just imagine it – the thrill of arriving at Paddington to find the Torbay Express waiting behind the locomotive *Caerphilly Castle*, freshly polished for the occasion, to whisk you off to Torquay, Paignton and Kingswear – a distance of 199.6 miles in three hours twenty-eight minutes – speeding non-stop through Exeter to get to those golden sands in double-quick time. On Saturday 27 July 1957, a peak day of travel that year for summer passenger trains, over half a million passenger journeys were made on the Western Region alone. According to British Railways statistics, in one hour around midday at Exeter St David's station twenty-six trains heading to resorts in Devon and Cornwall were counted, while further west at Newton Abbot, eighty trains passed through the station between 08.24 and 21.37 on their way to and from the seaside.

It's all very different now, when the few passengers taking the train for a holiday in British seaside resorts often have to endure changing from the comfort of a main-line train onto ancient wheezing diesel multiple units on forgotten secondary lines. There's not much special about travel by train to the sea any longer, where it can be an uncomfortable marathon to get to Scarborough, Skegness, Great Yarmouth, Morecambe, Bridlington, Pwllheli or Whitby aboard superannuated trains on often meagre timetables. Meanwhile, in a parallel universe, services to seaside towns such as Brighton, Southend, Bournemouth, Clacton and Southport are filled not with the bucket and spade brigade but perspiring commuters on their way to and from the office, condemned to long commutes by high central London house prices.

Worse, many of our most charming and beautiful seaside lines are gone for ever. No more the coastal delights of Whitby to Scarborough, the toy train to Southwold, the rickety wooden causeway on the 'Hayling Billy' line to Hayling Island, and Betjeman's favourite, the slow train alongside the wash from King's Lynn to Hunstanton, used by generations of the royal family on their way to Sandringham. Gone also are the tracks from Axminster to Lyme Regis, only operable almost up to closure in the 1960s by elderly Victorian engines because of the twisting curves which defeated modern locomotives. Disappeared also have most of the tracks on the Isle of Wight – the quintessential seaside railway – where vintage tank engines survived until Beeching. Who can now remember the delightfully named Tilleynaught to Banff branch in Aberdeenshire, where the last trains ran in 1964? Yet, with its route alongside silvery Scottish coastal sands, it was one of the most beautiful seaside railways in Europe.

Goodbye too to the main-line seaside specials, such as the Devon Belle and the Cornishman. Farewell, the Sunny South Express. The Broadsman and the Man of Kent are no more. Oh joy when you could load your suitcases onto the Brighton Belle and the Bournemouth Belle in anticipation of a glorious fortnight of freedom on the sunny south coast. These days seaside railway stations are mostly sad, truncated places, mournful with the cries of seagulls and the long empty intervals between trains.

Today's Blackpool is no exception, although the north station has at least been included in a plan to electrify the lines around Preston and Manchester. But most of the day there is scarcely a soul at unstaffed Blackpool South, with its melancholy wind-blown single platform and bus shelter. The place is so miserable that even the Tommy Cooper Joke Shop next door has closed down.

Acres of redundant sidings rust unused at Blackpool

North, where an ugly concrete ticket hall has replaced the magnificent double-arched iron roof, demolished in 1974. So diminished is the station that it occupies only the area of the excursion platforms of the old one – the rest has been given over to a bleak retail development now occupied by Wilko, a store flogging cheap homeware to the masses. All that remains of the glory days – though you must search to find them – are two cast-iron plaques set in the wall, bearing the elaborate monograms of the London & North Western and Lancashire & Yorkshire Railways, which jointly ran the station before their merger in 1922.

How could the fall have happened? Even after all these years conspiracy theories still abound among the regulars at the vast Albert and Lion pub on the seafront, a handful of shingle's throw from where the entrance to Blackpool Central once stood. For once you can't blame Dr Beeching, since the station did not figure on his infamous closure list. So whodunnit? How can it be that the site of one of the world's most famous termini remains mostly a wasteland more than fifty years later? And what lobbying went on in high places that led to the heart being cut out of one of Britain's most famous towns?

One culprit whose name is often muttered darkly is Sir James Drake, founder of Britain's motorway network, who back in the 1940s called for the station to be moved, deploring that the centre of Blackpool had been allowed to develop into a 'characterless mass' with railways, tram sheds, houses, gas and electricity works all vying for space. (It is hardly characterful now!) Another villain is Ernest Marples, the transport minister who overrode Beeching and gave permission for the closure, himself the controversial director of a national road-building firm. We shall probably never know the truth now.

Back at Blackpool North to catch my train home, it is

drizzling. Before the afternoon light finally goes, there's a last chance to photograph the old semaphore signals, soon to be swept away in the new electrification works. Suddenly I feel a hand on my shoulder and a surreal conversation ensues with a peak-capped man who turns out to be the station's jobsworth-in-chief.

J-i-C: 'Oi! You can't take a picture without a ticket.'

Me: 'But, I've got a ticket. Here it is . . . And look, that's my train over there.'

J-i-C: 'Well, you're too far down the platform.'

Me: [Very politely] 'Not sure that's right.' [I gesture at the DON'T PASS BEYOND THIS POINT notice, which is a good thirty yards away.]

J-i-C: [Fuming by now, jowls as red as the signals] 'Well, it's your fault, anyway. Look what you've done, making me come out in the rain and getting wet.'

As my train pulls away from the platform I think how sad that the railways, which brought so much gaiety to Blackpool over the years, should now be playing their part in dampening the spirits of this once great town. But what's that overtaking us on the parallel track? A Lancashire & Yorkshire Highflyer locomotive, polished like a blackberry, at the head of an excursion train, lights ablaze, bearing home a happy seaside crowd to the Lancashire valleys, folk who have had the time of their lives. Could it just be my imagination? One thing is certain – the queen of seaside towns doesn't discard her memories so easily.

Chapter Sixteen

The line that came back from the dead

It was the most romantic and scenic line ever to be axed in Britain. The loss of the Waverley route from England through the Scottish Borders was the bitterest of the Beeching closures. But now, miraculously, the old line has risen from the ashes amid glorious scenery . . .

W as there ever a more grief-filled moment in the two centuries of Britain's railway history than when the 21.56 Edinburgh Waverley to London St Pancras sleeping car train pulled out of the Scottish capital behind diesel locomotive No. D60? For service 1M82 on the evening of 5 January 1969 was to be the very last train on the legendary

98¼-mile Waverley main line – shut cruelly by Dr Beeching after a 107-year life. It was the longest and most scenic main line ever to be closed, and its demise devastated an entire region of Britain.

There was to be no slow fade into obscurity for this most heroic of main lines, perhaps more loved by its local community and revered by railway enthusiasts across the land than any other. The Waverley line went out in a blaze of high drama, as a band of people, led with missionary zeal by a pugnacious Church of Scotland minister, blockaded the tracks to prevent the final train from passing. Not some slow rusty puffer this, crawling over weed-grown rails on a run-down timetable, but a haughty express on its final journey between the UK's two great capitals. Eventually the train was allowed to proceed, but what an operatic night of defiance – more reminiscent of the railroads of the Wild West than the British Isles.

For many the Edinburgh to Carlisle line was not just a railway, but a symbol of the greatness, passion and romance of the Border country, with its massive castles, grand houses, rolling hills and rivers, a world-famous wool and textile industry, and a tumultuous history of conflict between two nations. This too was a battle played out between London and Edinburgh as one of Scotland's most emblematic railways was brought low by political machinations.

While arguments about why it happened have raged over the years, the end of the Waverley line was certainly the most traumatic, the most bitterly fought and by wide agreement the most socially damaging of any closure in British railway history. Romantic in every sense, taking its name from the Waverley novels of Sir Walter Scott, and stamping ground of the eponymous London to Scotland express train the Waverley, this double-track railway over the steep moorland gradients of the Borders has perhaps the ultimate place in the pantheon of trains now departed.

Departed indeed. Wasting no time after the final train had passed, the track-lifting crews with their wrecking machinery were ripping up the rails before the buddleia and bindweed had time to grow over the line so brilliantly engineered by the North British Railway between 1849 and 1862. Such was the glee of the officials in charge of the lifting crews that just days after the final train a group of journalists was invited to witness the rails being plucked from the ground in preparation for a new road. This orgy of *Schadenfreude* must be one of the most cynical exercises ever in the history of railway spin doctoring.

The track-lifting ritual in front of the press was designed to ram home the fact that no more tickets would ever again be sold in the manorial booking office at the busy station at Galashiels to farmers on their way home from market. There would be no more chatter from schoolchildren heading up the line from Fountainhill or St Boswell's. Elderly ladies from Eskbank would no longer take the afternoon service for genteel tea and cucumber sandwiches in Edinburgh's Princes Street. The capacious parcels office at Melrose, so close to Sir Walter Scott's home, would no longer be taking deliveries, even for the great writer's big house along the road at Abbotsford.

Soon there would be only memories of the steeply graded embankments and viaducts, which tested the finest products of the steam age to their limits. Few main lines in Britain have ever hosted so many grand locomotives. Ghosts of the machines that once powered through the Borders include the *Mallard*, which set the world speed record for steam in 1938, as well as several of her A4 Class sisters – frequently in their dotage in the days they ran here. Here too can be summoned up the shades of the handsome A1 Pacific *North British* or the British Railways Britannia Class *Robin Hood*, both regulars beating up the incline to Whiterope summit.

The line that came back from the dead

Memories abound of _Strang Steel_, a member of Gresley's famous B1 class, whose appeal lay in its curious name (actually a director of the LNER who might otherwise have vanished into obscurity). You might catch the spirit of _Wandering Willie_, one of the D30 Scott Class 4-4-0s, named after the characters from the Waverley novels, which pootered along the line for many years. Even as closure loomed, small boys at the end of the platform at Waverley station were able to cop the latest products of the modern era taking a canter down the line to Carlisle, such as the English Electric Deltics, the fastest diesels of their day.

As for the passengers aboard the Anglo-Scottish expresses, there was hardly a rival in the world to the panorama of scenic majesty through the carriage window, as the train made its way north from the Gothic magnificence of George Gilbert Scott's St Pancras. Here was a double dose of splendour as the train traversed the roof of the English Pennines via the Settle & Carlisle line, only to be transported through yet another feast of scenic riches on the rest of the journey into Scotland through the Borders landscape.

But hold on a moment – let's freeze-frame the nostalgia. Today, on a sparkling late summer morning 46 years on, I'm on the platform at Edinburgh Waverley station about to board a tartan-bedecked Class 170 diesel train – the very first service on the splendidly resurrected route of the brand-new Borders Railway. Almost every panjandram in Scotland is aboard the history-making 10.20 to Tweedbank – and not surprising, since the superlatives abound.

Here is the first new domestic main line to be built in Britain for more than a century and the longest line to open in Scotland since the Fort William to Mallaig railway in 1901. It was completed on time and on budget at a cost of £296m. At its peak there were 1,100 people working on the 30-and-a-half mile route, with 137 bridges refurbished or

299

built and 1,000 rails laid across almost 100,000 sleepers. Add to that more than 800,000 tonnes of earth were moved, at least two million man hours spent on the reconstruction - not to mention the 25,000 bacon rolls consumed by the construction team.

As well as the new civil engineering, some of the old Waverley line infrastructure has been brought back into use, reinvigorating memories of a grander era. The magnificent 22-arch Newbattle viaduct at Newtongrange is still as good as new after 160 years. Its stern sandstone piers have withstood decades of mining subsidence, and the viaduct was even used by the new railway contractors' spoil lorries, to prevent damage to the local roads. Environmentally minded builders gently bent down to scoop up rare lampreys from the local Gala Water and relocate them out of harm's way.

Today's track is as smooth as anything laid by the Victorians, although the seven new stations at Shawfair, Eskbank, Newtongrange Gorebridge, Stow, Galashiels and Tweedbank are rather Spartan – more reminiscent of a Glasgow housing estate, perhaps, than a rural railway in one of the most beautiful parts of the land. And unlike its Waverley route heritage, the line is single track – although the terminus at Tweedbank, just short of Melrose, has been thoughtfully laid out to accommodate the long steam-hauled excursion trains that the line will inevitably attract.

Just before the reopening I had taken the X95 First Group bus up the switchback A7 road that parallels the old railway along the long and winding road to Carlisle – a grim reminder of the callous way in which a whole swathe of Britain was cruelly deprived of decent public transport at the end of the 1960s. Here is the worst of slow travel, in which sizeable communities such as Galashiels, and Melrose were forced to rely upon for decades since the closure.

Hawick, 56 miles from Edinburgh and 42 miles from Carlisle with a population of 16,000, acquired the dismal accolade as Britain's largest town farthest from a railway station. Sadly, it still remains marooned since the new railway only goes as far as Tweedbank, just short of Melrose.

And the 'new' trains that serve the reopened line are modest second-hand diesel trains. By contrast, a century ago, the entire route could be traversed in supreme comfort aboard some of the finest and most softly upholstered corridor carriages of the day, complete with restaurant cars riding on cushioned bogies, serving some of the finest haute cuisine available on any train in Europe.

Still today, I must count myself lucky, since I'm ahead of the Queen who will arrive in two days' time on a special train hauled by the famous locomotive *Union of South Africa* to perform the official reopening. At the end of my journey I spend the night amid expanses of crisp, starched sheets in a four-poster bed in Walter Scott's gothic baronial home at Abbotsford, where owls hoot in the fir trees outside. But there is no nicer sound in the world than the early morning rattle of the trains running again in the valley below bearing travellers from Edinburgh, just an hour away.

We've come a long way since the day of the closure which, till this day is described as 'the rape of the Borders'.

Unlike the Settle & Carlisle line – the only surviving British main-line rival to the Waverley route for scenic grandeur, luckily saved in 1989 after a long and hard-fought campaign – the official axe fell swiftly on the Edinburgh–Carlisle line as the mandarins in London, set on closure, outsmarted the locals. The first indication of doom came in the 1963 Beeching Report, where the railway was identified as one, in the anodyne phraseology of the time, from which it was 'intended to withdraw passenger train services'. Beeching hammered an especially devastating nail into its coffin by describing the Waverley route as 'the biggest money-loser in the British railway system'. At this stage closure was not certain – several Scottish lines given the kiss of death by Beeching are still with us today, including the Far North line from Inverness to Wick and Thurso and the 'road to Skye' from Fort William to Mallaig in the West Highlands – but the local campaign against closure was too slow and too late.

On 17 August 1966 British Railways gave formal notice that the line would be shut from 2 January the following year. Reluctant porters expended buckets of paste sticking up posters at stations along the line announcing an end to their own livelihood and potential disaster for their communities. Disingenuously the managers in London argued that there would be no disruption to services between Carlisle and Edinburgh since trains would be diverted along other routes. This was to ignore one of the primary functions of the railway over more than a century, which was to serve the people of the Borders and the economy of the region.

A total of 508 official objections to the closure came in over the statutory six weeks, and a temporary reprieve was announced, with a public hearing held in Hawick on 16 and 17 November 1967. But it was to no avail. On 15 July 1968 Richard Marsh, the minister of transport, issued the final order that the line would close on Monday 5 January 1969. Never mind the massed ranks of the Scottish Economic Council, the Scottish Transport Users' Consultative Committee and the Borders Consultative Group, which had all declared that the line should stay open. Ignored also were the views of David Steel, MP for Roxburgh, Selkirk and Peebles, as well as Edinburgh grandee the Earl of Dalkeith. (His family had endorsed the horse-drawn Edinburgh to Dalkeith line of 1831, the city's first railway and the template for what was to become the Waverley route.) No comparable area of Britain had ever been stripped of its public transport since the start of the Industrial Revolution.

The outcry against closure reverberated across the region and beyond. But it was futile. Even a petition piped in across the steps of number 10 Downing Street, heralded with placards proclaiming THE 12 DAYS OF CHRISTMAS. RAILWAY MURDER WILL BE PROSECUTED failed to save the day. The battle for the Waverley line was over.

At least that was how the authorities saw it. But the fight didn't end there. British Railways, with what many regarded as complete insensitivity to local feeling, organised a special train called Farewell to the Waverley Route on 3 January, three days before the axe finally fell. Railway enthusiasts were urged to boycott it, and it was greeted by 400 protesters wearing black armbands carrying a mock coffin. The train was further delayed by a bomb hoax, and there were even reports of a plot to blow up the Royal Border Bridge on the east coast main line south of Berwick. However, the 400 passengers on the train were able to take their final nostalgic journey without further interruptions.

But the trouble continued. A final special on Sunday 5 January, hauled by one of British Railways' most powerful locomotives, Deltic Class No. D9007 *Pinza*, had a struggle to climb out of Riccarton Junction. Not surprising, since a group of north of England railway photographers had ensured that the rails were lubricated with grease for about 200 yards. The wheels slipped furiously as the locomotive strove to get a grip. The very last train on the line was the 21.56 sleeper departure for St Pancras, hauled by Peak Class diesel No. D60 *Lytham St Annes*, in the charge of driver W. Fleming from Edinburgh's Haymarket shed. In the second seat was Fireman G. Patterson. (In those days the fireman grade still existed despite the fact there were no fires to stoke

– certainly not on *Lytham St Annes*, which was then one of the most modern and powerful locomotives on the railway.)

Fearing demonstrations against the final train, local managers sent a pilot engine along the line in case of trouble – which, indeed, there was. Fog detonators had been placed on the tracks by local enthusiasts, spaced to replicate the beat of the cylinders of the much-loved Gresley V2 Class locomotives, which had been one of the modern mainstays of traffic on the line. But these were less of a problem than what was to follow. The exploding detonators were just the beginning of a night the like of which had never been seen in the history of the railways.

Cunningly, the authorities arranged for the final train to arrive at Hawick station ten minutes late at 23.27 so the stop would be minimal and it could pull away quickly from any protestors. But in vain. According to a report by the Berwick, Selkirk and Roxburgh Constabulary, there were 200 people on the southbound platform, and someone had booked a black-painted cardboard coffin onto the train as a goods parcel for delivery to Richard Marsh in London. It bore the words 'Waverley line – born 1849, killed 1969, aged 120 years'. The coffin was paraded along the platform accompanied by a piper, before being loaded with lingering ceremony into the guard's van.

Meanwhile there was another reception committee lying in wait further south at Newcastleton. When the pilot engine arrived ahead of the express, the driver found the level crossing gates had been blocked by a posse of angry villagers. Ignorant of the obstruction, the express, running behind it, continued on its journey south. What happened next is lyrically recalled by passenger Iain Purdon.

For this part of the journey, ours was the last revenue-earning train of any sort to traverse the line, and circumstances combined to make sure nobody would forget it. As we stormed through the rolling hills, lit in black and white by a ghostly full moon, graced with sub-zero temperatures and the odd snowflake, the night was lit by further showers of sparks from the wheels as the train frequently came to unexpected mysterious halts. It may be that the communication cord was in on the secret, but no one was actually seen to operate it.

Purdon continued with the drama, related by David Spaven in his book *Waverley Route*:

> Many houses on the hills were conscious of the passage of their lifeline. Against the bright background of lit doorways and windows could be seen Border folk, still up and about, watching the passing train. Some waved, others stood sullenly. It was the end of an era. What happened next was undoubtedly the climax of the drama. To a shower of sparks we came to a very decisive halt halfway down the platform at Newcastleton. The station lights were burning yet it was very difficult to see why we had stopped. Attempts to get out of the train to investigate were subverted by worried policemen and furious BR staff.

Ahead of the train a group of people led by the local vicar had chained and wired the crossing gates. Following a long tradition of troublesome priests, the Reverend Brydon Maben had straddled the tracks and squared up to the railway officials who attempted to move him. According to Maben's account, the driver of the pilot locomotive, now just in front of the express, said, 'Are you going to stand there?' Maben replied, 'I am going to stand here.' The local railway traffic inspector then told the driver to 'put pressure on the gates'. But the driver replied, 'If you want to drive the bloody engine, you can drive it yourself.' Maben recalled afterwards – perhaps not entirely in the spirit of Christian conciliation – that the traffic inspector was 'an idiot'. 'He nearly had one under the jaw from me, I can tell you.'

Peace was eventually brokered by David Steel (then a young Liberal MP and now Lord Steel of Aikwood), who was travelling in a sleeping compartment on the train. He recalls,

> The train halted and I was aware of my name being called. I opened a top window and there was a railway inspector standing with a swaying lamp looking at me. 'The people are blocking the line and you are the only one that will persuade them to move,' he said. I dressed hurriedly, clambered on to the line, and was escorted alongside the carriages in freezing darkness. [There was] what looked like half the population of the village – at least two or three hundred people.
>
> Newcastleton is a village newly created by the building of the railway and they felt more strongly than most about the loss of employment as well as transport. I was met by the parish minister. 'They'll expect you to make a speech,' he said. 'It's midnight and the temperature is about ten below freezing,' I replied. 'So it will be a short one.'

Too short clearly for the Reverend Maben, who responded, 'I suggest we stay here till we are forcibly removed' – whereupon he was promptly dragged away by the police to roars from the protestors. Eventually Steel got the crowd to disperse through a deal with the constabulary to release the clergyman with no charges. The final train eventually limped into St Pancras two hours late. For Steel, who was later to become leader of the Liberal Party, it was a lesson in diplomacy that would serve him well in the future.

The tribulations of its final day were typical of the challenges that had faced the line since its difficult parturition. The Waverley line, like many others celebrated in this book, was born out of the railway mania that gripped the land from 1844 onwards. Here was what seemed to be a perfect get-rich-quick opportunity, and Britain's track mileage simply grew and grew, with 4,128 miles added to the network in the space of eight years. But inevitably, amid what sometimes seemed like a great opportunity for small investors, the larger companies became dominant, using their muscle to squeeze out weaker competitors and blocking off rival routes in a giant game of chess.

Few line proposals suffered in this process more than that for the Waverley line, which was conceived in bitterness out of the rivalry between the two mighty railways that dominated access to Scotland from south of the border. The Caledonian, whose tentacles stretched into almost every part of Scotland, and the North British, its less profitable rival, were fighting for supremacy from their respective strongholds in Glasgow and Edinburgh. In 1846 the North British opened its main line between Edinburgh and Berwick-on-Tweed, but there was a problem in that further access into England via Newcastle depended on another mighty railway empire, the North Eastern, which would come at a usurious cost.

But John Learmouth, the ambitious founder of the NBR and a former provost of Edinburgh, had his eye on another way south – through the sparsely populated country of the Borders. In 1845 he spent £120,000 buying a primitive wagon way, the Edinburgh and Dalkeith Railway, and proceeded to drive it on to Hawick, altering the track from 4 feet 6 inches to standard gauge and exchanging horses for the latest products of the steam age. For two wet summers and three harsh winters, sometimes in blinding snowstorms, thousands of navvies slaved to build the tracks at altitudes up to 880 feet to arrive at Hawick on 1 November 1849.

But the Caledonian was already planning a devastating manoeuvre to prevent access to its stronghold at Carlisle on the west coast route into England, announcing that it would open its own line from Carlisle to Hawick via Langholm, the most populous town in the region. Since this was little more than a gesture to thwart the NBR, it was only to be a single-track secondary railway, but the canny North British outmanoeuvred its rival by proposing a double-track main line through Liddesdale along the valley of Liddel Water. Public support was shamelessly courted by the NBR chairman and local MP Richard Hodgson, who organised a huge party in Hawick in 1858 to get backing for his favoured route. He declared the day a public holiday, throwing a huge open-air banquet for 1,000 people with flags and bunting. Special trains brought guests from as far away as Glasgow and Edinburgh. After a year of parliamentary wrangling, the NBR won the day and the new Border Union Railway was born.

The first sod of the new line was cut on 7 September by Mrs Hodgson, the NBR chairman's wife, wielding a silver-plated spade. She was flanked by four navvies carrying a mahogany wheelbarrow shoulder high. But this was the easy part. Now the rest of the line had to be hewn from some of the most unforgiving and remote countryside ever to be encountered by any railway in Britain. Even the celebrated Settle & Carlisle was never more than two miles from a road.

Armies of navvies marched across the hills, taking their shanty towns with them, building massive embankments and viaducts. Many died during the construction of the dramatic

Whiterope Tunnel, 1,208 yards long and 1,000 feet above sea level. Four hundred gallons of water poured every minute from a stream that ran through the mouth of the tunnel, and weather conditions were so unpredictable that the men had to work either semi-naked or wearing heavy overcoats – sometimes alternating within minutes. At Hawick up to thirty men slept in a single hut, twenty-eight by twelve feet, with two or three navvies sharing each bed.

Further south the NBR constructed what was the most remote major junction on the railway network. Located in the midst of bleak forest plantations and blustered by harsh winds sweeping across the Cheviots, Riccarton Junction (all change for the branch line that wandered over to Hexham in Northumberland), which opened in 1863, was a purpose-built railway community of some thirty cottages, with a three-road engine shed, carriage depot, two signal boxes, a gas plant and a smithy. This hamlet, entirely without road access, was one of the strangest places on the network – an enclosed world that was effectively Planet Railway. Here everything was railway-connected – physically, commercially and spiritually. Close to the station was terraced housing for the drivers, firemen, signalmen, porters, fitters, cleaners, gangers and everyone else for whom the railway provided a living. Two much grander three-bedroom houses were built for the stationmaster and a teacher. Following the social hierarchy of the era, the teacher had an inside toilet, while the less-exalted stationmaster had to make do with one outside. Human needs were served by daily deliveries by rail to the Riccarton Grocery Branch, Hawick Co-op Society shop on the platform. Next to it was the sub-post office and later a telephone kiosk, while the station buffet doubled up as the pub. In later years a train paused three days a week for people returning from the cinema.

Younger children went to school in a superannuated

railway coach parked behind the station. Older pupils were packed off to Newcastleton or Hawick aboard a special carriage attached to the 6.30 a.m. freight train to Edinburgh's Millerhill freight yard. Illness and death were also catered for. If a doctor or minister of religion was needed, a locomotive was prepared and dispatched hastily along the line. Thankfully, the railway provided a concession for those who had departed this life by carrying coffins free of charge to the closest town with a funeral parlour. Only in 1963, just six years before closure, did the community of 130 people get its first road – an unmetalled track provided by the Forestry Commission.

Despite the heroic efforts to bring it into being and the legendary status accorded to it by railway enthusiasts in later years, the Waverley was always a sickly child that never quite thrived. Journey times were slower than its rivals, hampered by its many gradients and sharp curves. No less a personage than Queen Victoria complained about a journey over the route from Aberdeen to Windsor aboard the Royal Train. Even a partnership with the Midland on that mighty railway's route to London via Leeds, using carriages and dining cars that were among the most luxurious in the world, wasn't sufficient to attract the necessary traffic. The fact was the area served by the Waverley route had no heavy industry, and the line was limited to local merchandise, agricultural materials, livestock and coal.

Its dismal financial performance, where receipts at stations rarely even covered staff wages, are recorded in David St John Thomas's *The Country Railway*: 'The North British Railway Border Union line had eleven stations in the lean windswept miles between Hawick and Carlisle. In 1920, the peak year for railway traffic, before the age of mass motoring and with few buses hardy enough to search there for traffic, the annual passenger takings were as little as £147 at

Shankend, £249 at Harker and £281 at Kershope Foot.' It got worse after the grouping of the railways in 1923, when the Waverley was absorbed into the London & North Eastern Railway.

Sensibly, the LNER concentrated on the east coast route through Newcastle, with its slick streamliners such as the Silver Jubilee and Coronation making the Waverley line expresses look like plodders in comparison. By the 1950s 80 per cent of local livestock traffic, once a mainstay of the Waverley, was going by road. By the 1960s there were only two through expresses to London – the daytime Waverley and an overnight train. I once travelled on this service from London to Edinburgh and recall stretching out full length in an otherwise empty compartment, waking up at dawn to admire the magnificent Borders scenery in solitude.

Since the track lifters passed, the Waverley line has slumbered, with the vividness of memory slowly fading. But despite the best efforts of the wreckers of the 1960s, some of its grandest artefacts survive today as permanent memorials in the landscape. None finer perhaps than Melrose station, with its elevated position overlooking the town and the abbey. With its fine Flemish gables and elaborate bay windows intact, the building survives in the slightly less romantic guise of a childrens' nursery and a pizza restaurant, and – even more humiliating – the Melrose bypass now runs where its platforms once stood.

Still, it was lucky to survive, having been rescued from dereliction by an English architect, and is now regarded as one of Scotland's most important station buildings. Equally indelible are the elegant Redbridge Viaduct across the Tweed at Galashiels and the grandstanding Shankend Viaduct further south, whose fifteen semicircular arches, each sixty feet high, march for 199 yards, brooding over the moorland landscape like some prehistoric monument.

But these days there's no talk of prehistory since, mile by mile, the Waverley line (or at least its northern part) is rising inexorably from the dead. Now fast modern diesel trains speed half-hourly down the tracks on schedules that the North British pioneers of old could only have dreamed of. Today's newly engineeered railway is not the product of Victorian chancers and risk-takers but an injection of public money by the Scottish government, flexing its muscles in an increasingly devolved Britain. Still, the dream is just as bright as it was for the line's Victorian forebears – with no greater believer than Hugh Wark, project director of the new railway and with the pedigree of having upgraded the London–Glasgow route.

'We haven't just built a railway here,' he tells me as the train speeds through Newtongrange, next to the fossilised winding gear of the National Mining Museum – a perfect juxtaposition of the old and new industrial Scotland. 'We've put right an historic injustice. The Borders line is back on the travel map of Scotland once again – where it should have remained.'

Will the day ever dawn when the rails stretch all the way from Edinburgh to Carlisle again? Who knows? Even today, amid the windswept ruins of Riccarton Junction, huddles of enthusiasts can frequently be found paying homage, collars turned up against the weather and ever hopeful that the express trains might one day power over the entire length of the Waverley route once more. Is that the wind in the hills? For the dreamers it could be the approach of a sparkling green Gresley Pacific pounding out of the mist up the gradient at the head of The Waverley. And who's to say they are wrong? On the line that came back from the dead, anything is possible.

Acknowledgements

Though you might imagine that the people who run our fast-paced modern railways would be too busy with the present to bother with the past, quite the opposite is true. I've had huge support in writing this book from today's train companies, many of whom are only too keen to recall their legacy and heritage. Special thanks to Mark Hopwood and Sue Evans of First Great Western, Ken Gibbs and Damien Henderson of Virgin Trains, John Yellowlees of Scotrail, Lucy Drake of Eurostar, Tim Shoveller, Emma Knight of South West Trains and Emma Wylde of the train division of the travel company Belmond. East Coast Trains, whose head of communications John Gelson is a true friend of railways past and present and sponsored my travel from London to undertake research in the National Railway Museum at York.

Thanks too to a host of others – generous not only with their wisdom but also with large tranches of their time. Richard Burningham, Anthony Coulls, Peter Davis, Philip Haigh, Brian Janes, Chris Milner, John Robinson, Russ Rollings, Gordon Rushton, Ross Shimmon, Andy Thompson and Christian Wolmar read and commented on the manuscript. All sorts of support and guidance were also given by a diaspora of folk who might be termed Friends of the Railways, including Paul Bigland, Hazel Bonner, Neil Buxton,

Rupert Brennan-Brown, Richard Clinnick, Ian Dinmore, Barry Doe, Roger Ford, Nigel Harris, Anthony Lambert, Paul Prentice, Jo Guiver, Hassard Stacpoole, Alexa Stott, Michael Whitehouse and Dawn Wolrich.

I owe a huge debt of gratitude too to Michael Max, one of the most prolific collectors of railway lore and literature, who allowed me to use his magnificent private library before it was sadly dispersed. Likewise the staff of the British Library at St Pancras, the Search Engine archive at the National Railway Museum in York and the National Archive at Kew, who were always patient in my requests for the most abstruse information from the past.

Biggest thanks of all to my ever-supportive wife Melanie, to whom this book is dedicated, and to my son Edmund. Many were the ideas he contributed in conversations late into the evening after homework was over. And, as always, I've had unflagging support from my publisher Trevor Dolby at Preface, who had the inspiration for this book, and my agent Sheila Ableman, always calm as I raced headlong along the tracks to my destination.

Finally, a cautionary note. I recently asked a leading celebrity with a widely known interest in railways why he didn't write books on the subject. They would clearly be popular, I suggested to him. 'You know,' he replied, 'there are so many *experts* out there in the railway community that I'd be terrified about getting things wrong.' Well, I've taken that risk with this volume. So I hope readers will bear with me in my aim here – not to produce a scholarly work of history or topography, but to enter imaginatively into the world of the railways of the past and to summon up for the modern reader at least the spirit of the trains now departed.

I take full responsibility for any errors, and I'd be delighted to hear comments and suggestions from you, the readers, many of whom will be vastly more knowledgeable than me. Please get in touch via michael@michaelwennwilliams.co.uk. All comments will be acknowledged and corrections incorporated into future editions of the book.

For this revised and updated new edition of the book, I am delighted to be able to include maps for relevant chapters – for which I am grateful to the cartographer John Gilkes. The map section begins on page 321.

Sources and further reading

It's surprising given the never-ending outpourings from publishers of books on trains that there has been relatively little of what you might call *writing* about railways. Sure, if you are seeking something entitled *Track-Tamping Machines of the Early BR Era* or *Pictorial Memories of Golden Days at Snoozington Junction* then you may find plenty of what you need. But I'm inclined to agree with George Ottley, the bibliographer of railways, when he wrote, 'One's first impression upon entering a railway bookshop is that nobody *reads* books today, for so much of what is on sale consists of albums of illustrations with captions and a brief introduction the only textual support.' 'Middle-depth writing' – let alone solid scholarly publications about Britain's railway heritage 'in the fullness of all its aspects, woven in the weft and warp of social and economic development' – had, according to Ottley, drowned in a sea of egregious pap.

While this may be a bit strong, it's certainly true that the best-written books – and the ones that have inspired me in writing this volume – derive mostly from a more literary era of publishing. I include C. Hamilton Ellis's *The Trains We Loved* (George Allen & Unwin 1947), *The Fascination of Railways* by Roger Lloyd (George Allen & Unwin 1951), *Lines of Character* by L. T. C. Rolt and P. B. Whitehouse (Constable

1952), *The Railways of Britain* by Jack Simmons (Routledge & Kegan Paul 1961), *The Railway Age* by Michael Robbins (Routledge & Kegan Paul 1962), Bryan Morgan's *The Railway-Lover's Companion* (Eyre & Spottiswoode 1963) and *The Country Railway* by David St John Thomas (David & Charles 1976), as well as the many volumes from the 1940s onwards by the prolific O. S. Nock and Cecil J. Allen.

This doesn't mean there hasn't been some good writing in later decades, notably the definitive *Fire and Steam* by Christian Wolmar (Atlantic 2007) and the compendious *The Railway Station: A Social History* by Jeffrey Richards and John M. MacKenzie (Oxford University Press 1986). More quirky but nevertheless a good read are *Platform Souls* by Nicholas Whitaker (Victor Gollancz 1995), *Parallel Lines* by Ian Marchant (Bloomsbury 2003) and *Eleven Minutes Late* by Matthew Engel (Macmillan 2009).

For most of my sources I've drawn on an eclectic range of original archive material, personal memoirs, individual railway histories, face-to-face interviews – and discovered many gems in the following volumes.

Cecil J. Allen, *The Titled Trains of Great Britain* (Ian Allan 5th edn, 1967)

Anonymous, *The Railway Traveller's Handy Book* (Old House reprint 2012)

Robin Atthill, *The Somerset & Dorset Railway* (David & Charles 1967)

Martin Bairstow, *Railways of Blackpool and the Fylde* (Martin Bairstow 2001)

George Behrend, *Gone with Regret* (Lambarde Press 1964)

George Behrend and Gary Buchanan, *Night Ferry* (Ian Allan 1985)

John Betjeman, *London's Historic Railway Stations* (John Murray 1972)

Gordon Biddle, *Great Railway Stations of Britain* (David & Charles 1986)

Paul Bolger, *The Docker's Umbrella* (Bluecoat Press 1992)

G. A. Brown, J. D. C. Prideaux and H. G. Radcliffe, *The Lynton and Barnstaple Railway* (David & Charles 1964)

Ernest F. Carter, *Unusual Locomotives* (Frederick Muller 1960)

Ian Carter, *British Railway Enthusiasm* (Manchester University Press 2008)

R. Davies and M. D. Grant, *Forgotten Railways: Chilterns and Cotswolds* (David & Charles 1975)

W. J. K. Davies, *Light Railways* (Ian Allan 1964)

Andrew Dow, *Dow's Dictionary of Railway Quotations* (John Hopkins University Press 2009)

J. M. Dunn, *The Stratford-upon-Avon & Midland Junction Railway* (Oakwood Press 1952)

John Gahan, *Seventeen Stations to Dingle* (Countyvise 1981)

A. E. Grigg, *Country Railwaymen* (Calypus Books 1982)

Alan and Christine Hammond, *The Splendour of the Somerset & Dorset Railway* (Millstream Books 2010)

Chris de Winter Hebron, *Dining at Speed* (Silver Link 2004)

John Hadrill, *Rails to the Sea* (Atlantic 1999)

C. Hamilton Ellis, *Four Main Lines* (Allen and Unwin 1950)

Derek Harrison, *Salute to Snow Hill* (Barbryn Press 1978)

Brian Hollingsworth, *The Pleasures of Railways* (Allen Lane 1983)

Peter Johnson, *The Shropshire and Montgomeryshire Light Railway* (Oxford Publishing Co. 2008)

Arthur Jordan, *The Stratford-upon-Avon and Midland Junction Railway* (Oxford Publishing Co. 1982)

R. W. Kidner, *The Colonel Stephens Railways* (Oakwood Press 1936)

Stuart Legg, *The Railway Book* (Fourth Estate 1988)

Chris Leigh, *Portrait of the Lynton & Barnstaple Railway* (Ian Allan 1983)

Colin G. Maggs, *The Last Years of the Somerset & Dorset* (Ian Allan 1991)

Andrew Martin, *Belles and Whistles* (Profile Books 2014)

Barry McLoughlin, *Railway Heritage: Blackpool and the Fylde* (Silver Link Publishing 1996)

John Minnis, *Britain's Lost Railways* (Aurum Press 2011)

Bryan Morgan, *The End of the Line* (Cleaver-Hume Press 1955)

Sean O'Brien and Don Paterson (eds), *Train Songs* (Faber 2013)

Robert Prance, *West Country Railway Memories* (Oakwood Press 2013)

Kevin Robertson, *The Leader Project* (Oxford Publishing Co. 2007)

W. Heath Robinson, *Railway Ribaldry* (Great Western Railway 1935)

Robert Robotham, *The Waverley Route: The post-war years* (Ian Allan 1999)

T. W. E. Roche, *The Withered Arm* (Branch Line Handbooks 1967)

Muriel Searle, *Lost Lines* (New Cavendish Books 1982)

Frank Shaw, *My Liverpool* (Wolfe Publishing 1971)

Jack Simmons, *The Railway in Town and Country 1830–1914* (David & Charles 1986)

Jack Simmons, *Railways: An Anthology* (Collins 1991)

Roger Siviter, *Waverley: Portrait of a famous route* (Runpast Publishing 1996)

David Norman Smith, *The Railway and its Passengers* (David & Charles 1988)

David Spaven, *Waverley Route* (Argyll Publishing 2012)

David St John Thomas and Patrick Whitehouse, *The Great Days of the Country Railway* (David & Charles 1986)

Gilbert Thomas and David St John Thomas, *Double-Headed* (David & Charles 1963)

Eric Tonks, *The Shropshire & Montgomeryshire Railway* (Industrial Railway Society 1972)

Robert Tufnell, *Prototype Locomotives* (David & Charles 1985)

Keith & Susan Turner, *The Shropshire & Montgomeryshire Light Railway* (David & Charles 1982)

Peter Walton, *The Stainmore and Eden Valley Railways* (Oxford Publishing Co. 1992)

David Wroe, *An Illustrated History of the North Cornwall Railway* (Irwell Press 1994)

Maps

Maps

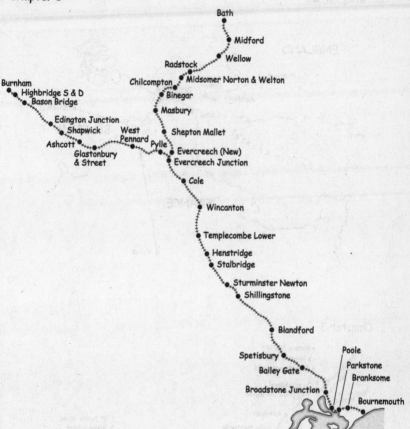

Chapter 1

Bath
Midford
Wellow
Radstock
Midsomer Norton & Welton
Chilcompton
Binegar
Masbury
Shepton Mallet
West Pennard
Pylle
Evercreech (New)
Evercreech Junction
Cole
Wincanton
Templecombe Lower
Henstridge
Stalbridge
Sturminster Newton
Shillingstone
Blandford
Spetisbury
Bailey Gate
Broadstone Junction
Burnham
Highbridge S & D
Bason Bridge
Edington Junction
Shapwick
Ashcott
Glastonbury & Street
Poole
Parkstone
Branksome
Bournemouth

Chapter 2

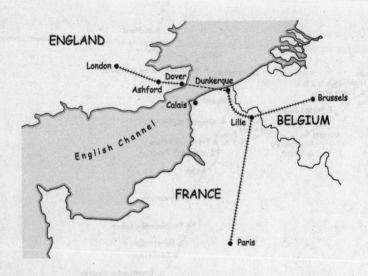

Chapter 3

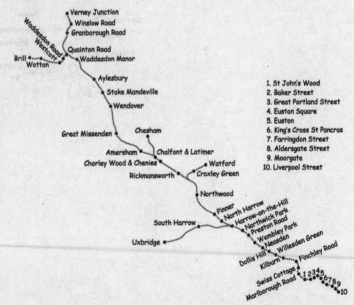

1. St John's Wood
2. Baker Street
3. Great Portland Street
4. Euston Square
5. Euston
6. King's Cross St Pancras
7. Farringdon Street
8. Aldersgate Street
9. Moorgate
10. Liverpool Street

Chapter 4

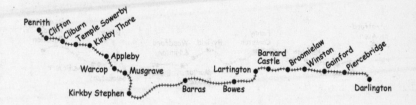

Penrith • Clifton • Cliburn • Temple Sowerby • Kirkby Thore
Appleby •
Warcop • Musgrave
Kirkby Stephen •
Barras • Bowes
Lartington •
Barnard Castle • Broomielaw • Winston • Gainford • Piercebridge
Darlington

Chapter 6

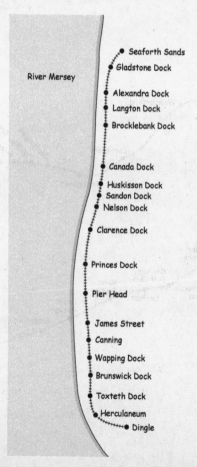

River Mersey

• Seaforth Sands
• Gladstone Dock
• Alexandra Dock
• Langton Dock
• Brocklebank Dock
• Canada Dock
• Huskisson Dock
• Sandon Dock
• Nelson Dock
• Clarence Dock
• Princes Dock
• Pier Head
• James Street
• Canning
• Wapping Dock
• Brunswick Dock
• Toxteth Dock
• Herculaneum
• Dingle

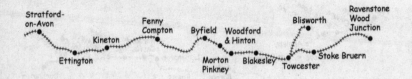

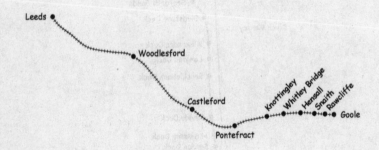

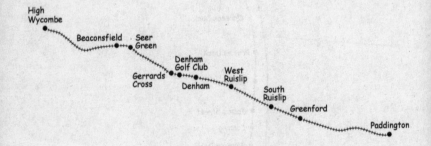

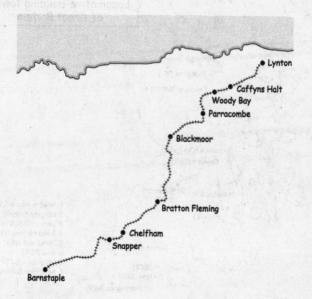

- Lynton
- Caffyns Halt
- Woody Bay
- Parracombe
- Blackmoor
- Bratton Fleming
- Chelfham
- Snapper
- Barnstaple

Chapter 10

Locomotive-building towns of Great Britain

Lochgorm (HR)
Inverurie (GNSR)
Greenock (CR)
Cowlairs (EGR)
St Rollox (CR)   St Margarets (NBR)
Kilmarnock (GSWR)

Gateshead (NDR)
Maryport (MCR)
Shildon (SDR)
Darlington (NER)
Barrow-in-Furness (FR)
York (NER)
Horwich (LYR)
Earlstown (LNWR)   Bury (LYR)
Edge Hill (GJR)   Doncaster (GNR)
Sheffield (GCR)
Crewe (GJR)
Stoke (NSR)   Derby (NMR)
Wolverhampton (SBR)   Melton Constable (MGNJR)
Bromsgrove (BGR)
Wolverton (LNWR)
Caerphilly (RR)
Swindon (GWR)
Cardiff (TVR)   Bristol (GWR)
Highbridge (SDJR)
Ashford (SECR)
Eastleigh (LSWR)   Brighton (LBR)

1. Newton Heath (LYR)
2. Longsight (MBR)
3. Gorton (MSLR to GCR)
4. Miles Platting (LYR)
5. Stratford (GER)
6. Bow (NLR)
7. Longhedge (LCDR)
8. Nine Elms (LSWR)

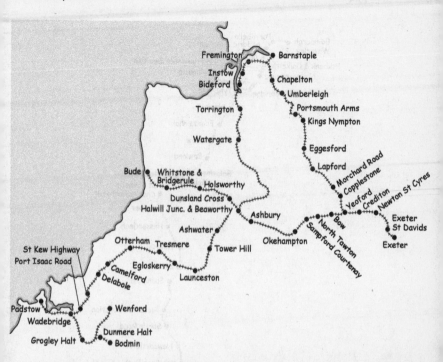

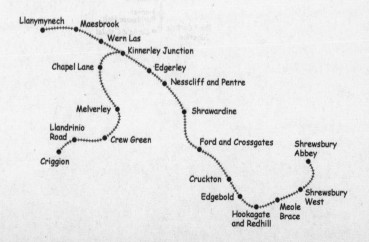

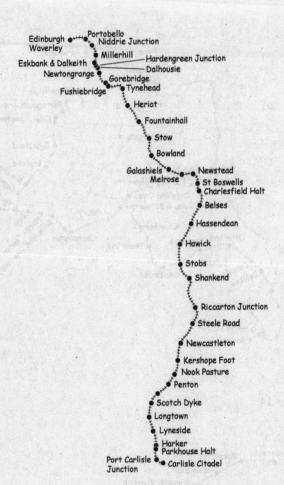

Portobello
Edinburgh
Waverley
Niddrie Junction
Millerhill
Hardengreen Junction
Eskbank & Dalkeith
Dalhousie
Newtongrange
Gorebridge
Fushiebridge
Tynehead
Heriot
Fountainhall
Stow
Bowland
Galashiels
Newstead
Melrose
St Boswells
Charlesfield Halt
Belses
Hassendean
Hawick
Stobs
Shankend
Riccarton Junction
Steele Road
Newcastleton
Kershope Foot
Nook Pasture
Penton
Scotch Dyke
Longtown
Lyneside
Harker
Parkhouse Halt
Port Carlisle
Junction
Carlisle Citadel

Index